Up on the pub veranda Womba Billy the teamster raised his bloodshot eyes to the sun and beat his chest and roared. The wet season was over, and for everyone in the tiny port of Derby—including Womba, who had spent the Wet getting drunk and thinking he was a scrub bull—life was beginning again. Black men and white men were preparing to wander far and wide through the rugged Kimberleys and the vast Northern Territory. Many of the white men were answering the call of gold, as news came of finds, particularly in the developing goldfield of Tennant's Creek.

Ion Idriess was one of those who set out from Derby with the ending of the Wet. This is the story of his wanderings and what he heard and saw along the way, at a time when wireless and air and motor transport were rapidly changing life in the North and North-west, but when the age of the pioneers, of heroic journeys, terrifying loneliness, and violent death, had not yet passed away.

ION IDRIESS

ETT IMPRINT has the following books back in print in 2021:

Flynn of the Inland
The Desert Column
The Red Chief
Nemarluk
Horrie the Wog Dog
Prospecting for Gold
Drums of Mer
Madman's Island
The Yellow Joss
Forty Fathoms Deep
Lasseter's Last Ride
Sniping
Shoot to Kill
Guerrilla Tactics
Trapping the Jap
Lurking Death
The Scout
The Wild White Man of Badu
Gold Dust and Ashes
Headhunters of the Coral Sea
Gouger of the Bulletin
Ion Idriess: The Last Interview
Man Tracks
Men of the Jungle
Outlaws of the Leopolds
Over the Range
Tracks of Destiny

TRACKS OF DESTINY

From Derby to Tennant Creek

ION IDRIESS

ETT IMPRINT
Exile Bay

This 3rd edition published by ETT Imprint, Exile Bay 2021

This book is copyright. Apart from any fair dealing for the purposes of private study, research, criticism or review, as permitted under the Copyright Act, no part may be reproduced by any process without written permission. Inquiries should be addressed to the publishers:

ETT IMPRINT
PO Box R1906
Royal Exchange NSW 1225 Australia

First published by Angus & Robertson in 1961. Reprinted 1962
First electronic edition by ETT Imprint 2021

Copyright © Idriess Enterprises Pty Ltd, 2021

ISBN 9781922473936 (pbk)
ISBN 9781922473943 (ebk)

Cover: Bush mechanic sorting out a little problem in the Territory, 1935

Cover design by Tom Thompson

To Grace George

our own proof girl "Georgie", who throughout the battling years has been so patient and understanding with so many impatient Australian authors, including me

Sam Irvine, pioneer driver of His Majesty's Overland Mail. His run was 600 miles up north into the Territory, 600 miles back.

CONTENTS

CHAPTER		PAGE
I.	THE DROVER OF GOATS	9
II.	THE NEW LIFE	15
III.	COMING OF A NEW ERA	22
IV.	THE VALLEY	28
V.	WHERE THE WILD MEN ROAM	32
VI.	THE WOMAN-STEALER	37
VII.	WHILE DEATH CREEPS NEAR	42
VIII.	THE MASSACRE	46
IX.	WYNDHAM DAYS	54
X.	THE OLD DOC	59
XI.	OUT WHERE HE-MEN REFUSE TO DIE	62
XII.	WHAT DOES IT FEEL LIKE TO BE DEAD?	67
XIII.	THE PORT OF PLENTY-O'-TIME	71
XIV.	WHERE WOMEN CAN BE AS GOOD AS MEN	77
XV.	ABOARD THE BIRDUM FLYER	81
XVI.	PINE CREEK NIGHTS	86
XVII.	SORROWS OF THE OPIUM TRADERS	90
XVIII.	"SOOL THE WOLVES ONTO 'EM!"	97
XIX.	AS TIME PASSES	102
XX.	THE LADY ETHNOLOGIST	108
XXI.	WE COME TO THE TENNANT'S	114
XXII.	THAT ARMOUR-PLATED BAR	120
XXIII.	TO DONALD MACKAY	125
XXIV.	IRONSTONE AND SPINIFEX	131
XXV.	THE BLIND MINER	136
XXVI.	THE RISING SUN	141
XXVII.	THE GUNS	147
XXVIII.	GOLD!	151
XXIX.	WOODY AND THE PETER PAN	157
XXX.	A STUDY OF BALLISTICS	161
XXXI.	THE ALICE BRIDES OF YESTERYEAR	165
XXXII.	THE STONE AGE STEPS INTO THE MODERN	170

CHAPTER	PAGE
XXXIII. THE BLACK PHANTOM	176
XXXIV. THE PURSUIT	181
XXXV. HE WHO WALKS IN THE NIGHT	188
XXXVI. THE HEAT IS ON	193
XXXVII. "FINISH!"	197

Michael Terry refuelling his truck for a 1928 expedition into the Northern Territory.

I

THE DROVER OF GOATS

Under a blazing Centralian sun, the red dust wavering under the little hooves as the goats mooched steadily along. Red dust on the lean face of the drover carefully shepherding his charges.

"I've got to," he muttered, "out here where water is scarce as ice-creams in hell. No wonder I'm talking to myself. Nursing a mob of goats across this track to Hades and Gone. Who'd 'a' thought it?"

Who indeed, in this year 1932-3, along that seldom-used track from Mount Isa south-west through North Queensland and down across the Territory to a forlorn spot on the Overland Telegraph Line called Tennant's Creek?[1]

"Name of some old explorer bloke most likely," the goat-drover told himself. "Good luck to him, anyway, good luck to any bloke who finds a waterhole in a creek out here! And now here's me—with a mob of goats!"

Later O'Brien would laugh at the memory. "I used to wonder if I was going crazy, then I knew I was. Eating spinifex grubs and talking to myself while droving a mob of goats across Australia. A cattleman won't be seen droving a mob of sheep, but here was a goat droving a mob of goats!"

Since then I've wondered if O'Brien's ghost has gazed down amazed at the modern town of Tennant's Creek, perhaps puzzling over the whereabouts of that faint track, which is now a broad road leading out through the dust haze south-east from the Tennant's, a road along which roar huge touring cars to and from that other wonder town of the wilderness, Mount Isa.

But the drover of the goats would never know it in this life. His was the ticklish job of getting those goats alive across those hundreds of miles of sunburnt space. And he wished to arrive alive with them.

Fezal Deene devoutly hoped he would. For Fezal Deene, the sombre-faced Afghan, must live also, but he must live by the Prophet. And in this most isolated spot of this infidel land the safe arrival of those goats meant that his own hand would now kill his own meat; no unclean hand would touch it.

O'Brien, an Ishmael himself, had taken this undignified droving job because a whisper had come floating across the sun-scorched wilderness, a

---

[1] "Tennant Creek" is now the form of the name officially used, but at the time of these happenings it was usually called "Tennant's Creek", or just "the Tennant's".

bare rumour murmuring through the haze of distance, "Prospectors have struck gold somewhere near Tennant's Creek in the Centre!" A following rumour then was that the enterprising Fezal Deene was actually transporting a battery there to crush stone for the gold-miners. So that wild rumour must be true. The job of droving the goats meant confirmation to O'Brien. Eagerly he accepted. Thus he would reach this new find if any, and actually be paid for the trip.

"I'd go hopping to hell along a road of criss-cross saws to reach a new goldfield," he declared, "let alone drive a mob of goats across a desert!"

Which it wasn't, actually. But it was a cruel, sparse land to those who did not know their way about. And thus he crossed it in hopes of finding gold. He would find lead, poor chap. Four ounces of it—in his belly. Such things happen. You never know.

While I would give away my chance of gold. Such things happen. You never know. I didn't, of course.

While that shepherder of goats was drawing nearer the centre of Australia I was a thousand miles farther on, on the shores of the Indian Ocean at the little Derby port of the West Kimberley, eager to get a start on to return down over the Territory-Centralian track for home. But big blue clouds ominously piling up again warned, "Not yet! More rain coming!"

"Pull off the track for a while and come in with me on Tennant's Creek, Jack," suggested Jack Noble one day.

"Not on your life, Jack," I replied. "I'm bound for the Big Smoke. And every post is a winning-post."

"But there's gold at Tennant's Creek, Jack, and that's dinkum! I've seen it. It's only just found. It's such a hard-to-get-at place that there'll be no rush for quite a while. But in time there will be. I'm making straight back there after the Wet. There *is* gold there, Jack. How about it?"

"I'm for the gold of Pitt Street." I laughed. "I've had the spinifex and the mulga and the witchety grubs—for the time being, anyway."

And thus I threw away a fortune. For a thousand miles south-east amongst that same spinifex Jack was to find Noble's Knob. Fortunes came out of it. Jack got his whack, quite a little pile, too. But good-hearted Jack could not hang on to fortune. Few of them did. Only a very few in any mining field ever do.

For untold ages past the fierce sun in that Central Australian wilderness had been beating down upon many a fortune encased within those harsh brown ironstone hills. Already I'd ridden through them, unaware of the wealth deep hidden on either side. Yet again I would drive through them, and miss out again—as did many another man.

But we don't know these things.

Big, easy-going Jack Noble. Adventurous, taking things as they came unless he heard of a new gold strike. It needed but the merest whisper and Jack was packing his swag and away, across to the other side of the continent if need be. At such times Jack would keep going. Just keep going on and on. He would toil like a galley-slave, too, so long as he was looking for gold. Otherwise an easy-going mate, so his friends declared, maybe a bit too easy-going at times. With a big virtue—Jack never forgot a friend. Even now he'd left the early opportunities lying around those distant hills of gold to hurry all the way back to Derby, a thousand hazardous miles, a thousand to return, just to bring the news to three or four friends who had done him a good turn during difficult times. (I wasn't one of these particular staunch old friends.) He had come all this way to try to convince them of the find and urge them to return with him and grasp the chance of fortune—a certainty, as it turned out.

But that problematical gold was a long way away. Here in Derby all hands were eagerly awaiting the end of the Wet so that we could begin travelling again, could begin the work of the Kimberleys, the sheep and the cattle work, the droving east and west, the cattle shipping on the west coast at Derby, the pearling fleets sailing out from Broome, the meatworks opening up to hectic life again away north at Wyndham, the mounted patrols riding out to visit those dozen pioneer settlers "Over the Range" and make sure all was well with them in their rugged isolation, more isolated actually than many pioneers of the early days down south. That, and the prospecting being done by a few diehards in that rough country from Hall's Creek south to the Black Elvira, and "Freeney's" oil-drilling camp round about Noonkanbah station, made up the work of the Kimberleys.

Each day now leaden skies were brightening with shafts of sunlight into clear, sparkling blue. The wind beating in from the turbulent Gulf came now with a less savage howl, even died down now and then. The so few, so precious womenfolk, pegs between teeth, arms and hands reaching up to the line, with roving eye for the chance of a shouted word of gossip, were thankfully hanging out the washing in the blazing sunlight. Cockatoos were shrieking on the big fat old baobab-trees whose gorgeous canopy of flowers and scent would soon make the little post office gay. A rainbow bird swept by with his coat of many colours flashing in the sunlight as he sped to an important meeting with his lady-love, to choose a safe, cosy gully bank to burrow into and build and furnish their new season's home. Yes, there was a quickening of fresh life now all over the Kimberleys.

Soon that welcome visitor from distant civilization, the first little steamer after the three months' wet—longer, should it have proved a nasty cyclone season—would come battling its way down to us through the whirlpools in the Gulf, forty churning miles of them. Yes, soon now the rains would die away, the Kimberleys come to life again. Young Henwood from Noonkanbah station came riding down the Yeeda road, heading now for the post office—a good sign that. It meant that the road to the Crossing, the one and only inland road to Fitzroy Crossing, two hundred miles eastward, must be drying up fast, now opening the way to the big inland stations. Two business-like black trackers, felt hats set at rakish angles, belts and riding boots polished, came riding down from the police station—first sign of the early patrols. The cattle-spearers Over the Range, and those beetle-browed Tarzans so quick with club and spear, would watch the signal smokes, ready for a quick dash to their mountain fastness when the patrols came riding again.

Swift and ready with spear and nullah were the wild tribesmen Over the Range. I know, for I've ridden with the patrols, and watched the wild men themselves unearth the skeletons of their victims.

But here in Derby the tiny port was bathed in brilliant sunshine. A lively girl came by riding on a prancing chestnut. A roar up on the pub veranda showed old Womba Billy greeting the coming of the Dry in his own bovine fashion. Old Womba, the donkey teamster, had been "wet" for these last two months and more, and was only now waking up to the fact that the Dry was coming fast. He roared again as he held baboon-like arms up to the life-giving sun and thumped his barrel of a chest. He swore he had been suckled by a wild lubra and reared by her with her own piccaninny, which I believe was fact. Anyway, he was a blood brother to the natives out along the Fitzroy and they thought the world of him; he had given them the reason to many a time. Womba in native language means "old man", and out among the tribes he held all the power, except in strictly tribal matters of the cunning Old Men.

Happier with the aborigines than with the whites, he was a short, nuggety barrel of an old fellow seasoned by seventy Nor'-west summers, a gruff, suspicious, though moderately kindly old chap in the sober season, but dangerous and with a raging strength when drunk. When properly "seasoned" after the first month or so of the Wet his speciality was to imagine he was a wild scrub bull intent on protecting his cows. At that stage he would tear off his old grey flannel, hitch up his belt, fling away his boots, and announce his "bulldom" by beating his hairy chest with ironwood fists while roaring a challenge. Lowering his bullet-shaped head, he would come charging down upon any yarning groups of men within sight of those little bloodshot eyes of his, his belief being that he was "horning in" on enemy bulls who had come snorting round intent to steal the pick of his cows. He would scatter any group of men at such times; there were no holds barred, and it took good men and a hectic battle to quieten him. As he was so thick and round and lively, with a stomach tough as an ironwood stump, it was no use kicking him in the guts. That only made him froth at the mouth with laughter. When he was really on the rampage they used to put him to sleep with a blow on the back of the neck with a hunk of wood or a bottle. He was a holy terror when in the near horrors, any unlucky man who received that head of his in the stomach was butted helpless, he was horned and gored to such effect that he was a sick "bull" indeed for a fortnight afterward. No wonder that at such dangerous periods the boys sought to skittle the old bastard"—quick-feller!

At this present moment Womba, yawning up at the sky, cared nothing for the black and brown-yellow bruises and gravel rash causing his tough old face to look as if it had been laundered by a steam-roller, the ugly-looking cuts and scratches marking his powerful body, the mat of hair plastered to his chest with dried blood—his usual "dress-suit" at this period. All these were the result of "bull-fights" at those times when his mind nightmared into the borderland of the horrors while "putting in the Wet". But now his face was working with some milder animal instinct as with bloodshot eyes dazzled by sunlight he stared up at the heavens so vastly blue and drank in the message of creative vitality and renewed life. In a very few days now Womba would begin to look almost human again, after he'd had a mighty bath and strolled along to Jack Knopp's store for a new flannel and trousers. Thus Womba also, like the early shoots already peeping from shrub and tree, was growing happy again now that the Dry was coming.

Good old Womba, beloved of the aborigines. From the mouth of the Fitzroy right up to its mountain source he was known to the Old Folk as "Old Man of the River". Savagely rough with the tough, savagely inclined young bucks when he needed to be, still he was protector to any who came running to him for help, and throughout the years there had been many. If it was in his power to help he always would, even against the white police, or even against the Old Men—in so far as he dared, for the one thing he dared not interfere too deeply with was the penalty imposed by the Old Men on one who had broken the tribal law. But even against those implacables he had managed, just occasionally, to save a young girl who had offended against the law. Womba had bought the old devils off somehow or other, but to the natives such release was a miracle. No wonder the younger aboriginals in particular would do anything at all for this tough old human gorilla.

Personally, I could cheerfully have shot the brute at times. When you've got to camp under the same roof for several months with half a dozen unpredictable volcanoes more or less like Womba you get mad occasionally when suddenly forced to defend yourself. But now the Dry had come and we all loved one another—even the cook looked human.

Came days of brilliant sunlight, horsemen now in the sodden track we called a street. And over at the police station there was swift movement, before we expected it—trackers running in horses. For which I was sorry. You see, friends of mine had "escaped", when there was no need for them to have escaped at all. For they had been brought in from the wild bush by a patrol for medical treatment only.

I had ridden with that patrol and saw that these wild tribesmen suffered from terrible diseases—leprosy, and diseases which I, at least, believed worse. They were almost certainly doomed—this was before the days of that blessed penicillin, and the antibiotics—but they would have received some sort of treatment at the Native Hospital, and with treatment, of course, there would be a chance—a faint chance.

But the call of the Kimberleys, the fascinating country away Over the Range, had proved too great. For the Wet was nearly over, the Dry was fast coming.

By day they sat with faces to the ranges, those rugged King Leopolds, sniffing the breezes from the wild north. Those breezes day by day bringing them the swelling waves of perfume bursting from the water-tom gorges, the untamed valleys far Over the Range, the scent of the big swamps and that craggy sea of mountain-tops, all bursting into vegetable, animal, fish, reptile and bird life with the coming of the Dry, their tribal land being born again under the magic of the sun-god. By night they looked up and they had never seen those golden stars far up there twinkling so alluringly over their immemorial tribal grounds—never! Lying there motionless within that iron-walled compound, eyes staring up to the sky, they heard faintly the "honk-konk, honk-konk" of the wild geese bound in swiftly vanishing flight Over the Range to the rich swamps and lily lagoons with their lotus and golden grain. Then days of streaming sunlight came when their dreamy eyes clouded over, and they glanced at one another, the pain of hurt animals deep in their misty eyes.

Then from far away Over the Range came that ghostly call to exiled ears, that triumph call, that call of the wild from mountain crags, "*Kok-kai-e! Kok-kai-eee!*"—the hunting call of the munjon, the wild Kimberley aboriginal.

And that very night, last night, they had answered.

II

THE NEW LIFE

They could not help answering, of course. But I was sorry. You see, I had helped bring them in, had given the children a lift on such days when the travelling was long and rough and their feet had at last grown weary. I had come to know and like those tribesmen and their swift-eyed, wild women and wilder children. At first these children of the untamed forests had looked upon harmless me as something more than frightening, as very terrible. On the first occasion when I dismounted and lifted a sore-footed little girl into the saddle she went stiff in my hands, clutched the mane of that gigantic, fearsome beast, and screamed and screamed. She nearly frightened the life out of the old horse, let alone me; I had to cling to her with one hand and the bridle with the other to prevent the terrified horse from plunging away until a laughing tracker came hurrying up to lend a hand. Of course, a horse was a monster to that child, but when a feared white man lifted her up upon it she snatched at its mane and fastened her legs round its neck while screaming to her agitated mother that her last hour had come. Whether she, the horse, or I got the worst fright I'll never know.

That, to me at any rate, was a wonderful trip, riding the farthest nor'-west ranges of the West Kimberley in company with a police patrol seeking native killers who had speared quite a number of tribesmen in vendetta, in intrigue fanned by clash of jealousies, and by command of tribal law, and inviting the desperately sick to come back with us to receive the white man's medicine.

Over twelve hundred miles of that wild, primitive country we rode and walked, eventually with a long line of sick patiently trailing along behind, buoyed up with pathetic faith in the magic of the white man's medicine. Some had been brave enough to trudge out from their tribal lands and follow us back over the King Leopold Ranges right to Derby, a "white man camp" of unknown tenors to them. It was the black trackers, laughing at their fears, who had persuaded them to come all the way.[2]

But the patrol was over. And now had come the call of their own wild lands and they had gone—to their death, I knew, for their witch-doctors were powerless against these diseases. The big tragedy was that those who did safely return would now spread disease amongst their healthy people.

Thus six of the lepers, including the Big Leper, whose soles had dropped off his feet, escaped from the Lazaret, determined to walk back to their own

---

[2] This patrol was described in *Over the Ranges*.

country. The Big Leper, of course, was soon left far behind. On bloody feet he still hobbled after them into the night. At dawn the trackers Davey and Toby rode swiftly in pursuit. They caught only the doomed men, though they had travelled fast. Those men preferred death in the bush to treatment at the white man's hospital.

And death came to one man, old Jungolongoh. Poor chap! During the patrol, when the natives brought him down from the hills far away on the Sale River, Fred Merry the settler had remarked, "Look how he is trembling!" Merry had tried to convince him that he would soon return to his own country, that the patrol would only take him to the white man's country to see a wonderful doctor who would cure him; that then he would return in health and strength to his own country again.

I remembered now how he had stood there dumbly, his piccaninnies crying, huddled together a little distance away in the tall grasses by the Sale River, gamely holding their ground in awful fear of these two strange white men and the police trackers and all these snorting great horses and mules. In sheer terror they had crouched there with protective arms round one another, their tearful eyes all for their dumb father. In vain Fred Merry tried to assure them that if father would only go away with the police patrol the white doctor would cure him and within a few moons of time he would return, while if he stayed he would surely die. At last, in a dumb fear, Jungolongoh had come.

But now Jungolongoh had "escaped" with the others away into black night. Neither he nor the others, of course, could realize that it takes time to cure a bad disease. In their haste and in the darkness, and with this distressful disease upon him, he became separated from his hurrying mates. Next morning the trackers saw by his tracks that his diseased feet had swollen, very fast. Soon they were riding erratically upon those tracks that began edging away in wavering spirals, then in long, hesitating circles. These experienced men glanced meaningly at one another, for such tracks told plainly that Jungolongoh was going mad in his fear and distress. He was lost now by his mates, who would push on in fear of pursuit—for it is the law of the wild aboriginal that in time of distress he who cannot keep up must fall out and perish. The leper would be fearful also because he was passing through enemy country between Derby and the Range; he knew well that he would he hunted and fall to the spear of enemy tribesmen if his tracks were seen when daylight came. For that was the law too. Poor Jungolongoh! In worse and mounting terror as age-old superstition closed in upon him, he was lost and crippled and alone with the Spirits of the Night.

Then the trackers pointed as the tracks grew all bloody. Jungolongoh had started to run this way, then that, crying out in the darkness that the debil-

debils were after him. Here and there in frantic terror he had wrenched a limb from a mangrove-tree as a weapon of protection. His tracks led them right to the deep, gloomy creek. There he had slid down the steep, muddy banks—heavy black mud, these are—sliding down from black night into blacker water. As the crocodile grabbed him he snatched at a mangrove branch, but it broke.

Billy Adcock's store was a popular yarning place for all hands, men and women—there were only about three score women, if that many—while they waited eagerly for news that *Koolinda* or maybe *Centaur* had been sighted steaming north from Broome, for news of Jack Shaw or Bevan Evans, the mailmen bullocking their way through from the inland, for news of early horsemen or truck or patrol getting through from Fitzroy Crossing. One bright morning Steele's car from Yeeda station honked by with a wave and yell of *"Yak-ail Yak-ai!"* from the driver. Of course, Adcock's dog had to fly barking after the car and get beautifully splattered with mud.

"Even if that dog had caught that motor-car he wouldn't know what to do with it," mused Maitland Buckle.

"No," remarked a pleasant-featured wife, a bit broad in the beam. "Like that old fool of a husband of mine, chasing the young blondes."

"That's how I lost *my* hair," said Maitland cheerfully. "Like that ambitious dog, running against the wind. And I never caught one. Don't you worry, mum, hubby won't catch one either."

"I'm not worrying," replied mum decidedly, "but that old he-goat would, if he did catch one!"

"You're right, mum," declared Buckle solemnly, "as you can tell him when he comes crawling home to you with a flea in his ear. It's a sadly overrated pastime," he went on solemnly, "though I'll admit it was redheads was *my* downfall—an' how! I was always trying to catch one until I got caught."

"How she must have wished you'd got away!" laughed an impish brunette.

"How could I," demanded Buckle, "when she left me with not a feather to fly with?"

"My hobby's beer," said Jack Knopp, smiling.

"Sure it's not 'still waters run deep'?" suggested a young woman slyly.

For the likable Jack Knopp was a very quiet chap, a bachelor, though well capable of keeping a wife in comfort. And I'd heard folk wondering why he didn't take a trip south with this most interesting idea in view. For there were not nearly enough girls to go round in Derby, this tiny cattle port of the

West Kimberley nestling by the mouth of the "Old Man" Fitzroy. Barely one hundred and fifty folk clustered here where the turbulent waters of King Sound fought the brown floods that every Wet rushed out against their tumultuous battalions from the broad mouth of the Fitzroy. Just two stores and two pubs here, the Port and Scott's Club. No such luxuries as a barber's shop or a dentist or a chemist or a newspaper shop, of course, no such fal-lals in this he-man's land. Just one hundred and fifty folk clustered here, white and coloured, living in cheerful amity in their great isolation, a friendly little crowd indeed. The few marriageable girls were swiftly snapped up. And, believe me, they were pretty girls, lively as untamed fillies, and could dance and sing the night through when they got the chance, then turn to and do the cooking and washing for the whole family with a smile. And in the bushland back country, among those million-acre stations, there were only six white women, their frontier homesteads far apart, in all the West Kimberley.

"A woman here," croaked Mick the Frog hoarsely, "is worth her weight in gold."

"Meanin' it would take a bullick a week to keep her," growled old Bullocky Johnson decidedly. "No good ter me!"

"*You* wouldn't know what to do with her, anyway, you elongated, grey-whiskered old telegraph pole!" declared Maitland Buckle. "You're like the dog that chased the car."

"You're all the same!" broke in a buxom lass against the old bullocky's fierce retort. "You think you're great, wonderful he-men all done up in giant's whiskers! You've *all* got the same brains as the dog that chased the car; all your brains are under your belts. No wonder every mother advises her daughter to feed the brute!" She got our laughs, though the wiry-whiskered, tall old bullocky strolled indignantly away, escorted by his tiny, supercilious dog.

Three flash aboriginal stockmen rode by with gleam of teeth to some laughing feminine tribal Sally coming from down by the mangroves. Those stockmen seemed part of the lively animals they rode.

"Meeda station boys." Buckle nodded with deep satisfaction. 'The stations will start mustering very soon now, it's the end of the Wet. Notice that boy on the chestnut, that flash coon with the yellow neckerchief and leggings polished with goanna fat until he can see his chocolate face in 'em? He's from Mount Hart, away out at the foot of the Range. His brother and he went on walkabout at the beginning of the Wet before this. His brother was speared through the chest in the Isdell Gorge. Those Isdell nigs chased this fellow for miles in great fun, howling for him to stop, yelling that they only wanted his kidney fat—how tasty it would he when they guzzled it down their gizzards! They howled out to him that he could keep all the rest of him, they didn't want *him*, they only wanted to chew his kidney fat. But that lively fellow didn't stop—not that they expected him to, but they were quite certain they could leisurely run him down in their own country. They didn't, their invitations only seemed to make him run faster and farther. He got away from them in the night, anyway, and his kidney fat still greases his own kidneys. But they ate his brother's kidney fat, and his kidneys, too. Wolfed 'em raw, for, as you know, it's only raw meat that can transfer the strength of the victim to the eater."

With a wild yell a horseman appeared from nowhere, leaving us dodging a splatter of mud. A triumphant yell from the vanishing horseman as Mick the Rager wiped a dob of mud from eye and whiskers.

"Damn an' blast him!" growled Mick. "May he break his flamin' neck before he reaches Oobagooma!"

"Bert Orr is too good a horseman for that," chuckled Maitland. "Anyway, a slap of mud in the kisser couldn't hurt *you*!"

"Ter hell with you, too!" snarled Mick.

'Why didn't you jump back on those big splay feet of yours," asked Bob Graham, "instead of standing there swearing with mud in your eye?"

"Yah!" growled the bad-tempered Rager. "I've known the time *you* didn't jump out of the way quick enough, either. I only stopped a blob of mud in the eye, but you stopped an ounce of lead in the ribs."

Which retort referred to a hair-raising twenty minutes a few months earlier on a lonely out-station up river, where Bob Graham was working all alone. A stranger came riding along, was cordially welcomed, invited to a billy of tea, a feed, and a shake-down for the night. And then, without warning, he sprang at Bob, jagging at his face, his eyes, with fish-hooks, of all things in the world! Bob fought him off, the man pulled a gun, Bob dodged as the maniac aimed, then fired, and Bob reeled to the thump of a bullet. But he bored straight in and closed; it was the only hope, for this was truly a fight to the death. It proved a desperate struggle, with the only witnesses a camel and excited cockatoos screeching from the tree-tops. Bob won, he had to. Completely done in, for hours and hours he felt as if he could never move again.

This bullet was the "ounce of lead" of Mick the Rager's retort. Bob still carried that ounce. He carried another ounce also. But he could still laugh, and work, and fight like a thrashing machine when necessary. He had proved it yet again during this Wet when the boys had become a bit "obstruculous".

A mother was hopefully pegging washing on the line. Across the road Fred Rankine stepped out of the tiny "Tick-tack" office and gazed up at the now brilliant sky. I knew the youthful postmaster was gratefully drinking in the pure, sweet air of the rejuvenated Kimberleys. Out of the corner of my eye I saw old Womba Billy squinting at the sun as, quite sober now, his gorilla-like figure waddled across to confer with fellow-teamsters by the wharf shed.

Ah! So the *Koolinda* at last must be expected! Womba and his teamster mates with their blackboys would soon be riding away to their inland station camps to muster their donkey-teams for the road. What wonderful teams they were!

I glanced up the road to where children were playing in the sunlight by the big old baobab-trees. And there was Sam Waycott busily greasing his truck.

Donkey-teams? Trucks? A hazy picture, a vague premonition flashed before me—the end of an era! Old Womba Billy and his greybeard mates—were they on the way out? And the donkey-teams, and the horse- and camel-teams? And old Bullocky Johnson and the bullock-teams? Was this nearly the finish of the environment that bred characters such as Mick the Rager, Bunch-'em-up Gardiner, Kelly the Rake, Bindi-eye Walker, the Bony Bream, the Living Fossil, the Vivid Alligator, Dirty Mac the Teamster, and Chunder Loo. Long and brown and skinny Chunder, with his enigmatic grin and his slouching walk, had got his nickname from his resemblance to a well-known advertisement of the day. He would fight, though, if you said so. I can see him now, that long skinny form trailing over his shoulder the whip he seldom used, mooching along beside his team of eighty donkeys, five abreast, the lumbering wagon with a towering load of Noonkanbah wool, parrots screaming in the big river trees, native companions trumpeting and dancing on a sweet green flat beside the old Fitzroy. Chunder was a better man with language than the whip, but he reckoned he was a gentleman for all that, the proof being that, if ever he wanted to, he could harness his donkeys without swearing. There were plenty of other characters those days in the Nor'-west: the Dumbbell—wood from the neck up, so his friends declared, though now and again I used to suspect he was not quite so dumb as believed—the Freshwater Admiral, the Sawfish, the Croaking Frog—and he *could* croak, too—Paddy the Flat, Kelly the Rake—I've met his brothers or namesakes in each State—Blue Bob the Bastard from Borroloola, the Koolinda Chicken, the Prying Mouse, the Living Centipede, and numerous others.

Would the internal-combustion engine really change such utterly isolated places as the Kimberleys? Men still doubted it, but some were uneasy. And now a little aeroplane was flying up from Perth, two thousand miles away, with the mail each week to this little town where there had not been a mail a month, and none at all during the Wet.

Two purposeful aboriginal horsemen came riding along to the store, well mounted and well clothed in flannel, khaki trousers, leggings, slouch hat. These were police trackers, Old Larry and Davey. The sergeant was busy up at the police station, we knew, the boys running in the horses and mules for long patrols over the Range.

And the aborigines—were they doomed, too? Would these few wild ones soon he wild no more? Those few munjons, those aboriginals still living in their wild state just here and there in little corners of the continent, were helping to kill themselves off in ceaseless vendetta and feud. If these unfortunate prehistoric few could only be brought to see, to realize, and help themselves guard against, the fact that tribal feuds, that disease introduced by personal contact and by sea and air travel, were killing them out so tragically fast!

Was the aboriginal doomed? As the horse and donkey, mule and camel, the teamsters and greybeards of the era?

With an unhappy feeling I glanced up at the skies. But they were wonderfully blue and sparkling bright, smiling down on me and all the world with everlasting promise of life—new life.

III

COMING OF A NEW ERA

The day the *Koolinda* berths with stores and the shearers on her first voyage after the Wet is a great day, with every soul in the township, aborigines and all, and all the Derby dogs, lining the little jetty that had been cut out of the dense belt of mangrove-trees lining the bay. But what lively activity aboard immediately the little vessel tied up! An already loaded truck was slung overside, packed with three or four surprising things—motor-cycles, and all ready loaded to ride off on. And this in the land that was still the Land of Lots o' Time. The shearers strolled down the gangway, along the jetty, and across the "street" to Billy Adcock's store, some along to Jack Knopp's by the Meeda turn-off, others across to the pub. At the stores they bought only a few things they'd "missed out on", for most had brought their goods ready packed from Perth. Those strolling into the pub sought only a couple of drinks while their mates bought their goods from the store. How very different—!

A lively wool-classer among them yelled out a greeting and a joke to us onlookers.

"Louey Cicerago." Maitland Buckle nodded. "There's a story behind him, but he only laughs. Well-educated bloke, and he can sing and dance and juggle with the best of them on the boards. He *has* done the vaudeville shows; he's been a journalist, too, but now he travels up and down the coast wool-classing. Up here with the end of the Wet, works his way back down south through the stations, and lands in Perth with a big cheque just before next Christmas. A good wool-classer, but like all the shearers, leaving us up here to put in the Wet.

"You know Louey's a piebald, don't you? Well, he is—whopping big splotches of greys and browns and whites all over his body. He reckons Peter will be puzzled how to class him when he knocks on the Pearly Gates. He reckons, too, that if Peter sends him down below Old Nick won't have anything new to show him. That's because Louey was blown up. He and some of his mates went down a dark cellar during hot weather in Onslow to bring up a keg of rum. The keg was leaking, the cellar full of rum vapour. When they struck a light the whole business blew up. Louey reckons he's surprised many an audience with a conjuring trick, but that was the biggest surprise *he* ever got. One of his friends was killed, the other dying. Even though Louey was in a hell of a state he drove this man forty miles to medical help."

The last of the shearers stamped out of the pub and store, piled into the last truck, and were away on the road to Yeeda station. How very, very different from their ways only a season or two ago!

Then, taking their time in our Land of Lots o' Time, the shearers would camp round the port for a week or more before the last of them rode or followed a wagon to the stations inland up along the Fitzroy. Besides enlivening the little port, they used to bring quite an amount of business, too—spending money there, buying stores, livening the place up. But now, how different! Times were changing indeed.

Ah, well! Thank goodness the Dry had come again, anyway. The seasons weren't changing. Or were they?

Tired of trying to give away the localities of gold-mines, Jack Noble set out on his return to the Tennant's about the time the crocodile was eating old Jungolongoh. Jack Noble would travel along the one main Kimberley road two hundred odd miles east to Fitzroy Crossing, where his friends Alex Scott and Arthur Gardiner kept the store, and his friend Fallon was manager, then on another two hundred miles to Hall's Creek, whence my tracks followed his. Thence Jack carried on to historic Wave Hill station. The test would come with the next stage. Probably he would take the Tanami track, southward, then on through the heat-haze across waterless sands and spinifex to the soak at the Granites, then through more heat-wave and desolation eastward to Tennant's. He would arrive at about the same time as the drover of goats from far away in the opposite direction, from Mount Isa. If all went well, of course. For he would not arrive at all if anything went wrong along that track, which can he truly awful in a dry season. From Derby to the Tennant's that route would be roughly one thousand miles.

As for me, from Hall's Creek I would, and did, turn north, bound for business at Wyndham. Thence, when Fate and Chance and Transport decided, to Darwin. For travelling left much to chance, only a few years back in the Kimberleys. But how interesting it could be!

Near the Hall's Creek track, securely propped up against the massive trunk of a huge tree, reclined a dead horse, well sun-dried. Such a startling, grotesque thing must attract every passing eye—in a grim, thoughtful sort of way.

You see, southward, towards the desert fringe, the sun beating down there will sun-dry a carcass bone hard, should it be stretched out upon the right sort of earth. I well remember when I was in Egypt our horror and amazement at seeing lines of dead men, dead Tommies, stretched out after a terrific storm had scooped away the sand covering them. These "natural mummies" were soldiers killed in a battle of General Gordon's day. Of course, it seldom rains in that Egyptian desert. There are just the bare desert sands and the sun. I have heard it suggested that there may be some chemical in the sand which helps preserve the bodies. I do not know. It is a fact, though, that in places in that desert bodies buried in shallow graves may be uncovered by sandstorms many years later in a perfect state of preservation.

It is not generally so in Australia, of course. However, sometimes a carcass will be wonderfully preserved in a hideous sun-dried form. And that was what had happened to this horse.

You see, out there they don't like a man who ill-treats his dog or horse. Nailed to the tree-trunk above that fearsome caricature of a horse was a board upon which was painted in bold, heavy letters:

RIDDEN
TO
DEATH
BY

—and followed by a name we both knew.

"That bloke will go reaching for his gun when he hears about this. My travelling mate nodded grimly. "I've known men to be shot for less than this in these lonely old dry gullies around here."

"The Mounteds would have their trackers out and run him down," I said confidently. For Hall's Creek Mounted Police station, only a mile away, had built up a sternly efficient frontier record.

My mate was boiling the billy by a cotton-bush already heavy in yellow flower. He grunted, jerking his chin towards the wilderness that ran south to the desert fringe.

"Things have happened away out there," he said quietly, "that have *never* been found out—never will be!"

I said nothing. He knew the country, the men, and the natives. All I knew was that "out there" was as wildly primitive as the "day it was born". At its southern edge you stepped out of the desert fringe onto the Great Sandy Desert, a real desert, stretching some nine hundred miles south. But just here there was no desolation. A tangle of heavily wooded hills and ravines, gullies and well-grassed flats, watered creeks, plenty of game and bird life. As my somewhat solemn-visaged mate sorted out the tucker-box I was watching the big black cockatoos busily, quietly knocking nuts from the topmost branches of a heavily foliaged tree. Before I learnt things, I used to think what fools the big birds were, for they worked so hard, so efficiently with that sturdy nutcracker beak, that twist of neck, strong tug of head, and the big nut would simply fall down to earth. Just a rain of big, greeny-brown pods, fat nuts falling down to thump on the earth all around the tree. In my earlier days I used to think the busy birds were wrenching off the nuts hut, not being able to hold them, finally flew away in disgust.

Of course, I knew better by now, had learnt long since that practically everything that any creature in this world does, it does for a purpose.

In three days' time, provided they were nice hot days, those cockatoos would come flying back—this time to settle *under* the trees. For by now the warm sun would not only have finished ripening the nuts, but would be on the point of bursting open that steel-hard casing which protects the baby nut until it is able to burst out upon the earth and take root to start growing up into a tree—provided that no hungry thing, black cockatoos included, should pounce upon it and eat it, of course.

"Better get your tucker before the ants get it!"

As I came back to the hungry present my mate was listening, and then even I heard advancing hoofbeats as a horseman appeared among the timber.

"Old Mick O'Connor," said my mate with a grin, "and a long way out of his country. Looks innocent as a schoolboy caught raiding the pantry. I'll bet the stock he's looking for are not his own."

However, it's not etiquette to mention such a little oversight in the Kimberleys—or it wasn't in those days, anyway. Grizzled old Mick rode up, dismounted with that charming grin, trailed his horse's rein, unbuckled the pannikin from his saddle ring, and squatted on his heels beside us to take his place at the festive board as a matter of course. Old Mick was doing well, in his own quiet way, farther nor'-west, out in the munjon's country. By some means or other, by good health and good luck plus initiative and action, he was "building up a mob" and, if he did not get speared or otherwise disposed of by accident or intentionally, it was pretty certain he would end up a real cattleman with a million acres dinkum. It was all in the game, of course.

But somehow or other memory always coupled Old Mick with a fine friend of mine, old Inspector Tuohy away south of Broome, across on the Nullagine side. A travelling inspector of police over a vast district he was warmly liked by white and aborigines alike all over that scantily populated area. He and Old Mick met for the first time one day along the Nullagine road. Mick was making for that picturesque little wayside hotel hidden among the broad river trees. Mick was very partial to a noggin or two when it was within reach, he had now ridden twenty miles on this hot day to enjoy the drinks he was lifting to his lips in imagination as his horse neared the pub. And now came this stranger riding along, sure and he'd be good company. Then his eyes narrowed, even though the inspector was in civilian togs. Mick's face was a mask as both men reined in.

"An' who might you he?" inquired Mick guardedly.

"Oh, I'm only a person travelling about bringing tribulation to the community," answered the inspector mildly.

"So thin," said Mick instantly, "ye'd be Irish!"

"Yes, thanks be to God!" and the old inspector raised his hat.

"Ah! An' then," said Mick with a twinkle, "Ye'd only be bringin' troubles to the haythen. For bedad, an' I'm Irish, too!"

"Don't worry about it," replied this stranger. "Ye can't help being that. Live it down."

"Ah, h'm!" mumbled Mick. "An' is that so? Well, now, bedad," he added suspiciously, "an' what country do you come from?"

"The best in all Ireland."

"Bedad! An' what country may that be?"

"Tipperary."

"Oh, Tipperary is it? An' I come from Clare. An' what do ye think of that?"

"I don't think of it at all. It's not in Tipperary, an' never counts."

"Oh! An' ye're very sure of Tipperary?"

"I am."

"An' will ye have a drink with me?"

"No." Then, smiling at Mick's dumbfounded face, the inspector added, "Before ye demand to fight me, let me explain that I'm a wowser. So there! Let there be peace."

"Oh!" mumbled Mick and in a daze shook his horse's rein as the inspector rode on past with a cheery, "Will be seeing ye! But *not* at the pub!"

Which left Mick staring after him more bewildered than ever. For those sounded ominous words.

Of course, I don't mean to infer that Mick had been "up to something". As the old inspector said to me later, with a smile, "Sure, and I'm certain his conscience must have been crystal-clear on such a lovely mornin'."

But away out here old Mick had no fear of riding right up to an inspector of police, though he *had* unexpectedly ridden right upon us.

The meal over, we lit up and slung the tucker-box in the car. Old Mick stood up, casually picking his teeth with a bloodwood splinter, wiping ants from the seat of his pants with a horny paw, and mumbling, "Thanks fer the feed", all at the same time. He reached out for his horse and swung easily into the saddle as my mate let in the clutch and said, grinning, "I suppose you're riding down to the station to have a look at the new cook."

"No," replied Mick unconcernedly, "I've seen her. She's as raw as uncooked potatoes. Rather have the Fairies of the Glen meself."

As we struck north on the Wyndham road my mate casually remarked,

"Those lively little lubras of the lily lagoons have been of service to Old Mick, and I suppose to all the old hands, many and many a time. Saved their lives, too, at times, when the munjons have come in from the hills all het up to kill. One little Fairy of the Glen saved Old Mick's life twice from the same disgruntled warrior, and at great risk to herself. All hands out here would be very sorry to see the abos die out—for more reasons than one, too."

From this little outpost of Hall's Creek, deep in the hills towards the Territory border, we took the track directly north, actually a road now, to Wyndham, the port of East Kimberley. A rugged pathway of frontier romance to me.

Members of the Forrest 1879 Expedition, including Alexander Forrest (sitting centre) and the remarkable tracker Tommy Dowler (lower right).

IV

THE VALLEY

That rough, "primitive" roadway was, over centuries unknown to us, trodden by the horny feet of Stone Age men, and before them, no doubt, by animals. The Giant Kangaroo and the Diprotodon and other museum pieces would perhaps be the first to make thumping big tracks down that valley, lumbering heavily along from their lush pastures down to water. The first aborigines would follow in their wake—even as they do today, or rather did in those years "when my beard was black". For the simple reason that 'roos and wallabies "hop out" a path to water and thus flatten out pricks and burrs, which suits the abo's feet when he happens to be going that way.

Hence, some thousands of years at least before the coming of the white man, aboriginal tracks were plain down along that so picturesque valley.

The first white men to tread the earth of the Kimberley region were, as usual, the explorers, but away south-west from here, landing at King Sound, and forming Derby. The first party to penetrate *deeply* into the Kimberleys was Alexander Forrest's expedition of 1879, riding east from King Sound for hundreds of miles inland, through the Kimberleys and into the Northern Territory. On his return to the south Forrest reported finding what he believed to be probably gold country, and good pastoral country.

Two prospector mates, Phil Saunders and Adam Johns, so Warden Lamden Owen leaves on record, followed on that expedition's tracks and found gold at a locality later named Hall's Creek. Just then, right at the pinnacle of success, Johns fell desperately ill of malaria. Saunders struck camp, loaded the sick man and their goods on horses, and struck out doggedly for Palmerston (Port Darwin), five hundred miles north-east.

He made it, it is not known how to this day—five hundred miles with a desperately ill mate all through rough and unexplored country, thickly populated with hostile natives.

Several years later the Western Australian Government sent out another expedition to the Kimberleys. This expedition, too, reported the probable chance of mineral and pastoral country.

Prospectors Charlie Hall and Jack Slattery followed on, in the track of Geologist Hardman's map. Four hundred miles inland they found (and reported at Derby) payable gold near where Saunders and Johns had found it, at a rocky creek henceforward known as Hall's Creek, close by the spot where so many years later the mummified body of a horse was so securely propped up against the old gum-tree.

From the Forrest Expedition of 1879 to the "Rush to the Kimberleys" took a few years. Presently, the unlucky (though so lucky to be alive) Saunders claimed the Government Reward for the discovery of a goldfield in Western Australia. Warden Owen writes in his reminiscences, "Saunders claimed the reward, but, for some reason nobody seems to understand, his claim was disallowed." Which seems to me to be a wonderful case for the present-day query, "How lucky (or unlucky) can you be?"

Meanwhile, a group of New South Wales grazier-adventurers had already commenced the great treks which grew increasingly famous, from New South Wales with mobs of cattle up to the far nor'-west of Queensland, thence on to the Barkly Tablelands. Thence on again well into the Territory, and yet again to the Ord River and the East Kimberley. The Buchanans and O'Donnells and Duracks, the Kilfoyles, Gordon, Doherty, O'Connor—these and other old diehards made the first great treks.

The Forrest expedition really started the Rush to the Kimberleys, for the very term "good country" meant just the same to the land-seeking pastoralist as "gold" means to the prospector.

And the prospectors pushing eastward inland from Derby and the land-seekers pushing south from Cambridge Gulf and west from Queensland "struck oil" apparently at nearly the same time. The prospectors found their gold at Hall's Creek, the pastoralists the rich lands of the Ord and elsewhere up towards the Gulf, nearly three hundred miles north, then other lands extending down south to Hall's Creek and the Margaret.

Without venturing too closely into pioneering history, I believe it was the land-seekers who rode my valley first—half a dozen or so venturesome white men who sailed from New South Wales in a crazy little boat with a score or so of horses, and at last landed away down the practically unknown gulf vaguely named Cambridge. Just about where they waded ashore would very soon be known as Wyndham.

Soon the pioneer stations were established. The Macdonald brothers from Goulburn in New South Wales, droving their herd through four States, formed Fossil Downs station on the Margaret, quite close to Hall's Creek. The Duracks from Queensland came riding along the Ord and formed Lissadell and other stations. W. O'Donnell pushed southward at about the same time—and right in the nick of time, for the diggers had found gold and here was a hungry market for beef where otherwise a market would he a thousand miles away.

Within two years ten thousand men had passed through Hall's Creek, which was remarkable if you think of the slowness of news in those days, the slowness of travel, the unexplored country, the distances, and no supplies to he obtained on the way.

Revising this chapter for the last time before publication makes me grin. For on the table beside me is an account of the "pirate ship" *Santa Maria*, which has just landed her passengers in Brazil. Her exploits have entertained the world for the last ten days.

Well, the first of the Australians to travel by sea in the Kimberley Rush came in a pirate ship, the *Ferret*. It was a craft of one hundred and fifty tons, very different from the palatial liner *Santa Maria*. The *Ferret* was stolen at Glasgow and got clear away, her new crew sailing all they were worth for South America, with a horrid vision of their necks being stretched at the yardarm. But fortune favoured the "brave", and the little runaway reached the shelter of the Argentine safely, where her adventures really began. The world of that day followed her adventures with amusement—people seemed to think that pinching a ship from Scotsmen, from Glasgow itself, was quite humorous and that the vile perpetrators deserved to get away with it—if they could! However, I don't know the real innards of the seizure of the *Ferret*. She was safe with her monkey tricks when once in South American waters. In course of time, though, her new "owners" grew cocky. They accepted a highly payable cargo for Australia, and thus in this new country most unexpectedly met their Waterloo. The *Ferret* was seized by the authorities in Melbourne, and presently sold to the Adelaide Steamship Company. She sailed the coast of Western Australia and brought the first shipload of men to Cambridge Gulf in the Kimberley Rush. Where they landed the port of Wyndham was formed.

Though the region was so remote even to Australians—even today I would not be surprised if many Australians do not know the location of our Kimberleys—many diggers came from distant New Zealand. The first ship brought three hundred and fifty, with their supplies, and one hundred and sixty horses, from Wellington, New Zealand.

And now that valley would be trodden in earnest. The few land-seekers riding south along the hunting pads of the aborigines to scatter and vanish, and now the horses of the wild and woolly Kimberley Rush pouring down that same valley. Soon it would be broadened by the pads of camel-teams, finally by dray and wagon, then by the hooves of mobs of cattle stirring uneasily as the fateful smell of the wild munjons came creeping around them in the night. Some heart-breaking happenings there, when to a shower of spears, followed by piercing yells, the mob rose as one and stampeded in maddened terror away into the night. At times, too, the valley has thundered to gunfire, for the wild men, very numerous then, were not afraid to attack armed whites or the Afghan camel-teams as well as spear and drive off their animals. Thus the track was formed throughout hectic years, formed into a road—though no doubt the Romans of two thousand years ago would have sniffed in disdain.

The Kimberley Rush soon faded away, the diggers vanished, leaving the wild hills and valleys almost as they were. At the time of which I am writing, though, the Wyndham Track was one a motor-truck could rumble over, though the driver had to know his way about and how to handle the car to get through crossing broad streams that are raging torrents in the Wet, while the Sandy Bow has its quicksands even in the Dry, dodging boggy patches where possible, up and over rock-bound ridges, then rolling downward again over northward to creep into the valley that will lead it right to the sea, nearly three hundred miles north from Hall's Creek, with a bare half-dozen pioneer homesteads along the track breaking the monotony of untamed bush.

A road of ever recurring interest to me, while as to the valley itself every mile, every ridge and peak to either side, holds a story—oft, like Joseph's coat, of many colours.

V

WHERE THE WILD MEN ROAM

Dawdling along, for nobody knew when the boat would call in at Wyndham, camping where fancy called, we pulled up one sunset by Growler's Gully. Away back in the fastnesses there, Major some years earlier had gone on the rampage, sullenly mad against the whites, fiercely ambitious then to emulate the deeds of the notorious Pigeon, otherwise Sandamara, in the West Kimberley. Pigeon, with Captain and his band, had set out to drive the whites from the West Kimberley. He and his chief men could use firearms and played merry hell throughout the West Kimberley before being gradually decimated by police posses, until they were finally cornered and shot to pieces. Pigeon, mortally wounded, died firing his last cartridge, shouting curses to the trackers to throw him more so he could fight on.

Major, intelligent, aggressive, and a fine type of aboriginal, could handle firearms also. He decided to "clean up" the East Kimberley, to wipe out the few scattered whites, to succeed in the East where Sandamara had failed in the West. So Major shot Scotty McDonald in Growler's Gully at Mount John, then shot Fettle, then Jordy at Black Gin Creek by Lissadell. It took some time for the first news to drift through, then a patrol set out from Wild Dog police camp, another was quickly organized at Wyndham in the extreme north and another at Hall's Creek away in the south. Major gathered a mob round him, killers and cattle-spearers; his two best and gamest men were Nipper and Dippy, both handy with firearms. "Major's mob" came swarming out of the labyrinth of gorges whose cliffs and peaks embattle both sides of this valley. They killed the genial Kelly owner of Texas station, and by then the patrols were gathering and riding fast. But for the next two years the fear of death hovered all over the East Kimberley.

A terrible time for the half-dozen white women inland living in frontier homesteads a hundred miles apart, quite alone except for station blacks at such times as the worried husband had to ride away mustering. To add to the terror, not only the wild blacks but the semi-tame station blacks were all excited by the continuous raids of Major, Nipper and Dippy, who with their ever-growing gang were becoming more and more aggressively bloodthirsty as the months passed, howling their certainty that the last day of the white man had come. Inside the blockaded little homestead at night-time, with for company the Chinese cook and a muzzle-loader he probably could not handle, the lonely white woman spent frightful nights at times. For Major's gang, knowing every inch of that rough territory, could move with appalling swiftness. Camped here tonight, within twenty-four hours a hundred miles away. No one ever knew where they would turn up next.

Listening to the stories of the surviving white women who had lived through those hair-raising times, I used to marvel how they managed to carry on.

Major never succeeded in becoming the menace that Pigeon was, but it took the settlers' posses and police patrols two years to run his gang down. He worked from practically inaccessible hideouts within both sides of the range that form this valley. His men would come out into the valley even by night, defying primitive superstitions, strike in a lightning raid, then melt back into the ranges, and from there, away up on the cliffs, they would dance and yell and shake their spears and jeer at the frustrated horsemen away below. At other times they would simply strike and vanish, and no one would know into which wall of the ranges and thus on into the valleys, the gang had disappeared.

But the ceaseless hunt gradually wore down their nerves. They became increasingly boastful as if to bolster up their morale, then repeated escapes made them careless. Major, forsaking the safety of his wonderful hide-outs, broke away down the Osman, boasting that no white police or settlers could ever catch him. But once he broke from cover the chase was on his heels— most grimly so, as he soon realized.

In desperate straits he sped on and out into the desert fringe, attempting to hoodwink the patrols and double back. But those magnificent fastnesses were away behind him. The horsemen clung grimly to the outlaws' heels, driving them south, ever south, away from the ranges. There was no turning back for Major's mob; they were driven down into the low country right by the desert fringe where the patrols closed in. Like Pigeon, they died with rifles in their hands. And Growler's Gully, its sombre shadows near overwhelming our cheery campfire, knew their stealthy footsteps no more.

Some thirteen miles past Mabel Downs homestead the roofs of houses glinted away down in the valley—unusual sight indeed in this rugged Kimberley bush. There were only three houses, but that was a crowd indeed out there.

"Turkey Creek!" grunted my cobber.

"Yes. What a scene for a Wild West camp a few years back when the teamsters and camel-men from Wyndham and from across the Territory border camped here! They even came right away across from Queensland. What wild and woolly gatherings these must have been—all at a whisper of gold found in some utterly unknown speck in the continent called Hall's Creek!"

"And the bumboats!" added my companion grimly. "Don't forget them. And the cattlemen riding through looking for land and clean-skins while the crazy miners fresh landed from those funny little ships kept plodding on down into the land seeking Hall's Creek. Worked out the best gold in less than three years, then broke camp and trudged west towards the coast and kept plodding on four hundred miles further to the sea. And hit it on the shore of a wild gulf we call King Sound now. No Derby then, and they couldn't walk on into the sea. So they turned south, those who could still carry on—goodness only knows how they did it—plodded on to the Port of Pearls, or rather the Port of Buccaneers, and right on down to the Nullagine. My God! What men have done in times like those! What they've gone through in the name of gold!"

"You're doing very well," I said, grinning. "Carry on."

"You barely even grasp *fragments* of the picture," he growled. "Oh well, to your menagerie here"—and he nodded to a little open flat by the creek surrounded by bush and ranges—"just add the Afghan camel-drivers and their Indian mates, then all the half-wild horse and camel boys of the prospectors and cattlemen, the bullock- and horse-teamsters and the camel-teams, chuck in a few score Chinamen to make up weight, and you have a devil's brew when the bumboats began unloading their poison. You've thrown away the prospector's pick and dish for book-writing, but nothing you might read in the wildest book could equal the things that have happened here at times. Especially when a big mob's been camped here, as occasionally happened after a boat had recently unloaded just north of Wyndham. The flat down there then would be thick with browsing horses and camels and stock, uneasy because now and then a breeze would bring them a whiff of wild blackfellow. There'd quite likely be a sprinkling of mules and donkeys, too, and all the dogs of white men, brown men, yellow men, and black. The various owners of everything would be riotously sampling the bumboat's brew along their camps by this Turkey Creek. Meanwhile the blackboys away out over the flat, shepherding all that stock for the various owners, would be riding round feeding the animals very uneasily indeed, knowing perfectly well that just out in the timber the wild munjons were creeping in, seeking a chance of a spear-throw from cover. When that bad grog spread through those camps, there used to be a bit of sniping going on from all sides, believe me. Where there were flighty horses with plenty of saddlery and plenty of space and guns and wild blacks and even wilder grog there used to be some wild happenings at times. But those days are gone. And the motor-trucks have come."

And I really believe my grizzled old travelling partner sighed, if it were possible for a tough old gorilla to sigh.

I had been admiring the setting for those wild years. The broad, timbered valley running straight on into distance where a big blue range shot right across it, with down below the tiny post office of the overland telegraph line, with Mrs McMurray in charge, and beside it Mrs Rhatigan's cottage, and opposite them across Turkey Creek the neat little police station. The valley walled in by picturesque ranges, the Pink Range standing out a deceptive line of flat tops, walling the valley there with precipices. My eyes never got tired of glancing along there, for there was always change at any time of the day. Some days at midday the valley walls would start to ripple with faint colouring gradually shimmering into pink, and every now and then into yet deeper tints, developing a glorious reddish glow towards sunset. Some days the sky artist, the sun, would spray his cliffs with gold. Sometimes his fancy would turn to fire. It seemed to depend upon the strength and intensity of the rays he splashed upon his rocky canvas; it depended, too, upon drifting clouds that deflected rays, or diluted them, or threw gliding shadows down and along and over the painted walls. In the Dry season, to glance across those miles was to see a picture being slowly, gracefully painted in colours that never dried, colours ever living, ever changing day by day, but always there until hidden by the curtain of night—only to burst out with the dawn into fanfares of moving, glowing splendour.

But just now, as our truck pulled up by the creek, those cliff-walls were miles of deep purples splashed here and there by dull fire, while across the valley, high up, there gently climbed straight up towards the sky a thin pencil of smoke from a native look-out. So from time immemorial the aborigines had smoke-signalled their news.

Our own "signal" was that there was still no news of the boat from Wyndham, only one hundred and thirty-five miles northward now. And the "signal" came via the little box of a post office here by the overland telegraph line, the only means of immediate contact with Perth, some two thousand miles south. This the Western Australian overland telegraph line, of course. There is another great overland telegraph line running up through the Cape York Peninsula of Northern Queensland, while the daddy of them all is *the* Overland Telegraph Line, the continental line running up through South Australia and the Northern Territory to Port Darwin. These telegraph lines were a heaven-sent lifeline for the isolated north of the continent until the coming of the radio and the aeroplane—and afterwards, too. What untold stories there were in those whispering wires! Of the idea and the preparatory exploratory parties, of the building, then of the men who manned the tiny telegraph stations so far apart throughout the lonely areas. One story here at Turkey Creek was of Rhatigan the linesman. A good man, though wild and woolly. Hot-tempered, too, and liable to be a devil in drink.

Way back, when he was a constable in Wyndham, duty took him aboard an incoming boat. There was plenty of drink aboard. And when Rhatigan really woke up, a week later, the little vessel was just tying up at the Derby wharf.

"An' is *that* so?" said Rhatigan as he rubbed the back of a hairy hand across a fevered brow. "An' here I am in Derby, the blessed capital of the West Kimberley, while all the time I should be hundreds of miles north in Wyndham, blessed capital of the East Kimberley. But I'm a million miles away in Derby. An' right here be where I resign."

Which he did, pronto. However, men were scarce up there in those days as they are today. Rhatigan was offered a job as linesman up north at Turkey Creek, and accepted.

A tough consignment to the right man. Apart from taking a good chance of being knocked about or worse in some wild brawl when the teamsters or coloured wanderers were playing up when a bumboat happened to be in, the linesman had to "ride" those lonesome wires stretching through wild bush and right down the valley from Wyndham to Hall's Creek. Keeping those wires in repair was a gruelling job in some seasons. For, quite apart from natural accidents, such as trees falling across them in the tropical storms, the telegraph wires suffered because they were the first thing a man in desperate straits made for. Whether perishing of thirst or fever, or crippled by accident, or savaged by blacks, he would try to reach the wires and cut them. Then he would hang out, if he could, under the wires until some distant linesman came jogging along to find the fault and repair the wire. The wild munjons, too, would expertly cut the line by monkey-climbing a pole and hammering through the wire with a rock. With a good length of it they would then hurry away back into the hills. The wire, of course, made wonderful spearheads, hooks, and quite a number of handy things, far superior to similar ones made of wood or bone. And then aggressive hillmen resented being disturbed, especially by one lonely linesman, even if he did have a tame blackboy riding with him. With excited vim, they would declare they'd cut out that blackboy's kidney fat and wolf it if they could only catch him.

What cared Mick Rhatigan for the numbers of such troublemakers, what cared he for their yells and spear-brandishing? Provided they were not too well sheltered by hilltop, rocks, or timber, he would set spurs to his horse and gallop straight at them, firing from the saddle.

His narrow escapes were legion, but he dearly loved a fight. He certainly got plenty.

VI

THE WOMAN-STEALER

But Rhatigan fell foul of the telegraphist, the postmaster. They camped only a hundred yards apart and often had no other company for considerable periods—just the two of them, and the horses, and a dozen half-tamed blackboys, at times when the lone mounted policeman was away with his trackers on patrol, and when no supply teams were passing through. The little telegraph hut faced Rhatigan's camp down there by the creek in the valley, lively with bird life and often scented by flowers, all walled in by purple cliffs which were the abrupt faces of the wild ranges peopled by healthily aggressive Stone Age men and their agile families. You'd think two men living in such isolation, with the very real chance of being speared or tomahawked any hour of the day or night would both help and guard one another.

Not a bit of it. There came periods when they scowled at one another in such a way it would have turned the milk sour, if they'd had any milk.

Then one day the postmaster made some sarcastic remark to which Rhatigan took immediate exception. And it was on.

A man in a bush camp with only himself for company day after day for months at a time often gets half sulky with himself. These two were happier, for they had each other to snarl at. They had also those blacks willing enough to do an odd job for a plug of tobacco or a broken bottle to make knives out of, half-tamed hillmen who could never be really trusted. As for the munjons, these thoroughly wild men knew far and wide that if they approached the camp any closer than a clearly defined circle down round the flat, they would probably be fired at. If the wild people wanted contact with the whites at all the definite rule was that it must be through the horse-boys.

There was a truce now only when the policeman was in camp. But when he rode away———!

So the two lone white men, a sour-looking pair now, were "not speaking". Not on grunting terms, even. When Rhatigan of necessity occasionally strode across to the little telegraph station for orders, those orders, as he fully expected, were thrown at him. He would snarl back in reply and insultingly show his back as he strode away to his horse and job.

One day Rhatigan from his camp was glaring across the creek at the postmaster glaring back from his tiny veranda. The postmaster deliberately put his fingers to his nose—and *wiggled* them!

With a wild Irish howl Rhatigan leapt inside camp and snatched his rifle. As he emerged the postmaster leapt for his door, slamming it behind him as Rhatigan sprayed the post office with bullets.

However, little exchanges of opinion like that are liable to enliven even the best-regulated camp, if the liver and environment are favourable.

Rhatigan's luck was remarkable in that he survived for so long, for miraculously he escaped what could have been serious accidents in other ways; more than once, too, his contempt of danger and of natives brought him within an ace of losing his life. Perhaps his narrowest shave was his greatest surprise; he knew nothing about it until it happened. Quite innocently, and for a wonder to his dismay, he was caught up in a native vendetta. And by that sulky, beetle-browed, hook-nosed swine, his own aboriginal horse-boy, Joe Wynne, aided by another trusty horse-boy, Nipper, who had been in his employ for some years past. Fancy trusting such ungrateful, murderous ! What a fool he had been!

So thought Rhatigan, too late.

It all came about through the immemorial pastime of woman-stealing, which has brought woe upon mankind since untold thousands of years before Helen of Troy. And this risky sport caught the, for once, innocent Rhatigan within its toils.

This-a-way: Joe Wynne, who wormed his way into being one of Rhatigan's trusted horse-boys, was really a member of a coastal tribe near Port Darwin, away over the ranges on the Northern Territory coast to the north-east.

What then brought him from the coast down into this inland Kimberley valley, where by tribal law death awaited the trespasser?

Brains, and hatred, and vengeance.

In happy years gone by his coastal tribe had accepted an invitation to the yearly ceremonial corroboree of the Making of the Young Men. The visitors could come inland only as far as the meeting grounds and at the agreed time. Similar rules were observed by the inland tribes venturing north to meet them.

Well, then, a venturesome young warrior from Turkey Creek travelling north to the ceremonies with those inland tribes was soon to be widely nicknamed by the few scattered whites as "Hopples". That is, when he would become leader of "Hopples's Mob" at about the time a certain wild Irish-Australian took over a linesman's job at Turkey Creek. Before that, though, this boyish warrior was merely a wary but fightable young buck with an eye to the main chance, his agile person gifted with the priceless knack of a quick get-away.

And the main chance came in the primitively attractive sloe-eyed girl wife of another wild young warrior, that same young warrior who by and by would adopt the "white-feller" name "Joe Wynne" to help him make use of the white man's ways when he was ready to claim his vengeance.

And now, shielded by the excitement of the corroboree, that wide-awake young warrior, Hopples, got clean away with that slippery young wife, back to his tribal fastnesses in the ranges beside Turkey Creek.

Ah, well!

Joe Wynne, that hoodwinked and murderously embittered young husband, had to return with his tribe to the coast according to tribal law when the ceremonies were over. Back in his own tribal lands he brooded as time went on. It seemed hardly possible for him to make his way inland, then away down into that unknown valley, through those alert and hostile tribes; inevitably he would be tracked and speared well before he could snake his way down to Turkey Creek and beyond, let alone before he could find his man within the surrounding gorges.

This solving of a particularly ticklish tribal problem was yet another and very early proof that the aboriginal has brains.

There appeared to be only one chance, a long and arduous way, to wreak his vengeance. This wronged warrior must first learn the white man's language and ways, must put aside for the time being his aboriginal independence, and work for white men. Then, and then only, when he had gained their confidence, could he penetrate into his enemy's country, and only then when in the company of, and thus protected by, white men.

Even so, he had to be as secretive as possible. And patient.

He secured a station job on the coastal fringe and worked until he was known as a sullen, but good worker. Then, seeking opportunity, he took another job on a station yet farther inland. Finally he got a job on a station right down in the valley near the Turkey Creek district, the wife-stealer's tribal country. It was down there, somewhere within that labyrinth of ranges, that recently he had heard his enemy was camped. And at this particular station and time he heard yet further news.

That lively young warrior, the wife-stealer, had, so it seemed, developed with the times, too. He proudly admitted he was now a bit of an outlaw, and with a "white-feller name" he was now the boss of "Hopples's Mob". He *was* Hopples! And he knew all about firearms. With a cheerful grin he admitted to losing his precious stolen firearms through a "mistake" on his part, but cheerfully assured all interested that he would soon steal plenty more.

Grimly Joe Wynne, the vengeful stockman, thought of the long, long time before he had succeeded in prevailing upon his white employer to teach him, then allow him the use of a rifle. It appeared he would need that knowledge now.

How quickly he and his enemy had learnt the white man's ways, even to throwing aside the spear for the repeating rifle, the terrible "thunder-stick" that but a few years earlier could put a whole tribe to terror-stricken flight. But now———! Savagely he snarled, with a twitching of his trigger finger.

At last Joe Wynne got his big break, secured a job with white man Mick Rhatigan, the telegraph linesman, right away down there in Turkey Creek!

Brains, will-power, cold-blooded determination had accomplished this—from the Stone Age into murderous civilization at a step.

Joe Wynne was now not only on the edge of the very heart of his enemy's country but was also safe under white protection, so long as he did not leave it. For here was a tiny telegraph office, and Rhatigan's little home, with just across the creek now the neat little police outpost with mounted, armed white police in charge—J. F. Flinders, P.C. 943, and J. Cullen, P.C. 1094, with their frighteningly efficient black trackers, Sandy and Joe, and their horse-boys.

Yes, thought Joe Wynne grimly, here he would be secure in his enemy's country until the time came for him to strike. After which, of course—but he shrugged *that* away.

Joe Wynne set to work to dig himself in well and truly at this job. And Mick Rhatigan gradually came to more or less trust him. This slouching, low-browed Joe Wynne was of the sulky type, given to long-continued brooding before he bounded into action. He was not trusted by the few cattlemen who had come into contact with him. But Rhatigan prided himself on knowing men, and especially believed he could "pick" a native. Other men disliked this silent, wary-eyed son of a God-knows-what. Well, then, Rhatigan liked him—or employed him, anyway. From the start this boy had been willing and anxious to please, which suited Rhatigan. "An' if he ever," Rhatigan declared, "so much as chucks a mornings-after scowl at me I'll belt the flamin' daylights out of him!"

But Joe Wynne did all he could to please his uncertain-tempered, violent-fisted boss.

Rhatigan really did trust Nipper, for Nipper had worked faithfully for him for some years past. He was pleased to see how well these two boys got along together, for it made life easier for him.

With Nipper's aid and from the Turkey Creek blacks as time went on, Joe Wynne picked up more and more information about the "run" and habits of Hopples's Mob. The increasing depredations of that now notorious, elusive little mob were freely discussed by whites and blacks alike—with delight by the aborigines, and with uneasy foreboding by the whites, who vividly remembered Major and Banjo and their hit-and-run gangs.

Meanwhile Mick Rhatigan, the Turkey Creek linesman, was constantly riding up and down the lonely telegraph line keeping it in order, and with him rode his aboriginal horse-boys, Nipper and Joe Wynne. Thus Wynne travelled up, then down, this picturesque valley along which the telegraph line runs between the Painted Ranges, this line which marked the border of his enemy's country. As they rode along, when the quick-tempered linesman did not have his eye upon them, Wynne used to scowl towards the ranges where grim peaks pointed out by Nipper marked several favourite hideouts of Hopples.

With a delicious awe did Nipper point out landmarks shadowing those gloomy fastnesses. For this up-and-coming bandit, Hopples, was now an aboriginal hero, beginning to attract to him notorious tribal killers and cattle-spearers. It was his ambition eventually to launch out against the whites as a bigger and better Major or Banjo, those aboriginal heroes who had "shot up" the whites, then "shot it out" with them. And so now it was with a fearful curiosity that the tribesmen whispered Hopples's name and deeds round the campfires at night. As Nipper murmured all this information to him in awed tones that already deep frown upon Joe Wynne's brow grew still deeper. He began to realize that he had a far harder nut to crack than he had bargained for. The more impossible vengeance now appeared, the more savage he grew inside; he had to close his mouth tight lest that stern white man see his grinding teeth.

Slowly but surely he gained Nipper's confidence and began to work on him with a really devilish cunning. Then, at the right moment, he poured out all his troubles. And Nipper's eyes grew wider and wider. Hopples! This fiercely whispering warrior beside him in white-feller clothes was hissing out words that meant he was tracking Hopples of Hopples's Mob to kill him. To kill Hopples—Hopples the Killer!

But Wynne knew how to work upon the instinct for tribal vengeance bred in the aborigines over thousands of years. Listening to him, Nipper was soon sharing his feelings, knowing just what *he* would do should any renegade steal his favourite woman. As primitive instincts stirred hotly within him so the terror of Hopples's name slowly began to fade. Most fiercely then Wynne poured out his lust for revenge. Nipper nodded, frowning understandingly. Every aboriginal understands that uncontrollable, burning thirst for vengeance. Then, in hoarse, snarling tones Wynne asked Nipper's aid in vengeance when the time should come.

Nipper promised.

And the time came.

VII

WHILE DEATH CREEPS NEAR

A bright day in the Kimberleys. The Wet was fast drawing to a close, really these were the first new weeks of the Dry. The earth was green and bursting with new-born life and promise.

Death seemed out of all reasoning where everything was so much alive. Mick Rhatigan at Turkey Creek quite cheerily swung his long, sinewy form into the saddle with a wave and a nod to ride off. Behind him mounted his horse-boys, that cheery Nipper and his surly mate Joe Wynne, driving before them the pack-mules loaded with camp swags and tucker. There was a tracking job ahead, for horses were missing, lured away by the captivating scent of sweet new grasses. As they rode through the bush they scattered, each man glancing down for tracks upon the still soft earth. By agreement they met again at the Big Waterhole at Mistake Creek at sunset, and camped. None of the three had seen any sign of the horse tracks. The following morning Rhatigan ordered Joe Wynne to go out towards Buttler's Bottle-tree to seek the missing horses, Nipper to seek in another direction, while he would search the flats down along both sides of Mistake Creek. The blackboys left the camp on foot, leaving the mules and packs in camp.

The very few whites along the valley right from Wyndham to Hall's Creek dubiously considered this low-browed, surly boy of Rhatigan's a dangerous native, and now he certainly looked it, creeping through the bush, face set in a harsh frown, brooding sullenly, everlastingly, on his revenge. But today there was an unconscious, stealthy spring in his step as he stared down unblinking, on the earth, his shaggy face lit up with animal cunning as he sought tracks—*not* horse tracks. For he was now right in his enemy's country, and his enemy, like the season, was moving, the time of his brooding, like the wet season, was past. Ah! So hard and long had been the time, straining all the aboriginal's stock of patience and cunning to get just where he was. The man who had stolen his woman, his first girl, that wonderful girl of so long ago—that hated man and his friends were now camped not far away. He knew! He stared down when he cut their tracks, his teeth grinding, his features diabolic. So long ago! Ah, but now Rhatigan, having seen neither horses nor tracks, came plodding back to camp in the afternoon. His blackboys Nipper and Joe Wynne appeared about half an hour later. They had seen tracks, but not those of the horses wanted, so Nipper assured the linesman. But he now felt certain they would find them tomorrow, morning time.

The next morning (Monday 29th) the linesman left camp early, having ordered the boys to make a thorough search high up Mistake Creek and along both sides of it, and having given them their lunch to take with them. Rhatigan then rode away in a westerly direction towards a blacksoil plain he knew of. Sweet grass would be springing up there, and the horses might have made for it; their instinct tells them where the sweetest tucker grows.

Joe Wynne and Nipper walked away from camp—not far. Joe Wynne grunted, they stood stock still, staring at one another. Quickly the glare in Wynne's eyes was reflected in the eyes of Nipper, their breaths now coming deep and fast as suddenly they crossed and locked their arms in the Squeezing Vengeance Grip of the aboriginal. Nipper's mouth gasped open wide to the heat of Wynne's fanatical grip and blazing eyes, as there came faintly to them through the hushed bush silence the thud of hooves going away. Rhatigan was now well away from camp.

With a final glare into one another's eyes they broke their armlock, with the stealthy caution of panthers stalking prey they crept back to camp.

In a moment Joe Wynne was kneeling beside the pack-bags.

"Get rifle from swag quick!" he grunted urgently. "I finish Hopples's Mob *this* time! Finish altogether!"

He seized a Winchester .44 rifle and a bag of cartridges from Rhatigan's swag as Nipper snatched out the .32 repeater Winchester. Then ran out into the bush, and very soon came upon the missing horses. They had them already "planted", of course. The day before they had driven those horses to a handy little hide-out Nipper knew of, taken off their bells, and hobbled them short.

Quickly they saddled up, mounted, and rode away. All the rest of the day they rode along ever ascending timbered spurs, higher and higher up into the ranges. It was in that direction, according to native rumour relayed to Nipper down in Turkey Creek, that Hopples's Mob were camped while preparing for a raid. Those native sympathizers who had given news to Nipper had not the faintest idea what the mind of the "foreign" aboriginal Joe Wynne was preparing for.

And it *was* up there, cosy in a secluded little fastness, that Hopples's followers were camped, quite happy and cheery, powdering up ochre to decorate their bodies so they would make a brave show when they swooped down on their lightning raid into the valley. They would certainly liven up that "white-feller camp" down in Turkey Creek *this* time, and they were confident of securing "plenty" firearms and arming themselves "white-feller fashion"; then they would show all hands just what they could do. Hopples, their trusted leader, joked and laughed as his men worked over their spear-points, all hands in a rollicking good humour. Well armed with spears and nullah were the fighting men, but Hopples was proudly armed with a stolen revolver. And, unusually enough, he could really use this difficult weapon. Tiger was his lieutenant, a proved fighter, too. Good men, though of lesser degree, were Mundy, Yarri, Wallaby, Charlie, and Ben. With their lubras Hopples's Nellie, Tukayurka, Mona, Long Nellie, Elsie, Gipsy, and Manjun — and a few children, this little band of nomads lived together, raided together, hunted together, and were hunted, ever ready for fight or flight as circumstances should suggest. For pursuit, attack, and vengeance hover always over native life. Hopples's Mob were not strong enough yet to break out as the "Big Heroes", Pigeon and Captain, had done, or as Major and Banjo. But Hopples had great hopes of gaining recruits with the success of the coming raid, a well-planned surprise attack, his most ambitious plan as yet, to raid a white man's outpost. For he knew, of course, that the tiny settlement was "bare", there were no travellers or teams or any sign of such within miles of Turkey Creek. In a happy confidence Hopples's men and women laughed and joked over their preparations, enthusiastically watched by the highly impressed, big-eyed children.

This was all told later by the pitifully few survivors.

Not even the harsh, mournful call of the black cockatoo warned them of enemies ever creeping closer up along the scantily timbered ridges. But even if they had known of the two horsemen they would have laughed that number-to scorn. The only enemies they thought of now were possible police patrols, but they knew there was no patrol anywhere at all handy.

By sundown Joe Wynne and Nipper were high up in the ranges. They hobbled their horses tight, then crept along a little farther on foot and quietly camped. No fire, of course.

Meanwhile, far away down below out in the flat country, Rhatigan came riding back to camp. He had found no sign of the horses along there on that blacksoil flat, and he felt puzzled and strangely uneasy. Surprised at no sign of a campfire, he concluded and hoped his blackboys must be camping on the tracks of the missing horses. Hobbling his horse, he set about preparing his evening meal. It was some time before he noticed that the pack swags had been interfered with. The rifles were gone! He stood stock still, listening, his alarmed face, his wary eyes, slowly turning to all points of the compass. But only the sigh of the night breeze whispered uneasy premonition in his ears. Hastily he searched in a circle well out from the camp. Just as darkness fell he found faint sign of horse tracks leading away — towards the range!

What a fool he had been! After all these years, ever to trust black boys!

Swiftly he stamped out the fire. Crouched under cover well away from the camp, he would spend a sleepless night, hand to revolver at every creeping sound.

In the timber far up there in the cold range, the faint smell of campfire smoke in their nostrils, Joe Wynne and Nipper were right back to the aboriginal primitive again. In whispers they discussed their plans, then Wynne's teeth gleamed as suddenly they glared into one another's eyes— they heard the distant, smothered laugh of a lubra. Hopples's camp was just over the little rocky rise ahead, just over on the other side, where the steep head of a gully began.

Down there in that sheltered gully the little party of men, women, and children were unconcernedly cooking the wallaby and rock python and smaller game the hunters had brought in with the sunset. They would sleep, though lightly, sheltered down there from any cold wind of the night.

Alas! Some among them would sleep deeply—tomorrow night.

Camp kitchen, in the West, 1928.

VIII

THE MASSACRE

In that chilly coldness which comes just before the dawn, Nipper sneaked away. He had to go the farthest, creep up over the rise in front, then cautiously down along the gully hank until he was past the sleepers, then drop down into the gully itself. Thus he would be "behind" them and the bottom of the hill. Cautiously then he must begin to work his way back up along the gully. Wynne would give him time, then sneak up over the rise, creep down into the head of the gully, and carefully work his way down along it.

A plan perfect in its deadly simplicity. For with every step they took they would he approaching one another, with the sleeping camp somewhere between them, deeply asleep down there in the gully darkness. It is in the numb chilliness just before dawn that the aboriginal sleeps with a dull heaviness. When the alarm came these startled nomads would run either up or down the gully, into death from Wynne's rifle or Nipper's, whichever way their startled wits and feet took them. Then, should some try to escape by leaping the precipitous gully sides, they could be shot back like scampering wallabies trying to leap up a cliff-face.

Though Nipper and Wynne's stealthy movements were timed perfectly a dog snarled warningly with the first steel grey of dawn. Instantly Nipper fired a shot to demoralize the sleepers, who, instinctively snatching spears as they leapt to their feet, glared from sleep-sodden eyes, the women hissing urgent commands for quietness to their children as they snatched them to their arms, listening in heart-thumping alarm.

Bounding down the gully with levelled rifle, Wynne saw Tiger's startled head come peering round a wild pear tree. He fired, and as flame stabbed into the still gloomy gully it showed Tiger falling, his face all screwed up as frantically he clawed the earth. As the lubras shrieked, Hopples, Mundy, Charlie, Yarri, Ben, and Wallaby jumped round and went leaping down the gully right into the rifle of Nipper.

"Stop!" he yelled to the crazy stampede as frantically Wallaby slipped spear to woomera, but stumbled sprawling at the feet of the bounding men. Nipper fired again at Hopples, coming straight at him with revolver levelled. He missed, and Hopples's bullet parted his hair, putting the fear of death into him as Hopples leapt aside for another shot.

"Run!" Nipper yelled urgently, warningly as he swung the rifle barrel round towards Hopples. "Run! Wynne get you!" and Hopples leapt back up the gully again after his vanished mates.

Nipper had been too frightened to fire again lest a second later the frenzied men overwhelm him, but his quick-witted warning had turned them back and saved his life. He was panting from fear, though, as he admitted later. But he had wounded Wallaby and put the others to flight. Glaring round, he breathed thankfully, then ran forward with rifle levelled at Wallaby, crying, "Jump up quick time!" The wounded aboriginal sighed, lifted stealthy hands from his spears, hauled himself erect, and walked unsteadily up back towards the head of the gully while Nipper quickly scattered the spears, then ran off into the timber seeking the crouching women, doubly excited now by the echoing in the gully ahead as Wynne fired right and left.

Wynne sped down the gully after the last four runaway men. These raced away as if the fiend was at their heels. Hopples, lower down the gully and in safety, pulled up panting and wheeled round. The revolver was shaking in his hand, but rage and bravery were now overcoming the nerve-breaking alarm. He heard the thump of feet and ran towards them, his lips set in a snarl, his revolver wrist growing steady. The runaways dashed past him with the now blood-crazed Wynne in close pursuit. Hopples crouched down with levelled revolver, but Wynne had seen him and, as if tripping and falling, really leapt aside among the bushes to suddenly appear with levelled rifle yards away to the right. He fired as Hopples swung round, and Hopples rolled and plunged away into the bushes, mortally wounded. Wynne swiftly ran him to earth and shot him dead.

Nipper had cornered most of the lubras, who, clinging to their small children, were huddled in a terrified group round the wounded Wallaby. Wynne now came striding in amongst them, glared down at Wallaby, and mercilessly killed him.

"Pick 'em up firewood quick time!" he shouted. "We burn him Tiger and Wallaby!"

The terrified lubras scattered for wood.

"Take best-feller lubra!" he snarled at Nipper. "Go back! Bring 'em up horses. Quick!"

And Nipper, now thoroughly scared of this killer he had helped unleash, obeyed quickly.

Wynne watched the lubras working for awhile, then shouted, "Pick 'em up spear! Quick-feller!"

At a trembling run in the now fast brightening sunrise they collected the scattered weapons, a young lubra choking down cries like a wounded animal as she bent to collect Tiger's spears. Their hands trembled superstitiously as they picked up the weapons of the three warriors who would need their loved spears no more. Wynne's tigerish eyes missed nothing, his face twitching in a cold fury. He chose a hiding-place between two boulders and snarled at the women to hide the weapons there, with a half-formed idea that they might come in handy for his own use later on.

"Walk up longa gully!" he snarled, and they crept fearfully ahead before his rifle muzzle. He forced them up to the ridge where Hopples was lying staring blindly up at the now bright dawn sky. Meat-ants were already breakfasting at his bloody wounds.

"Put stones and spinifex longa him!" he snarled.

He stood there just above them, glaring as they piled bundles of the resinous, fiercely burning spinifex upon that stricken body. Wynne stood there, breathing deeply. His blood-lust was not satisfied. At long last he had killed his enemy, but sight of these women maddened him yet again. Several of these women were Hopples's women, and Hopples had taken *his* woman.

Now *he* had Hopples's women!

His face growing diabolical again as he watched the terrified women collecting and throwing the firewood over Hopples's body, he rose slowly and jerked his rifle down the gully. They faced him, the sticks dropping from limp hands, their dark faces taking on a greyish hue, then they stumbled down the way that steadily pointing rifle barrel was insisting—down the gully. They had only gone a few yards when Wynne whipped the rifle to his shoulder—fired. At Hopples's Nellie first—she screamed, stumbled, and fell drunkenly forward on her face. He swung the rifle at Long Nellie, it took two bullets to finish her. To the vicious crack of the rifle shots again echoing down the gully the other women were flying screaming through the timber with the tiger now close on their heels. He fired again and Gipsy flung up her arms and fell. He blazed at the others vanishing amongst the timber, then stood panting, glaring round. There crouched before him two girls, their terrified eyes gazing up as a paralysed rabbit might gaze. He shot little Elsie. Mona put her trembling arm round the convulsive body. Wynne shot her through the head. Her arm was still round Elsie when the trackers found them days later.

Nipper had come up with the horses. "Quick-feller!" shouted Wynne as he leapt into the saddle. "Track 'em up! Shoot every feller before they tell 'em white police!"

Too late! Yarri and his fellow runaways had not ceased running from the moment Hopples fell. And aborigines, for speed and sustained endurance in running, have no equals in the World. And the way was all downhill with an awful fear urging their flying heels.

Far away down there Mick Rhatigan, after his uneasy night, had cooked an uneasy breakfast, concluding that maybe he'd better ride back to Turkey Creek and report this strange disappearance of his horse-boys with the rifles. Bad—bad indeed. They had not attempted to shoot him during the night, as he had believed they would. What then, was their idea?

Very relieved to find his riding horse feeding quietly near by, he saddled and rode away. Soon he cut the tracks of horses—his own! And not making back towards Turkey Creek and home, but away back up to the ranges! His practised eye on the tracks told him the horses were being ridden. He decided now to solve this mystery on his own. An anxious frown clouding the bewilderment on his face, he glanced swiftly round, made sure his revolver was in working order, turned his horse's head back up along Mistake Creek, and began slowly but steadily to follow up die tracks.

Barely eight miles away along the valley the hunted natives, eyes staring from their heads, raced into the tiny police outpost at Turkey Creek, gasping out the news. A few shouted orders and horses were run in, saddles thrown on, and Constable Cullen, with trackers Sandy and Joe, was riding fast for Mistake Creek. In less than two hours they had picked up horse and native tracks, then Rhatigan's dinner camp of two days before. Quickly they were in among the foothills, riding fast as a distant shot rang out. Cullen reined in instantly as they cocked their heads, listening.

"Unsling rifles!" he ordered. "Don't shoot, unless Joe Wynne or Nipper shoots at you first!"

He spurred ahead and they were away at full gallop, to burst out amongst the timber almost on top of the startled Rhatigan, who had been trying to place the location of yet another shot when he suddenly heard the galloping hooves of the police horses. He had been feeling decidedly nervy, a quite new experience for Mick Rhatigan, and now he shouted in his relief and waved an arm, but more shots rang out ahead, and the policeman and trackers galloped on. They raced up over the brow of a little rise and there before them, kneeling down, was Joe Wynne in the act of shooting a dog. He glanced round amazed at the riders almost on top of him, then sprang up and made a wild leap for his horse. The animal plunged away, but Wynne was in the saddle as Cullen's horse collided with him. As he fell the policeman snatched the rifle and the trackers, Joe and Sandy, galloped up. Next instant the four horses were plunging together in a rearing, wedged-in mass.

"Jump off and catch him, then search for his revolver. Quick!" shouted Cullen. "Throw me your reins!"

As the trackers leapt off Sandy's rifle struck the ground and exploded, and again the maddened horses plunged. In an instant Wynne had leapt round to the other side of his horse, snatched the reins and, springing into the saddle, was away and riding for his life.

"Stop!" shouted Cullen.

But Wynne was low over his horse's neck riding like the wind. The trackers ran back for their wheeling horses, to the constable's raging abuse, and then, half in their saddles, were after the flying runaway in shame for their clumsy work. Wynne had gained a surprising lead down a gentle slope and was riding like a demon, and a demon was flogging his horse.

They took a flat at the full gallop, Wynne spurring his horse for a sheltering line of timber distantly ahead. Cullen raced furiously after him for half a mile, then a gully yawned beneath him and horse and rider crashed violently, Cullen rolling over and over into the thrashing bushes. He raised his head as the trackers thundered by and shouted, "Catch him or shoot him!" He rose dizzily to his feet and staggered on after the vanishing hoof-beats.

Wynne was fast approaching that sheltering timber, but Death rode with him. Desperately he rode for life, up one more rise and down into a creek. Once up that bank, he would disappear into the timber. As his panting horse plunged up that last bank the trackers were racing down the rise. As Wynne's thrashed horse was pawing up over the creek-bank Tracker Joe reined in his horse, raised his rifle, took steady aim. Joe Wynne's labouring horse was struggling up the bank top, but in the seconds before it could gather fresh speed—"Crack!"

With a choking moan, Wynne spread his arms, toppled, clutched wildly, and rolled off his panting horse.

They rode back to where Cullen's horse had fallen, then quickly got on the tracks of Nipper. Within two hours they surprised and surrounded him. He hesitated—surrendered.

The reader may be interested to read extracts from the actual statements of some of those concerned in this incident. The aborigines made their statements in Pidgin English; these were written down and repeated to them, then typed when they appeared clear to all concerned, and after the aborigines had made their mark. The procedure, and the reason why, were explained to prisoners and witnesses beforehand.

Yarri. Nipper fire shot. All about been wake up. We jump up and run away. Joe Wynne push him back. Joe Wynne been shoot Tiger. We all run away. Charlie shot along arm. Me been go Violet Valley [cattle station] next day. Me and another blackfellow covered up Hopples. We all come back from Violet Valley.

Michael Rhatigan. I was taking .32 for Dick Harten to fix up. My shotgun carried on saddle. Found rifles gone—uneasy—laid down—fell asleep. Breakfast—got pack and riding horses—boys had others away. Decided to report—found boys' tracks first and horse tracks. Decided to follow up tracks. Heard shot—Cullen and trackers galloped past. Followed them up. Next saw Wynne with police in pursuit. Followed—but were galloping at their top pace, too fast for me.

Constable Cullen. Nipper said he took the revolver from Hopples. Asked if he knew why he was being put on the chain. "Yes," he replied, "belonging to shoot him boy." Reported to Flinders. March 31st, left Station with trackers Joe, Sandy—Mundy and Yarri. Went and found bodies, Hopples on top of a hill—body charred—right side and ear. Where Wynne started shooting first we found two bundles of spears in a tree a chain to the east. Long Nellie shot left side and arm and ankle.

Constable Flinders. Turkey Creek—Cunningham Postmaster reported. Constable Cullen investigated—found Charlie in camp shot in arm. Long grass. Mistake Creek eight miles from Turkey Creek, three miles through the hills. Joe shot about fourteen miles in direction of Lissadell. Nipper in Rhatigan's employ a number of years. Wynne was considered a dangerous native.

Mundy. I been camp high up Mistake Creek along other black-fellows. Tiger, Hopples, Wallaby, Charlie, Ben and me. Lubras Tukayurka, Nellie, Hopples's Nellie, Mona, Gipsy, Charcoal belong Elsie, and Manjun. Early fellow morning I see Nipper and Joe—I see Nipper first time he come from low down creek. Joe here come from high up. I see Nipper shoot Wallaby. Nipper shoot Tiger. Charlie, Ben and I run away high up. I fall down longa stone. Charlie shot along arm, we run away. I come back Mistake Creek dinner time went Micky. Micky and me go along camp two fellow bum camp. I come back Turkey Creek. I camp along Garden Creek. I been tell all about blackfellow I no see Rhatigan only Nipper and Joe Wynne. I set down on top watch for Joe and Nipper mustering the gins. Two fellow boys take them away. I saw no horses. He take them low down on Mistake Creek. I no see Rhatigan when they take the gins away.

Joe, tracker. Horse tracks—gins tracking too. Then chase Wynne—leading horse. Cullen fired when Wynne galloped—Sandy finish him off—we all go about to find Nipper's tracks. Cullen, Sandy you track up Nipper. Rifle, horse and Hopples's revolver. Next day Cullen, Sandy, Yarri, Mundy and I go long Mistake Creek follow all way up. Find where two boys camped. Follow up, find where all about blackfellow been camped. Fire longa Creek, two blacks half burnt, dog and 'roo. Dog shot along camp. Follow up creek, find blood along pear tree in deep gully. Yarri say Hopples shot here. Leave horse. Get up along hill find dead man, stone on top, grass, spinifex. Hopples. Shot side and head. Cover him with bushes and stones. Policeman Cullen send Yarri and Mundy to Police Station. We then go straight along where boy been shot before, find two mob spear along tree. Then Hopples's Nellie—face—shot stomach. Long Nellie—shot leg and side. Gipsy shot where we see Joe Wynne before. I find him two blackfeller shot together, Mona and little Elsie. Mona got arm round Elsie. We come up and go where we shot Joe Wynne. Policeman Cullen take cartridges from Wynne's pocket. We cover him—catch spear we see first time and go.

Sandy, tracker. Tracking—found coolamon and tomahawk—we find dinner-time track. Cross little creek—hear shot. Nipper say Joe Wynne been soolem him to shoot all about mob. Policeman Cullen take rifle—handcuff him. Nipper, next day—track two horses, blood on log.

Nipper. Camp along Bob Beattie's and sleep there. Morning—separated—Joe say "We sneak rifle, I want to finish Hopples's Mob"—Joe finish Wallaby—hit him along rib. Joe make the gins cut the firewood. We start away to go along Telegraph Creek, Joe tell me go long Junction look out horse. Joe talk me. I look one gin. We never see Mick [Rhatigan] all that time—Police boy catch me longa Telegraph Creek. Policeman Cullen and Mick there too. Joe Wynne talk all time want to finish Hopples. Hopples stole Joe Wynne's gin before. I sorry for Hopples. Joe Wynne belong Port Darwin. All time talk to shoot him blackfellow. Joe Wynne wanted the spears. He said he was going to clear out Lissadell way.

One dreamy afternoon I strolled down along this Turkey Creek and came unexpectedly upon a little camp of nomads squatting silently round smouldering fires. Lying on her belly in the ashes was a young lubra, softly, pitifully moaning. Bending over her was the camp idiot, methodically squirting blood all over her back. His arm was the syringe, he had cut a vein with a jagged piece of glass and was carefully but calmly plastering every inch of her back with crimson blood.

That poor, burnt back—I shuddered at sight of it. It is wonderful what the aborigines can endure, fantastic what they can sleep through when they roll on live coals when asleep. I've seen them with limbs almost burnt through.

I did not realize then, but believe now, that there was method in this cure. The warm blood from that poor unfortunate's arm would be soothing on the raw flesh, it would clot and thus form a protective and natural and probably even nourishing film all over this dreadful burn. Nature then could hurry up with repairs under the shelter of this covering, her healing juices free from contamination by touch or air-borne germs.

As to whether there was any superstitious reason that it should be the camp imbecile so freely giving his blood, I did not then inquire. But I don't think so. He just happened to be there, and felt proud to give of what he had.

Saying, "So long—we'll be seeing you!" to the three kindly little old white ladies who in past years had seen so much primitive life in this place, we were off again, heading north to plough through the Big Bow, hundreds of yards of sand and rocks, like dry rapids half-hidden among many trees, shady and thick along the watercourses. And there's a natural avenue of trees straight ahead, and at the end of these, through really miles away, there stands up like a stately statue Pompey's Pillar, a sign to occasional travellers that they are well on the way to Wyndham and the sea. The Pillar is a huge granitic rock perched on a little hill flanked by a peak to either side, with bare, rocky hills a thousand feet high leading up to support the Pillar.

"The nigs climb that rock like black monkeys," growled my mate. "It's a sacred rock to them, and a fine look-out; they can spy round about them and down the valley for miles and miles. On a bright, sunny day, to see a husky warrior perched motionless right atop of Pompey's Pillar is quite a sight." He spoke as if a bit ashamed of his sentiment.

Maybe he was thinking of Mrs Millard as we passed Dry Lagoon; a very popular woman, she had been drowned there not long before. She had been driving a truck with old Dick Harten and a station lubra aboard, and had got out to shoot some wild ducks, wading out after them as she'd done a hundred times before. She seemed to slip and didn't seem able to recover her footing. The lubra jumped out of the truck, splashed in after her, and hauled her out—with difficulty, for she was a big woman, but she was dead. She seemed drowned, but most hands believed a heart attack caused her slip in the water. Hard luck, with years yet of energetic and kindly life before her, to die so simply. For she had laughed her way through many a hardship. She used to dress in men's clothes as being more handy to work in, with a broad sombrero hat—"must keep my complexion!" she laughed, she who loved the bright, warm suns of the Kimberleys. She drove her husband's truck, and bushmen there declared she was every bit capable as a man. A very kindly person, beloved by the few inhabitants of the East Kimberley.

IX

WYNDHAM DAYS

No boat at Wyndham, but what odds? There's always tomorrow. Sunsets are glorious, the heavens a flame of scarlet and gold and orange blazing straight out over the Gulf in rippling farewells of brilliant joy behind the line of hills shadowing the opposite shore. Southward, which is left down the road—the street, I mean—loom miles away the cliffy tops of sandstone hills. The Bastion, abrupt little Gibraltar, its rugged wall wispy with insolent spinifex, its crest lightly timbered in silver tracery under moonlight, rises straight up from the backyard of this happy-go-lucky port of one hundred and fifty souls. Away north the Gulf stretches out through land to sea in mysterious reaches of water, violent when the big tides come surging down.

Dreamily quiet is this speck of a township sandwiched between the Arafura Sea and the rugged inland of a continent. On the dusty path fronting my friend's little shack looms the Tree of Knowledge, a nicely foliaged, friendly old tree round whose understanding trunk have been built the seats for the Oldest Inhabitants' Council.

If that kindly tree could only talk!

Here, under the stars, all the story of the Kimberleys was discussed, past and present, whites and aborigines, Afghans and Chinese, crocodiles and horses, camels and donks and mules, renegades and outlaws, explorers and pathfinders, cattle country and cattlemen, gold and the Ragged Thirteen and the epics along the overland telegraph line—just as if it had been yesterday. For the grizzled old relics who held the "chair" had been through it all. Alas! I believe the last one has slipped away "over the range" since then.

One evening, when a few of us tolerated "young coves" sat listening there, how I wished I understood shorthand! For, with a sniff of rum and a pound of Nigger Twist tobacco, half a dozen petrified old relics of the early days were discussing the early landings, while the grizzled aborigines squatting beside them broke in now and then with roars of glee.

Listening there, it was so easy to picture those hectic days when the crazy diggers from all manner of craft came sailing down the forty-mile Gulf to land on this wild shore before there was a Wyndham. With what startling yells yodelling from crag to crag, with what startled feelings the Stone Age men and their wild women and children gaped down from the heights of the Bastion, and from every vantage point all along the rugged Gulf! For the well-watered Kimberley, teeming with game, was then well populated with the folk of the wilds. How their canoes raced back for the shore at such terrifying sight! These amazing white men, with their black and brown and fiery beards, pouring overboard from these gigantic winged canoes, or canoes snorting smoke and flame, some among them forcing overboard enormous animals that with a mighty splash hit the water and came swimming to plunge ashore and shake their hides in a shower of spray. How the basking crocodiles in startled alarm must have turned their snouts to this alarming sight, then come slithering down the muddy banks to dive for shelter deep below!

Quite easy to picture such scenes as now were chuckled over here by white and black. For some of the old diehards had actually taken part in the first landings. I found myself admiring that "rip, tear, or bust" crowd of early diggers. They knew nothing except that gold was rumoured to have been found somewhere "inland" from a wild unexplored coastline called the north of Western Australia. So they landed here, in a place of magnificent wildness. Very fortunately, the scene of discovery actually was inland from this Gulf. But they had to find that locality.

And the aborigines at first were too terrified to help. For to them a horse or bullock or camel was some terrifying thing liable to snort and charge at any moment and devour them, together with their wives and families, while the thunder of these white men's "thunder-sticks" as they shot kangaroo or crocodile for food or sport scared the insides out of the bravest warriors. And what these warriors warned their womenfolk that these white monsters would do to them should they catch them was just nobody's business!

I've laughed at more than one moth-eaten old buck who, recalling such happenings would finally open his huge mouth and nearly swallow his screwed-up face in howls of laughter.

If those early aborigines could have written books how often we should have been surprised at their point of view! And at what they thought of *us*!

After landing, and sorting out their scanty stores and animals, these "white-men devil-devils" started off inland with all the confidence in the world, as if Heaven itself must guide their footsteps.

Surely Heaven must have done so, for their feet took them along round the Big Marsh then down southward to the valley up along which we had just come, and thus they found Nature's own pathway through the ranges. And thus their tramping feet and horses' hooves made the track to Hall's Creek.

But the casualty list was tragically heavy; some accounts say that more men perished in the Kimberley Rush than in any other rush in Australia, perished of hardship and thirst and accident and fever, and from the spears of the blacks. Fever was the worst killer.

It is difficult now to realize that the only port within hundreds of miles of them was a funny little place called Palmerston, which would become known as Port Darwin. No town within a thousand miles eastward, two thousand miles southward—and none there either, for you would have fallen over into the Great Australian Bight and got drownily wet. The tear-away waters there are frightfully erratic, the waves crash sullenly and with great force against that coastline of uninhabited cliffs, the tides roar up and down and in and out of the mouths of the underground caves, probably many of which run many miles inland right under the Nullarbor Plain. Yes, you would be very drowned, and bashed, and soggy if you carried on right away down southward there and fell over those cliffs in the dark. Or in the daylight either.

None of the gold-seekers did, at least that I've heard of, though some parties trudged farther in distance.

But that was all long ago, though it seemed only yesterday as the gruff old voices at "the Council" droned on while Chinese youngsters were squealing in hilarious play from a dimly lighted shop, and Chinese women were shrilly talking. A lone drunk's voice came noisily from the lone pub, the Wyndham Hotel, where the electric-light engine was noisily humming in vigorous competition and disdain. Several citizens in shirtsleeves, pipes alight, walked casually down the road, their figures distinct in the clear Kimberley starlight as they strolled by with a wave of a glowing pipe. Charlie Flinders and Alf Martin were there, on very serious business indeed, the final organization of the Wyndham Turf Club Annual Meeting coming off in a week or so. Charlie Flinders was the busy secretary, Alf Martin one of the vice-presidents, with others well known in the Kimberleys and the Territory.

It was difficult to picture the happy little crowd that would soon gather for Race Week and the event of the season, the Race Club Ball. From the adjoining Territory, from the East and West Kimberley, they were already starting out, some on journeys of hundreds of miles, by horse and the car of the day; camel-men would come lumbering there, too, cattlemen and miners and doggers, a sprinkling of government officials, and a few smiling white women who had been looking forward to meeting their fellow women for months past. Of course, there would be a mob of "flash", excitable black stockboys, a few Chinese citizens, and a few Afghan camel-drivers.

Like the shearers coming from Perth to Derby to "shear the West Kimberley" right down through the Nor'-west, right down south past Meekatharra even to Perth, like the shearers in other States shearing "right down" to Brisbane or to Sydney as the seasons come and go, like the cane-cutters and fruit-pickers and other seasonal workers, like the migratory birds setting out each year, some of those attending this "big race-meeting" were really beginning a yearly "migrational meeting". For some of the horses, and the half-dozen to dozen bookmakers would now follow the meetings, by buggy and car, right down through Western Australia to Perth, as the little townships and the stations in district after district organized their yearly race-meeting in turn. Thus those who followed the meetings would start either in Darwin or Wyndham and "follow the year" right down to Perth.

So that it was a very serious thing for the honour (and business) of the district, a big responsibility for the committee and honorary officials, for Charlie Hinders the secretary, and for Alf Martin, to make sure that the meeting of the season got off to a flying start.

That grizzled, shrewd, good-humoured Alf Martin had just "come in" from Victoria River Downs, the largest cattle station in the world, twelve thousand five hundred square miles. The kingdoms of some European monarchs were not as large as that. No one knew how many tens of thousands of cattle, what army of horses, roamed those fertile plains, those wild valleys and practically unknown watercourses and farflung miles of bush, which sheltered whole tribes of natives. The great station has been cut up a bit since then. The homestead is on the Wickham, a tributary of the picturesque Victoria River. Alf Martin was the manager then. Florence Martin, his daughter, was a wonderful rider, daring but highly skilled. She was the only girl in the Northern Territory who owned a pilot's licence— which would be a feat in these days, but then———!

Other than the recently pioneered air mail, the station's only communication with the outside world was by the little Australian Inland Mission pedal transmitter, that miracle machine to the Far Outback. The girl could tap out morse messages to Wave Hill station.

Fred Rankine, now stationed at Wyndham Post Office, with cheery Jack Christie the wireless man, strolled across to the Council to listen in. A mighty splashing just out in the Gulf from the wharf told of two bull crocodiles settling an argument—horrible, noisy brutes when in dispute. Otherwise all was peacefully quiet.

Thus, in the Dry, most nights at Wyndham.

"No word of the Darwin boat, Jack," said Doug Davidson cheerfully next morning. "You're lucky if you get away within the next fortnight. How put in time?"

"As usual," I replied. "Just loaf the time away."

"Right-oh. How about a stroll to the hospital? Meet the new doc. He's a 'modern', though, a pretty good man, not like some of those hearty old sawbones friends of yours." Doug grinned. "They're on the way out, Jack."

"Seems like it. Like the abo and the horse and the camel. The donkey and the mule, too, And even the 'Council'."

"Ah, yes, Jack," agreed Doug as we strolled along. "They've all done their job, Jack, a good job indeed, too. And, though it may seem surprising to say it, some at least of the little telegraph stations along the overland telegraph lines are also on the way out. Far more efficient instruments, new methods, you know. I suppose in the course of time even the internal-combustion engine must give way to some future discovery even yet more efficient. So far as those old sawbones friends of yours are concerned, well—tell me, now, Jack—if something *real* bad happened to you where would you hurry for repairs? To one of your old friends? Or to modern medicine?"

I thought for a moment, then grinned.

"Ah! Ha!" said Doug. "I thought so."

Still, those thoughts were a little regretful. I'd known a number of these "forgotten" medicos poked away in the very isolated places and, after understanding and making allowances for the strange ways of some, liked all I'd met.

One funny old cove had the rarest smile; quite often while seated upon a grease-splashed jam box I've enjoyed a yam and a smoke in his "surgery". There was no need of ash-trays, you simply knocked out the stub of your pipe on the floor. No difficulty about spitting on the carpet, either—there wasn't any.

"Be sure and blow your match out first," he requested mildly, "before you throw it on the floor among the papers—they're liable to catch alight. And this is the only surgery within five hundred miles of anywhere."

I'll say the papers were liable to catch alight! Accumulation of months of mail-days just thrown across the floor when read—if read. Splashed with candle-grease, too, and oil from sardine tins, and splashes of kerosene here and there where he'd overfilled the hurricane lamp. And what could be seen of the rough wooden floor, parched from many a dry season, was most liberally stained with rancid butter from times when he'd forgotten to put back the tin in the tucker chest. You see, butter melts quickly into oil when exposed like that under a hot iron roof. Beside a cobwebby window, on packing-board shelves that hadn't seen a duster since last wet season, or maybe years for all I knew, sat and drunkenly leant a forlorn array of dusty bottles and jars. He'd forgotten to replace a cork or lid here and there, thus allowing inquisitive flies and ants to drown and permanently bog themselves in the contents. A few dirty big old cockroaches lay along there, too, with their long gingery legs up in the air, which did not speak too well of the medicines they'd poked their greedy snouts into. This room, by the way, was the doc's surgery and office.

X

THE OLD DOC

"Aren't you afraid of your chemicals deteriorating in this hothouse?" I inquired of the Old Doc when I'd learnt he wouldn't take exception to little questions like that. 'The sun's heat through that window must fairly blaze on those bottles in the summer, let alone stir up the grease in those ointments."

"It's only goanna fat," he replied. "A touch of the sun will never do it any harm — much more likely help kill the wogs in it. The sun is a great killer of germs, as you know. Or do you know? The natives bring me the fat for a stick of Nigger Twist tobacco and I render it down in the frying-pan for the ointments. Though those cunning black bounders have sometimes palmed off on me the fat of a man they've killed, a very dead one, by the smell of it in the frying-pan, anyway. They don't like to waste anything." He cast a quizzical eye towards the dubious-looking liquids in the bottles.

"Yes, Mr Idriess," he went on — he was always meticulously polite, would never dream of calling me Ton" or "Jack"; he'd been well brought up, of course, "real refined like", and was highly educated, too — "Yes, Mr Idriess," he said again in his soft old voice and gently scratched his chin, "yes, I dare say the warmth of the day — quite often a hundred and seventeen in the shade here, as you know to your sweaty sorrow — the sun on the iron roof, plus possible after-effects through the sharp cold of night at times, quizzes the ointments and solutions up a bit. Puts body in 'em, as it were. I've experienced at times some quite miraculous cures," he mused, as if to himself.

"My heavens!" I thought. "Body! I'll say!" I could see for myself the bevy of drowned Cor poisoned) flies and mosquitoes and ants and the unclassified moths and insects which no doubt had come swarming in to the hurricane lamp through the open window in those hot, breathless nights. Those ointments would be peppered, too, with a modicum of dust and drifting dry-season pollen stuff and all that goes with it. Body, all right! How awful to have to use or drink any of that stuff! And yet, throughout this particular district, and it was a big one, a death through anything but accident or killing was an event.

Methodically he refilled his old charcoal-burner, with practised, nicotine-stained finger stubbing down the Nigger Twist tobacco into that well-charred bowl. Thick, greasy, black as the ace of spades, that aboriginal brand trade tobacco exuded more nicotine to the pipeful than an acre of ordinary poison weed.

"As a matter of fact," he remarked dreamily as he cocked a leg, scraped a match expertly along the right cheek of his corduroy pants and thus lit up, "the medicines and grease-spots I'm called to mix up for the boys *must* be pretty strong. They're tough boys out in those hills."

I knew they were. They had to be. Grizzled old veterans that you couldn't kill with an axe, middle-aged toilers tough as the steel-hard ironbark of their rocky hills. But I also knew that a lethal microbe can kill an elephant. How this dear old optimist of a doctor never killed himself by drinking his own "kill or cure" brews or turned up his toes through blood-poisoning because of the slip of a dirty lancet has often puzzled me. His favourite lancet was the one he cut up his Nigger Twist tobacco with. When he had to use it on a patient he gave it a rub or two on a rusty old file, spat on the blade, then gave it a rub on a half brick to "give it an edge". One sunny morning I happened to be yarning in the surgery when an old "wombat bull" came limping down from the hills.

"Got a hunk er steel in me hoof, doc," he growled, "an' me damn' fool of a gin has hammered it in a bloody sight worse. Yank it out before I go lame as a broken-down camel."

It was a "hoof" all right. Most of the boys gully-raking those hills don't wear boots until they come into town for the Wet, for Christmas, and many don't wear them even then. It took the doc patience, time, and skill to yank that splinter of steel out of that leathery hoof. He dabbed the jagged cuts with a mixture of tar and beef-fat and whatever else was mixed in it, and apparently then the hoof was all right. Accepting his quid from the quite grateful, grizzled old patient, he turned to me and sadly complained, running his cutting tool across his thumbnail. "I'm afraid I'll have to sharpen this lancet again, a shade more this time, it seems to be growing old, worn out."

"But you cut your *tobacco* with it!" I protested.

"That is the thing it is best for," he said in surprise.

'Well, then, when you use it as a lancet the blade must have a thick, heavy scum of tobacco greased over the edge. No wonder it's blunt."

'Well, yes," he agreed thoughtfully, "there's something in that. I'll have to give it a rub on the oilstone now and then—there's one about somewhere, I brought one with me from south when I came up here some years ago."

Half a century ago, I thought privately. "When you find that oilstone," I suggested mildly, "it might help if you first boiled it in good hot water. It certainly will be thick with grit, not to mention being heavily caked with oil, oil that has long since hardened nearly into stone. For that oilstone is lying over there in that corner where I rooted away all the rubbish the other day looking for the snake that went down the hole."

He strolled across and in mild surprise picked up the filthy-looking oilstone, cocked an eye at it as at an old, long-lost friend, and handled it almost fondly.

"I'm glad you found it," he said gratefully. "I thought the natives must have purloined it; some of them can pinch the eye out of a needle if you have not got eyes in your backside. I may not have been able to find this very useful oilstone had you not pointed it out. I'll give it to Louise to give it a thorough wash."

Louise wasn't his wife, by the way. She had long since given him up as hopeless. No doubt rightly so, too, in a way. That rather "classy" lady lived several thousand miles away, fortunately for her social ambitions. This understanding Louise was a wall-eyed, knowing old lubra who "did the washing". No doubt she'd chuck the oilstone in the tub with the doc's duds — when he remembered to tell her.

He was a dear old chap, gentle as a pet rabbit, and genuinely grateful for the recovery of the long lost oilstone. It really pained him when he see-sawed a blunt lancet into a festering wound and the patient gripped whatever he could lay his hands on and howled, "Gawdstruth, doc! Why don't you sharpen the bloody knife?"

I know, for I've heard them complain like that, and later the doc, in a puzzled tone, remarked ruefully to me, "I cannot quite understand them at times, Mr Idriess, though I've known them for so long. About an hour ago I treated my last patient. I was gentle as a lamb with that patient, and he roared like a bull."

"I heard him."

"Did you? I wonder why?"

"The whole camp heard him."

"Oh, I don't mean that! I simply mean I wondered why he was so agitated. I was very careful, very considerate during that little operation." He sighed. "Bless my soul, I was. And yet you would have thought the man was suffering a confinement!"

I could only murmur sympathy while privately aware that had I been that tortured patient, then at the very first jab I would have bolted out of the door, breaking a record for the hills.

XI

OUT WHERE HE-MEN REFUSE TO DIE

There was another delightful old medical character I was pleased to have on my visiting list, though never professionally, thank Heaven. He was stationed in yet another comer of the vast State, poked well away from all the annoying superfluities of civilization. Most friendly, too, so long as you always deferred to his "professional status". For a doctor is a doctor wherever he may roam "and, by God, don't you ever forget it!" Apart from insisting on deference to his position, this cheery old Bury-me-Quick was quite human, though he did go about bare-footed and with pants patched by a squint-eyed black gin—when they were patched at all. His "surgery" was closely similar in all respects to the other old character's, though this one was littered all over the place with empty tobacco tins in which he'd mixed his ointments. He had a perfect mania for mixing ointments in old tins and leaving them lying there with the stick he'd used as a mixer still glued in the tin. During an occasional epidemic he'd be short of tins and of course mix his ointments in the rusty old tin that he'd used before, though sometimes if not too busy he'd scrape out with a penknife what fragments of the hardened old ointments he could.

Thank goodness, all of that vast Nor'-west is very healthy. Just occasionally some unexplainable epidemic, maybe some obscure thing brought by coloured crews of the pearling fleets, would sweep like a raging bushfire throughout the aborigines of the Far North, and race mercilessly down inland through many of the stations. In common with all medical men, this old doc would help the abos all he could; he didn't mind how hard he toiled for the Children of the Sun, as for all others. But of course he expected his patients, be they white or black or yellow, brown or brindle, to take their medicines and ointments as and in what they received them. As a matter of fact, knowing how tough the aborigines are, he never gave the matter a thought. Daringly, but with a smile, I mentioned the little matter one day.

"What!" he stared back amazed. "A clean tobacco tin for an abo's ointment. Good heavens, man, they can chew bone! I've seen 'em swallow bloodwood charcoal just to help digestion. I've seen 'em sliced down the skull by a tomahawk and they only grin when you sew 'em up. You've got to hammer the hone back into place at times too; sometimes you've got to shove a wedge in, or lever it together with a flattened horseshoe nail or whatever damn gadget is handy. Clean out the tins be damned!"

Fearful lest I'd overstepped strict medical etiquette, I maintained a bashful silence.

Overcome by the enormity of the suggestion, he sat down on a wobbly stool and thoughtfully reached for his pipe. Not a Nigger Twist addict, he smoked Havelock (heavy). Frowningly he sliced at the plug, rolled the result in the palms of his hands. 'There may be something in it," he mused grudgingly, "about a clean tin for every patient. Though someone would have to pay an abo for cleaning them, and that someone wouldn't be me! The township couldn't save up enough tins for me, anyway; not many of us smoke these flash cuts of tobaccos that are coming to be all the rage with you city softies! Anyway, the aboriginal blood—the wild munjon blood, anyway—will just about defy anything, just gobble up germs and ask for more. What stray wogs they may pick up in these ointments wouldn't even be a morsel to the cannibal wogs that are already in 'em. Their blood is wog-proof!"

"How about the whites?" I asked.

"The whites?" He looked at me pityingly. "You mean these cast-iron gold prospectors," he growled, "with hoofs on 'em a camel could envy? You mean those hell-for-leather cattlemen with faces like ironbark and bodies tough as ironwood? Why, I wouldn't make fifty quid out of the lot in a year! And the teamsters are a darn sight worse! I never get a chance to slip a knife into one of them unless a wagon has run over him or his horse-boy chopped him over the head with a tomahawk. Don't you worry about the whites out there in the mulga. They're worse than the aborigines!"

He was right, I thought. The white men were beastly healthy, from a medical man's point of view, anyway. Strangely enough, apart from fever and another disease, it was the aborigines who suffered sicknesses by far the most.

"If their blood is wog-proof," I suggested, "then what causes these occasional outbreaks of widespread sickness, these epidemics!¹"

"H'm! That's a bit of a puzzle." He frowned up at a gecko lizard clinging like a fairy insect to the roof. "H'm, yes. A medical problem at present. Must be investigated. But that would cost a lot of money that we want for wars. It is far more expensive to kill people than to cure them, you know."

With a weary grunt he turned to the ointment he had been mixing, brushed the flies off it, chucked in a bit of brown powder, and started mixing again.

"Anyway, these ointments do 'em a lot of good 'way back there in those hills. And this patient's lucky." He grinned. "He's got three in one—the remains of the ointment I mixed in this tin months ago, the second ointment I mixed atop the remains of that, and this third ointment I'm mixing atop of the scrapings of that! These'll fix him! And I'm only charging him a quid for the lot, remember that!"

What I thought I didn't say. And if that ointment was going to a horse-boy, and the horse-boy worked for a teamster, and the teamster developed a cut or sore on any portion of his body he'd "dab on a plaster of the quack's body-grease", just to see.

As has happened countless times throughout many years. It was quite true what the South used to proudly boast, "We breed cast-iron men up in the North!"

By heavens, they did! Still do. However, there must have been "a something" in those old "kill or cure" medical days. The doc I'm writing of now had a really magical reputation over a very sparsely populated but still vast area as a great "Fever Man". His Fever Mixture was his pride, and was sought after far and wide. And there was no shadow of doubt that it was good indeed, to the gratitude and unyielding admiration of all the boys in the back country. Many a lonely teamster, racked with malaria under his wagon, with only a loyal horse-boy for company, has blessed the doc's Fever Mixture, as have many more cattlemen, let alone those wandering nomads generally operating away out in wild or semi-wild Aboriginal Land, the dingo-poisoners.

The Fever Mixtures and "X" Mixtures of those old-time docs in the really isolated areas helped to an extent never really recognized, because they were unknown, of course, outside the lonely places, helped in the pioneering of practically all the North, from Cape York Peninsula's east coast across the Gulf country and Territory right across the Kimberleys to the continent's west coast washed by the Indian Ocean. Each doc worked up some individual speciality of which he was jealous and proud. Almost always it was either a Fever or "X" Mixture, for these two ailments seemed the only health worries in the North. The old doc of whom I'm scribbling now made his famous Fever Mixture from iron and quinine in some proportion known only to himself, with a fistful of red pepper or other energetic ingredient chucked in; each doc was most jealously secretive of his "mixture". A spoonful of this particular darkish-brownish-looking stuff would fairly lift your head off. It was "dynamite", but as efficient as dynamite for its own purpose. The doc prepared the boiling Mixture always by the kerosene tin, and sent it out in beer-bottles, by the mailman, into the wilds to his patients among those great scattered stations, and to the isolated mining camps poked in rocky valleys amongst distant ranges, to bore-drain men, and to the so lonely camel-men who (or did then) patrol the long Border Fence.

The mailman, on return from his fortnightly or monthly trip as the case might he, would stroll up to the doc's with scribbled messages in his notebook from stockmen on station and out-station, from teamsters, mining camps, and doggers.

"Please send me along a bottle of that burn yer guts fever mixture of yours, doc. Better send a bottle of X Mixture too jest in case. An' make them strong. I'm pretty crook."

No need for the last invariable sentence. An overdose of the stuff would bring a bull camel to his knees.

One note the doc had just received when I happened to stroll along for a yarn was from a back river out-station camp, and it took a bit of deciphering. I knew there was something mighty wrong by that stubborn set of the old doc's jaw as he handed the crooked, faded lines to me.

"You call yourself a bit of a writer!" he snapped. "Now work that one out!"

So I read, laboriously scribbled on a scrap of brown paper in faded pencil: "Hey Doc send us out by maleman a bottle a that rib bustin poison youse call fever mixture. An a bottle of that hellfire X mixture—it's woresen ten loads of knee tremblers are rolled inter one. But fer the luv of Mike put labels on this time. An don't go drinkin your own poison an mix the labels like I knows on oncst befor."

Handing the note back to the doc, I said guardedly, "I'm afraid I cannot decipher this one, doc, the medical terms have got me heat. What is *your* diagnosis?"

"I'd let him know that right away if only I was within reach of him," replied the doc angrily. "A herring-gutted no-hoper of a bushwhacker besmirching my professional ethics! Me mixing labels! *I'll* mix him up a mixture presently, believe me. Anyway, there seems to be a hit of a mix-up here. I've never sent him any labels. Labels on his medicines! He'll want mulga daisies on his grave next!"

"But, doc," I said in mild curiosity, "if the bottles haven't labels on them, what medicine will they know to take for the different diseases?"

"Diseases!" The doc stared at me in a scornful sort of way. 'They don't get *diseases* out in that back country. They only get fever and the pox!"

It was some months later that I solved the mystery of the mixed labels. On my travels I met an indignant teamster.

"Here I am lyin' in camp haywire with fever. The mailman drops the medicines an' rides orf. My old nigger horse-boy is sufferin' from woman trouble, all doubled up in knots. I hands him the bottle labelled 'X Mixture', an' takes a good swig outer the Fever Mixture bottle. When me an' the nigger gets our breaths, erbout five minutes later, we both takes another swig. An' then I'm all tied up in knots with woman trouble, an' my nigger is goin' all haywire with fever!

Now what the———flamin' blazes do you make outer that?"

Later, when the returning mailman explained this tragedy to the doc he replied indignantly, "Serve him right! Insisting on labels! If a man doesn't know the taste of his own medicine then he can damn' well swallow it for me. It would cure him, anyway!"

It did, by the way.

Aboriginals jockeys, Western Australia 1905.

XII

WHAT DOES IT FEEL LIKE TO BE DEAD?

Regrettably enough in a way, but quite inevitably, those isolated characters of the Farthest Out medical world were on the way out with the abo, the horse and camel and donkey, just on the way out when the motor-car, then wireless and aeroplane, were coming in, as Doug had said. Doug Davidson was the Wyndham Commission Agent—"Always in commission", said Doug, grinning, "and you'd be surprised at what a man can sometimes pick up in this forgotten little comer of the woods."

"Even to a dentist's chair," added Martin, who was Roads Board Secretary, ambitious to build roads in a huge district possessing the one historical inland track, but, alas, no money. The few officials of both Kimberleys are great battlers for those rugged lands that surely will come good.

'What's the joke about the dentist's chair?" I inquired. "Are you pulling out crocodiles' teeth for tourists—ready for the happy day when tourists appear?"

"Not on your life," replied Doug. "It was a real dentist's chair built about the time Noah got his first toothache. It was the pride of the old doc's life, he used to admire it for hours on end, dreaming of the patients that never came. One glance at that monstrosity of ironmongery and wheels and levers and the most harrowing toothache would vanish. Even the natives would light out for the wide spaces. The doc had bought it second-hand on a trip south for eighty-five pounds, a big sum those days. He was retiring down south now and tried hard to sell it to the new doctor, who laughed at it as a medieval museum piece.

"At last, to appease the old fellow, most reluctantly the new doc offered him twenty pounds for it. The old doc glared at the new doc, rushed outside without a word, press-ganged a couple of passing abos, manhandled that old monstrosity down out into the yard, yanked it yard by yard up the street, bought a tin of kerosene, poured it over the chair, and set it alight, to the delight of all the abo and Chinese kids and dogs in the street. Then the old doc borrowed a sledgehammer, rolled up his sleeves, spat on his hands, swung the hammer and—'Bang Bang! Bang!' With each blow you could hear his grunt away down the street. But he kept on in a gasping fury until he'd broken that cast-iron atrocity into fragments." "To the grinning delight of the abos," chuckled Martin. "They collected all the pieces and traded them to the wild munjons inland to fashion into spear-heads."

"You were an especial pal of his," remarked Doug.

"I'll say!" replied Martin feelingly. "I've felt the lash of his tongue more than once. That tongue had a sting in it near as fiery as his medicines—the autocratic little old devil! Especially after the sanitary trouble, and that was always on. Kept worrying at it like a bantam tiger for months and months. He simply swore blind and blue and purple that there were only four weeks in any month, and that I simply could *not* make thirteen weeks in a quarter."

"Who won?" inquired Walker from our toy Commonwealth Bank.

"Oh,"—Doug grinned—"we were both pretty obstinate. I don't think it was fully settled up to the day he stamped up the gangway and shook the dust of Wyndham off his feet for ever and a day."

"Did he ever treat you professionally?"

"Not on your life he didn't—not after that sanitary trouble! Now and again, though, I'd have to get some Fever Mixture for the maintenance boys working down along the road. The drill then was to catch him in the street, not open up with 'Good day, doc!' but walk straight by and hiss out of the corner of your mouth, 'Bottle of Fever Mixture!' 'Hospital! Three o'clock!' he'd yelp back as he strode straight on. And I'd have to be on the doorstep of that little old hospital exactly at three o'clock to get that bottle, or bottles. One day, though, one of my men met with an accident and they brought him along to the hospital. He'd only broken a collar-bone as it turned out, but before I knew this I was anxious about him. So I stepped out to the hospital and knocked and the old devil came and glared at me.

" 'How is the patient, doc?' " I asked. He waved me aside in dismissal and snapped, 'That's *my* business!' So I got to hell out of it before he told me to."

"That's what he told the politician," chuckled Christie.

"Yes. A visiting politician thought he was doing a great stroke by coming near the place—just because we're out on the end of the world. In condescending good humour he strolled up to the doc and impressively introduced himself.-The old doc ignored the extended hand, just glared, and believe me he *could* glare.

" 'Ho! So you're a politician are you?'

" 'Yes, doctor.'

"The doc treated him to his famous wave aside and snorted, 'You ought to be exterminated!' and strode on."

"Why did he dislike politicians?"

"Goodness only knows," replied Doug. "He wouldn't know one when he saw one. I suppose we've all got to blame *someone*."

"Especially out in this country," said Old Martin quietly. "A man gets quaint ideas at times, if he doesn't watch himself."

I remembered that remark that night when strolling along the marsh, down past the little hospital. A quite different type of doctor there now, comfortingly "modern". This, like so many Kimberley nights, was cool and quiet, the air sweet to breathe and Scented elusively, the sky a hazy blue, the stars dim and without a twinkle, seeming drowsy for sleep. A half-moon made ghostly the marsh edge until it was lost in the gloom of water. Right away across there was the black line of mangroves. Distantly behind, a line of hills vaguely outlined against the sky. Here beside the road, on the left, rose the Bastion like a steeply sloping wall. Away up, a few small trees leant here and there as if growing from the cracks of a crumbling castle. Just dull moonlight ahead, the hum of native voices in quiet talk within the dense black shadow somewhere at the Bastion edge. Behind, the hazy lights of the tiny town.

And over everything, pressing gently down as from the sky, a faint breathing, as if all the world, as if all the universe were breathing, as if no man in all the world were quite alone.

Came a ghostly thought of the dead man. Only he wasn't dead—couldn't have been. And of the sun-tanned greybeard who so earnestly wished to know what it felt like to be dead, wanted to know before his time, he couldn't wait. He was a "blow-in" to Broome, the Port of Pearls, down the southern coast from Derby. This "blow-in" had come from goodness knows where, from unknown hundreds of miles probably. A stranger, wearing that "searching for the unknown" expression of face, almost frightening in its intensity.

"Who are you looking for?" inquired the publican.

"I want to catch up with that bloke who was dead for half a night. I want to ask him what it feels like to be dead."

"A border-line case," thought the publican. "Won't be long now."

But presently he realized the stranger was really seeking a "drowning" case of a year or more ago, a diver brought in by a lugger apparently drowned, believed drowned hours after "the body" was brought ashore.

"Ah, I see," said the publican. "But that diver wasn't dead, he recovered."

"He was dead all right!" insisted the stranger. "The doctors *said* he was dead."

"Yes, I know," explained the publican patiently, 'but he couldn't have been. He only toed the line—he *came back*!"

Finally the stranger disappeared, apparently trudging farther north, still fearfully anxious to know what it felt like to be dead. He had left the Port of Pearls firmly convinced that everyone was against him because no one would lead him to "the man who was dead".

And yet the publican had spoken truly. The "dead man" had only "toed the line".

I wondered at the army of men who must have "toed the line" since the world began, stepped to the very border-line, hesitated, then slipped back with a sigh, still not quite knowing what it "felt like to be dead".

It was while we were at Wyndham, or rather out on the King River, that most unexpectedly I heard word of that alleged gold find away down in the Centre.

"Weaver's struck gold!" called old Paddy Nolan as he came riding up to the pumping station. "Heard it from a bloke who heard it from over the wires."

"Struck gold—camped on it!" was that first laconic news. In time, though, it would be richly verified.

Weaver was a blind man, poor chap. He and his family had been camped a long while here on the King River by Mount Coburn. Hearing fragmentary news from Darwin, away east on the Territory side, he had decided, like a patriarch of old, to "up camp" with all his family and belongings and hopes and trek right down through the Centre to this Tennant's Creek. A thousand miles and more, soon into harsh, thirsty country, so very different to the sweet grasses, the pleasantly timbered hills, the plentiful game and fish and waterfowl, the beautiful waterholes of the King River.

And now this news of him had come, presently to be verified. No wonder it brought excitement and pleasure to this tiny community of half a dozen men and women. P. C. Marshall already knew it, though he had been patrolling away back in the "Bad Lands"; it is almost unbelievable how the mulga wire spreads news at times, even in country where the natives are still wild. With laughing greetings from the trackers to friends among the "King River mob" the patrol horses came noisily stamping towards the "Prisoner's Tree", anxious to be off-saddled and drink of the cool river water and feast on the luscious grass.

Marshall was prominent seeking Marshall and Klausman when their plane came down in that so wild country of the extreme Nor'-west corner. His experiences, like those of each one of the mounted men, would have made an exciting book. But now all the camp was pondering over the news of gold, wondering if it could really be true. And, if so, how could a blind man, a blind cattleman, have found it?

There was no one nearer than a thousand miles away to explain.

I wondered if Jack Noble had found his Golconda yet.

XIII

THE PORT OF PLENTY-O'-TIME

Ah! Distant smoke-haze of the little old boat coming at last. And next day we steam up that picturesque old Gulf, forty miles of surging waters hemmed in by wild, wooded hills, where adventure and romance and quaint things happened and were happening and would continue to happen every mile of the way, long before De Rougemont's day and after. For here it was that that world-famous adventurer rode his turtle, for which and for other alleged adventures he was labelled the World's Greatest Liar after Munchausen. Since then, of course, you've admired plenty of magazine photos of pretty girls riding turtles by the gambolling sea waves—maybe you've envied the turtle.

As a young fellow, however, I'd read scornful articles casting ridicule upon such a quaint pastime, declaring that it had never been, and could not be, done. Meanwhile I'd many a time watched Torres Strait Islanders and aborigines also "riding" turtle, not merely "play-acting" on a beach, but on the open sea where the lively turtle can swim and dive like nobody's business. He *has* to be able to, to dodge his enemy the shark. But I'd seen natives astride these huge, frantically swimming things, in laughing competition manoeuvring them in swimming and diving acts any way they wished. At times also, just for the fun of it, they forced the bulky, powerful creatures to dive and then to carry them back up to the surface—which is an incomparably different job to sitting atop of the old slow-coach when she waddles up the beach to lay an egg or two, anything from sixty up to one hundred and sixty at a batch. Yes, they do the job properly. If fowls were turtles how happy the poultry farmer would be!

Overseas, De Rougemont's pearling adventures had been laughed at, mostly by critics who believed pearls grew in jewellers' shops. For, after all, "the Baron" had really sailed on a pearling cruise or two. I'd found this out during much earlier wanderings along the Queensland coast from Cairns north. For in Port Douglas some folk remembered him well; he had started a small business there, calling himself "Henry Green". His real name was Henry Grien. His business failed and he took a job aboard a pearling lugger. I heard of him again in Cooktown during those happy wandering days when "my beard was black". And this solved for me the mystery I'd often puzzled over, or part of it—why a lot of the story of the Greatest Liar on Earth ran so true to fact. For he'd get plenty of experience in pearling aboard a schooner or lugger in those days when the Hell Ship sailed from Thursday Island, headquarters of the Torres Strait pearling fleets. He would see a little of native life also. As to the rest, he'd be toiling among real adventurers, and also hear numerous stories of the characters of those days—there were plenty of them, and some of them were living proof that truth can be stranger than fiction. Unfortunately for himself, De Rougemont hitched a string of other men's adventures to his own, and, talking far too much on some subjects he knew nothing about, he was eventually bowled out. But he made quite a stir in the world of that day before his pack of cards came tumbling down. He seems to have practically made the *Wide World Magazine,* an energetic journal that was just becoming popular and was enterprising enough to take a chance. The magazine declared, "These are the most amazing experiences man has ever lived to tell", which was agreed to by a breathless London. De Rougemont had the honour of lecturing on his "famous explorations" before no less august a body than the British Association for the Advancement of Science. And those scientific boys believed themselves no small potatoes, believe me.

So this lively little De Rougemont lit up the world's greatest metropolis with a bang while he lasted. I suppose if a man did the same thing today he'd make a fortune and be invited to do his stuff on all the television sets in the world.

Of course, some of the "facts" the romantic lecturer detailed to the rapidly increasing circulation of the *Wide World Magazine* were equal to the genuine Baron at his best. For instance, even today I grin, and can remember as a lad being doubled up with joyful laughter, while reading of De Rougemont's "flocks of wombats rising in the dusk". The thought of poor lumbering old piggy wombat rising in flocks in the dusk still seems irresistibly funny to me. De Rougemont, like many another man, did not know when to leave well alone. If, when he arrived in London, he had only spruiked the truth, as in his own little way he'd seen it, and given due credit to the stories of other men, he probably would have done quite well for himself. His main job out here, as it turned out, was butler to a Western Australian Governor of the day.

Anyway, some among the old Wyndham diehards stubbornly believed that De Rougemont really had sailed the Cambridge Gulf with the blacks and landed right here and trudged far into the interior. And they could retail his adventures in this Wyndham area as absolute fact.

Actually this is simple enough to understand. For while battling in Sydney De Rougemont had met and become very friendly with Harry Stockdale, and it was this bushman's stories that in this particular locality De Rougemont wove round himself. Stockdale was one among the pioneers who explored and helped open up the Cambridge Gulf and the country inland, and his stories were actual happenings. And a few among the early Kimberley hands, knowing such happenings as fact, still more than half believed that De Rougemont must have lived in this country with the aborigines.

He must have been quite a character in his own way, this De Rougemont, though this particular story about him I cannot vouch for. It could probably be simply enough verified should anyone be sufficiently interested, for this did not happen out in the Lands of Wild, Wild Men, and Wild, Wild Women, but in Sydney—right within Sydney Harbour, if it be fact. De Rougemont dabbled in inventions and for long, since his lone pearling experience, had been trying to "think out" a diving machine. As I heard the story, Stockdale financed him to make a model of his machine, which he did. Two men agreed to go down in the machine for a trial. They went down all right. And stayed there. So did the machine.

De Rougemont skipped away to New Zealand.

Anyway, De Rougemont would have needed the imagination of a Jules Verne to have foreseen what would actually come to pass over these same happy hunting-grounds of his. How he would have been laughed at and howled down had he written of the time coming when over this same fantastic country, this same wild and woolly coastline, huge man-made birds and their famous crews would come flying and disappear, would actually become lost and vanish in a mystery of unknown wildernesses. These happenings and others also would quite upset the happy-go-lucky routine of these forgotten lands.

Thus fact so easily can be stranger than fiction.

If a De Rougemont had prophesied that the swiftly coming Scientific Age would seek these same Kingsford Smiths and Ulms and others of their mighty breed by means of messages instantaneously flying through the air, then they would have put such a writer in jail or in a lunatic asylum as a maniac dangerous to society. And now today, just ahead of us, fantastic events will happen; there still are and ever will be "far more things in heaven and earth..."

When free of the wide mouth of the Gulf the bows dip eastward along that wild coast—at this time, anyway, very wild indeed—dodging the mazes of reefs and the shifting sands that the river mouths in tumultuous wet seasons move into unpredictable positions, making navigation close inshore dangerous.

It was a "morning time" under brilliant sunlight when we steamed into the sheltered harbour of the happy little port of Darwin, even then quite busy, though it seemed peaceful and pretty. A fine harbour ringed by low wooded cliffs, roofs that are landmarks peeping above the little jungle patches, and above the clumps of bamboo and palms and flowering shrubs. Little ships from strange seas at anchor, or sailing leisurely into harbour. Pearling luggers, too, a crocodile-shooter's cutter, several buffalo-shooters' little vessels now dreaming to the tide out in that sunlit bay. Ashore, the "mixture" of the town, with the citizens' bungalows creeping inland behind the business area, along the bush-clad roads signs of building activity that promise well for the future. An atmosphere of cheery optimism among the healthy sun-tanned citizens also.

White-suited chaps, and the boys with the grin who call themselves "the proletariat". The White Town cheek by jowl with Chinatown in Cavanagh Street, where there was a tiny shrine in every close-packed shop, little black-haired, piercing-eyed women in black silk pants (long-legged ones, don't mistake me) and toe-peeping sandals. A little woman in blue pants and long black coat-gown clatters past on wooden shoes. No hat, long black hair brushed severely back. Half a dozen big-eyed youngsters cling to her or trot along behind. In the dim recesses of shops a-glimpse of men and women toiling silently over ironing boards. On the doorsteps of some of the shops sit old Celestials, their locks scanty and grey, dull blotches on their nearly bald craniums. From a more prosperous looking shop a Chinese girl glances out. She has that expression that tells us she sees us, yet doesn't see us, and is not interested anyway. She is dressed modernly, is solemn of feature with staring brown eyes, but has grown the slim figure and independent walk that come with breeding under Australian skies. Darker-coloured people here and there drift in and out of the shops—several pretty coloured girls pass by with laughing chatter, a timid boldness about their stare. The lighter-skinned of the different mixtures are well dressed and quite conscious of their good figures.

The tang of incense, of joss-sticks smouldering, of smoked fish—the smell of the East is over everything. A Cingalese is sitting before his table, expertly carving pearl and trochus shell. Several times I was lucky enough to sit and watch a highly trusted expert peel a pearl, with marvellous delicacy of finger-touch peeling off tiny skin after skin to expose at last the full beauty of the pearl encased so tightly within. Many a time I had watched, fascinated, the experts away south in Broome. But you could see it in Darwin, too, if you were lucky. As also far away nor'-east at Thursday Island. I could always find plenty of interest in Darwin's Chinatown, but usually ended in the pleasant contrast of the "Big Store", A. E. Jolly and Company. The genial efficiency here was good to behold, and feel you had a share in. I was only an occasional customer, but the management and the boys behind the counter made you feel as if you really were "one of the mob".

I am told that "modern" Darwin is a smart, up-to-date port now. Time hurries on, of course. In my day it had a dreamy prettiness, but under the surface quite a lot was doing. The boys, and the women, too, of those "bow-and-arrow" days were battling along ceaselessly in laying the' foundations for that unbelievable prosperity of today.

Among the bungalows, along the roads, in the green jungle patches, too, were painted Nature's designs with the scarlet poinciana, scented flowers draping banyan and tamarind, the purple of bougainvillea trailing veranda and bush and tree, yellow of acacia and cassia hanging in lovely clusters, the whites and pinks of frangipani and countless other flowers and shrubs, perfuming the air and bringing gladness to the eyes.

There was the Abo Compound, of course, and Fanny Bay jail with its notorious aboriginal outlaws enjoying themselves in their own quaint way or, the novelty of the white man's jail having worn off, planning a do-or-die escape, or breaking their hearts in pining away for their tribal country. I already knew of, or had met, I think, all the most interesting ones, shaggy "bad men" of the wilds. I rather liked them. Naturally I should have felt very different had any one of them tried to hurl a ten-foot barbed spear through me, or split me up with one of those bullock-killing shovel-blade spears, the assegai of the wild aboriginal. It all depends on how you look at things, or on how the other fellow looks at you.

Along the white street leading towards the Residency comes a glimpse of the harbour's blue waters between the trees. Distantly across is Talc Head where Nemarluk turned at bay, staged his desperate wrestle with the redoubtable Bul-Bul, defeated the trackers, and again escaped. Down there towards the harbour is the long white building of the Government offices. Near by is a compact little barracks with a glimpse of smartly dressed men in khaki shirts and trousers, the broad-brimmed hats bearing the badge of the Northern Territory Mounted Police. Their thousand-mile and more patrols vie with the best work of the Canadian Mounted. Many patrols destined to become famous in the Territory's pioneering history have ridden out from there.

I enjoyed a grin and a whimsical thought one afternoon, "sticky-beaking" to listen in to a black tracker's point of view. It was a little crowd of coloured men standing gazing at the placards outside the local talkies, "Star Pictures". They are almost hysterically fond of the pictures. Among them glowered that aristocrat among natives, a tracker in uniform. He caught my eye when pointing with scorn to the over-saddled horse from which the cowboy hero was portrayed as firing guns and lassoing villains all at once.

"Me no more damn fool!" declared the tracker scornfully. "No more catchem man that way! Gib us blurry laugh."

And *he* would know. As I strolled on, idly I wondered what the highly modern civilized white man who made that picture would have thought of this criticism—from an Australian aboriginal who, less than a dozen years ago, was a Stone Age primitive, hunting in the wilds of Arnhem Land clad only in goanna fat and mud to keep off the mosquitoes, his weapons a handful of spears, a woomera, and a stone knife.

But a couple of laughing white women looking fresh and charming on their way to a tennis gossip caused my thoughts to drift away again—pleasantly so. But alas! Nobody loved me.

A warm afternoon, believe me, and the Victoria Hotel invitingly by the footpath. Cool inside, and cool beer. And the hostess, one of the dearest old girls in the continent—Mrs Gordon. With the quaint smile and the warm heart that never faltered. How many stories there are in the battling yet wonderful life of that pioneering old lady! What a shame her story and those of others like her have not been left on record for future generations! But, of course, writers were few and far between in those days, out there.

Phoebe Farrer (left) with her daughter Mary, Nutwood Downs station, about 1912.

XIV

WHERE WOMEN CAN BE AS GOOD AS MEN

Of the Territory pioneer women, perhaps the "daddy" of the lot is Mrs Phoebe Farrar, slim and young despite her years, and surely made of greenhide and lion's heart. For she was already a pioneer a score of years or so before the pioneer heroine of *We of the Never Never* took over at Elsey station. And *those* days were wild and woolly enough for sure.

As a child drover Phoebe was riding with the mob into the undeveloped Gulf country away back in 1882, even before I was born. And, believe me, a lot of water has flown under the bridge since I gave my first squawk to a delighted world. Not that the world has ever mentioned noticing the incident. Anyway, at the time of which I am writing Phoebe was still going strong, in the saddle from daylight to dark, throwing breakaway steers at the mustering, branding colts and calves, busy at all manner of station work, and sticking to it with the toughest of stockmen. I'd heard grizzled stockmen drawl admiringly, "Phoebe will outlast the best of us." And it looks as if she will.

When she married Bob Farrar, who himself was the son of a pioneer, they rode through the Territory land-seeking and eventually took up country which they developed into the well-known Nutwood Downs. This was in the days long before there were any such things as roads, of course, when the only lamp at night was the moon or the campfire. In an emergency, and when they grew "a bit comfortable", they had a slush lamp, which was generally a molasses tin half filled with sand, then having molten fat poured on top of it. A twist of wick from a rag of corduroy pants was thrust into it, and lighted. And there you had your slush lamp. When you blew or snuffed the wick out with your bare hand the fat hardened, of course. You simply lit the wick the next night, and as the fat slowly melted there was your slush lamp all dimly alight again, attracting to it, according to season, a thousand beetles and moths, all manner of often strange, sometimes beautiful insects fluttering in from the wide open bush. However, in those days pioneers considered they were lucky to have the fat to burn in a slush lamp.

Throughout the Territory the blacks were plentiful and in places 'bad", as of course they were for a good many years afterwards. Little the girl bride cared, though she was always cautious, quick as lightning, too, when need was. But quickly she came to understand the wild people of the forests and they took to her and spread the word round. Ever and anon a stockman was speared in the country they worked or travelled, but for a long lifetime she escaped, and her husband, too; they early developed that happy knack of getting along well with the blacks. And for years and years, for her long lifetime, this happy understanding was of priceless value. For when her husband fell ill with recurring bouts of malaria the whole responsibility of life, of the "young" station with its precious little herd, and of the family, fell full upon the young mother's shoulders. Booted and spurred, she was in the saddle from the first cold streaks of dawn, riding out from camp or the rude homestead with only blackboys for company. For years, throughout the work of the long day, her only companions were the half-tamed blackboys that she and her husband had "broken-in" themselves. And when her husband was lying helpless her tired horse would bring her back long after sunset to "knock up" the rude evening meal. She battled on when her baby came, taking everything in her stride. Of course, it would be years before she would see another white woman—twelve years, in fact. It was a tough life indeed, pioneering the Territory in her day.

When they had built up their precious score of cattle to a wonderful little herd of three hundred head, her husband located better land a mere four hundred miles farther west into the Territory, better watered land in unexplored bush at a locality to he called Ban Ban Springs. And in the movement to the new station the full responsibility of droving that precious herd of three hundred fell to her. At that particular time she could only muster a very scared half-caste stockman and one faithful old dog to help her. She got the mob there; the old hands swear she did not lose a beast.

Easy enough to write down. But that little trip was four hundred miles through wild, trackless bush. Often at camp at night, softly singing to soothe the uneasy herd as quietly she rode on her watch round and round the dark shadow of the resting mob, her ears were listening to the wild chanting rising and falling through the stilly timber, the rhythmic "Thump! Thump! Thump!" of warriors' feet in the war dance beside some nearby lagoon. The old dog resting warily with ears pricked, eyes ever following the shadowy rider, the dark form of the half-caste wrapped in his blanket beside the campfire's dull coals as he strove to snatch a precious two hours' sleep before his turn on watch. Four hundred miles of it. But then it was often so, many a time so, it was all in a lifetime those days. Many and many a time, especially when her husband was ill or away, she had to be out on the run mustering and branding stock and busy on the constant jobs of outback station life, her only human companions the half-wild stockboys. Yet she always managed these primitives, laughing boys one moment, the next liable to fly into a maniacal rage or into a dangerous sulkiness at any slight, real or imagined, from friend or foe.

Old hands assured me the first white woman she met in twelve years was Mrs Aeneas Gunn, she of the Never Never, when her husband came to manage Elsey station.

What a wonderful book in this pioneer woman's life! There was rich material, I knew, for other fine books all throughout the Territory. But collectors of such material were so very few. And, alas, time marches on.

We measured out some snakeskins along the bar. They were beauties, very handsomely marked, half a dozen of the best were heavily speckled in golden-brown. Carpet snake and python. Several of the boys had brought them across from Melville Island, where in seasons the crawlers were very plentiful. It was a tough life, of course, nearly all independent jobs those days were tough, but we never seemed to notice it. The boys got two shillings and sixpence a running foot for the skins; they'd get a lot more today for prize exhibits like those. However, the game was very precarious, for the skins had to be sent all the way to Sydney for market, and when they arrived the market might have closed. No buyers. Perhaps no more demand for years, not until the fashion for snakeskin came again.

Crocodile-shooting was precarious also. I had a go at it one time in the Territory when there seemed to be a market. That particular season, there were only two parties of us at it, east and west along that great coast, very different from conditions in the years since the last war. There were plenty of crocs. Every river mouth, every salt-water creek east and west of Darwin for a thousand miles each way was swarming with the ugly brutes. But we only got a pound for a first-class belly hide, and in a very short time the market again collapsed.

In recent years, with increased population, there has been a constant and hungry market and a great increase in price. Where we worked under primitive conditions the shooters (an army of them) have long since worked with modern launches and trucks, telescopic sights, spotlight for night shooting, and so on. The crocs have had a lively time, and have been well thinned out, believe me. A good job, too, for this means many a horse and bullock saved from a crocodile's stomach, and countless more fish to breed in the sea.

Cecil Freer and several of his buffalo-shooting mates were in town on business bent, taking mighty fine care to mix pleasure with business. I suppose the best known of the buffalo-shooters were the old originals, Joe Cooper and Paddy Cahill. Cahill was the first man in the territory to shoot buffalo from a galloping horse. Fred Smith and E. O. Robinson of Melville Island fame were old-time pioneer shooters. Certainly at that time the gun shooter was Cecil Freer of Wildman River fame. Son of a Territory pioneer, Freer had taken up country in the Van Diemen's Gulf, intending to turn it into a cattle station. Other buffalo men were Hunter and Gaden on the Alligator River, the Hardy Brothers on the Adelaide River, Mick Feeney, and a few others scattered here and there. There was plenty of space. Accidents, fever, occasional trouble with the blacks, perishing of thirst now and again, thinned their numbers. But since Cooper and Cahill there have always been shooters.

To Freer's reckoning, thirty thousand buffalo had fallen to his rifle—a score that Buffalo Bill would not have sniffed at. Every shooter must be an expert horseman. Freer was especially so, and was very keen at riding at the Darwin races; he used to win year after year, often riding his own horses. Full of energy, this lively little devil-may-care was stocking up a station with cattle in between the seasonal buffalo-shooting. The next time I would see Cecil Freer would be, of all places in the world, the Hotel Sydney. A far cry indeed, a very different life, to a buffalo-shooter's camp out on the Alligator. But of course he returned.

Cecil Freer very soon was to experience what he described as "the thrill of my life". Commander Bennet came along in charge of northern exploring work for Donald Mackay. Freer got the brainwave to charter the Expedition's monoplane to have a "look-see" over his far-flung domains by air. Of course, there were no settlements there, no such things as fences even, only the great black plains of tropical swamps and pandanus thickets extending on seemingly for ever. The well-known Captain Frank Neale piloted the plane, with Cecil Freer and Hutchins as passengers. Hurtling through the air over the Alligator River, then over the Wildman River where the plane zoomed down to just skim over the tree-tops, Freer looked out to see thousands of blue-grey buffaloes, *his* buffaloes, stampeding in all directions across the plain, chased by this great bird roaring just above them to hurtle by in terrifying sound.

Freer got such a kick out of it as they scattered mob after mob that he quite forgot to memorize the lie of the land to estimate the numbers of the herds they scattered. But the party saw enough to realize that what map they had was all skew-wiff, so far as the rivers were concerned, anyway. But it gave him a great kick, it was the first time also that he really gave a thought to "progress", to the difference between an aeroplane and a horse—to the difference in area of country he could travel over and the time occupied.

Amazing! But who'd 'a' thought if?

XV

ABOARD THE BIRDUM FLYER

Yes, I've known some happy times there, interesting times, too, in that quaint conglomeration of a port town, so mixed in its quarters, businesses, nationalities, characters, an intriguing background to the lively and likable citizenry so anxious for the Territory to be up and doing things. And at this time a mining boom inland was on, to which was added the great excitement of a truly remarkable happening, a Round-the-World Air Race. Sleepy, forgotten Darwin was now the centre for southern newspapermen to report the arrival of the planes, the aerodrome and the wireless of that day were busy, and huge stacks of "aeroplane juice" were all over the place. Darwin, of course, had never dreamed of anything so fantastic as this. The date, so far as I remember, was the year that Peter Pan won the Melbourne Cup for the second time. It's a different Darwin now, of course, for the Japanese had to come and blow that interesting little old place right off the map. And a fat lot of good it did them. And the same applies to Broome also.

A straight run now for me at last, to Sydney after a two-year roam-about, Darwin to Port Augusta, two thousand miles. Thence Adelaide, Melbourne, Sydney—say another three thousand miles from here to the Big Smoke. So aboard the little Puffing Jenny and we puff away south with might and main, Scotty at the throttle, on this one and only Territory train that will take us all the way to Birdum, some three hundred boisterous miles, just a hop, step, and jump in Territory distances. No doubt about the hop and jump either, for in that three hundred miles our noisy little steed will have three hundred and forty bridges to cross. All aboard are in shirtsleeves and good humour, cattlemen mostly, then after we rattle over' the "tall" iron bridge crossing the narrow, pretty Adelaide River there come aboard buffalo-shooters, miners, a dozen government officials, half a dozen Afghans, a sprinkling of Chinamen, and a mob of chattering abos, with their wives and wide-eyed piccaninnies, and dogs, of course. Among them is a "blow-in" or two like me—but they're to be found anywhere.

A deep blue sky above, with cockatoos like white flowers massed on the bloodwood-trees and screeching insults as we puff by, with many a *clickety-clank a-clank a-clank* announcing our rattling way through the timber all the way to Brock's Creek. Here all hands tumbled hungrily out for a bite at what they called the "Shanty", really Fanny Haynes's Hotel—a real old backwoodswoman, take it or leave it with Fanny, just as you like. If the mounted man were away on patrol Mine Hostess, of course, had to deal in a lonely place with naked blacks and some pretty tough old characters at times, blokes who could eat a tiger without troubling to spit out the teeth. So maybe it was just as well the lady could look after herself. And, believe me, she could! A square-built old girl, short and preposterously nuggety, she was always quite decent to me; maybe she guessed I was harmless.

A solidly built, good-humoured young fellow of sixty summers strolls aboard the puff-puff here—Harry Hardie, whose buffalo country lies sixty miles eastward. Making our own fun, we rattle along for the rest of the day, through hilly country sparsely timbered with stunted trees, and presently showing numerous old dumps and workings that tell hectic stories of Union Town and Pine Creek. A big old buffalo bull with magnificent spread of horns glares at us from the timber; he's on the prowl a good many miles west of his stamping grounds. Probably he is a victim of the merciless law of the survival of the fittest, an old bull driven away from the herd by the young bulls. The old fellow has lost his harem now and does not feel too happy about it. I sympathize with him, though I've never been lord of a harem. Cynically I wonder if the old bull's bovine mind is wondering whether this smoke-puffing monstrosity is another kind of bull buffalo coming to scatter the very daylights out of the young cows. Before he can make up his mind to charge we've thundered past, with the truckload of aborigines shrieking derisively at him.

We rattle into Pine Creek at sundown. A smart-looking mounted man on the platform and brown-limbed cattlemen in shirtsleeves run a quizzical eye over the passengers; the usual group of native stockboys are also keen to "eye us off". Low hills all around, and there's been gold in them, too, rich gold indeed among the stunted ironwood and bloodwood and box that stretch away into distance. The settlement is a line of low whitewashed buildings cosily painted by sunset on a timbered flat dimly edged by hills. All hands stamp out of the train, carrying swags and bags and with shouted greetings to friends across at the pub, the usual "eat-up", meeting, and "stay-at" place. We have just nice time to enjoy a wash before the evening meal. Half a dozen dusty motor-trucks in for "train day"—here again prophesying that in time the internal-combustion engine will overrun the bush.

This Pine Creek is one of the very, very few inland Territory townships. Another mounted man appears, he is seized upon by a noisy crowd and seems very popular. The genial Jack Mahony, with a wealth of Territory patrol history round him, especially that epic chase for Nemarluk in the Fitzmaurice country west of Darwin after the slaying of the crew of the *Ouida*. Nemarluk and his Red Band had led the patrols a wild chase for three years until they were broken up, only very recently. Mahony, with his mate

Morey, had worked, too, with other patrols cleaning up the massacre on the *Myrtle,* the *Olga,* and the *Raff* at Caledon Bay across the buffalo country eastward, the spearing of Constable McColl by Tuckiar at Woodah Island, the spearing of Stephens and Cook westward on the Fitzmaurice, the rescue of men perishing in the bush—it would take half a dozen books to record this agile man's adventures, as indeed those of all his mounted mates. Theirs was a rough life certainly but full of interest.

This little bush hotel at Pine Creek houses a low-roofed bar of bare iron.[3] For a while, three men behind the little bar serve out drinks as hard as they can go, then the boys adjourn to the eat-up room. A jovial throng calling jokes to mates, stamp of heavy boots, bumping of shoulders as we tramp along the low, narrow passageway. Besides us train passengers there is a "mob in from the bush". I wonder how they are all going to fit in. A buffalo-shooter, bushy eyebrows matching a walrus moustache, grunts as he sits his nuggety body on a crowded form. Dressed in khaki pants with broad belt and open-necked shirt showing a chest hairy as a doormat, he glances round with humorous brown eyes, seeking an opportunity for a joke. Noted for a cheery personality is this tough old fellow, Woods, an old hand at the game. He's now taken up cattle country, which they all do if they live long enough. His life story would be worth reading beside that of the original Buffalo Bill. Australians might not believe that, but few of us know the buffalo herds of the north, or the shooters either; we know little indeed of the life of our own north. Indeed, the stories of the few old-timers present here, and of the steady-eyed cattlemen who have put their stake and life in the country, would fill many volumes. I've often thought it a pity that such stories must inevitably be lost to future generations. Still, I suppose it has been the same in all young countries.

Among the grizzly miners present are a sprinkling of young fellows of the "modern" type just then beginning to spread out into the bush. Those of them game to push farther out from the tiny settlements into what are left of the isolated areas will be among the bushmen of the future.

This dining-room, a pioneer place, is a long, low room of bare iron painted green. Punkahs are suspended from the roof, but their cool breath is felt no more since aboriginals are not allowed to work in hotels and the white staff is too small for anyone to be spared for this duty. I wonder how many other hotels in Australia have thus used the Indian punkah for cooling

---

[3] I Hear that "The Creek" has gone all modern these days, and Albert Young and his wife, Mayse, have built a new two-storey hotel. At the opening last year, so mulga wire tells me, four hundred turned up for the opening, coming from hundreds of miles away. Good luck to such progress, and may the new hotel build up hosts of cheery memories for the new generations as did the "old place" for us.

purposes. A highly coloured battle scene hangs on the wall above these now bent-backed, busy bushmen, a red-coated figure of Johnny Walker does his Beau Brummel act from the old-time sideboard. Believe me, we are busy, elbow to elbow, all along those hard wooden forms round the three tables under the dull light of a carbide-gas jet. There is a glimpse of a table, too, set out on the tree-shaded veranda, while from those who cannot crowd in there comes good-humoured jests questioning the influence of fortune's favourites before they adjourn to bar or veranda to open their precious mail. These hungry ones must await a second sitting, and a third.

All hands, myself included, are good eaters, keeping "our" two girls very busy. One is a fair-haired girl in a red striped dress; her cobber is dark-haired, in a blue striped dress. Both are surprisingly pretty, cheerful, and competent with it. Quite animated, too, for they look forward to "train day" as do all the tiny township, as little old Cooktown far away used to look forward to the monthly steamer. But we are a hungry mob for only two girls to serve. A man who is a bit smart with lip service can pay his compliment and get his tucker, and perhaps his mate's without waiting unduly for it. Such competition is a brisk aid to appetite when it works, but leaves an empty feeling otherwise. For if a "smartie" pays a compliment but misses out, to the huge delight of blokes "slow on the tongue", then that brave feeling begins to thaw out as he waits for his tucker.

As a couple of diners rise with a satisfied grunt and cautiously edge their legs from under the table, in strolls the heavily built figure of Harold Nelson, the Northern Territory's one and only politician for all that vast area. Through frustrating years he has been a very good battler for the Territory too. With Nelson is the taller, still more heavily built figure of Sam Irvine, the battling mailman on the Birdum to Alice Springs run, one of the longest mail-runs in the world. Sam's life for years has been the contradiction of fighting flood and bog in areas that soon would he scorching distances where an ounce of water would be worth more than its weight in gold.

But now, sliding and expertly squeezing into those two warm vacated seats, our worthy travelling companions seize their eating tools and glance round in lively anticipation.

"Get her eye!" growls Sam. "You're good at spruiking."

And the Member for the Northern Territory "gets her eye".

After the evening meal all hands adjourn to the tree-shaded veranda, sheltered on the hottest day, now delightfully cool and splashed by starlight. Out come the pipes, then there is yarning of "the news", of what the train has brought from Darwin, both in humanity and goods, a little gossip of "Officialdom" spiced with good-humoured sarcasm, and talk of the pearling fleet, any good takes of shell, any killings among white or black or brown or yellow. Any news of the Roper and of the buffalo lands away to the nor'-east of "the Creek", of cattle and the great Victoria River Downs station to the west, of historic Wave Hill, Gordon Downs, and other pioneer stations right on west into the Kimberleys and away eastward across the Barkly Tableland, even into the Gulf Country and across the Queensland border. There was always someone who volunteered some "mulga whisper" of news from every point of the compass. A mighty field from which to draw their news, three thousand miles from east to west.

Even today we do not fully realize the vastness of our continent.

The Aboriginal tracker Bul-Bul, whose story is in *Man Tracks*.

XVI

PINE CREEK NIGHTS

Of course, they jovially asked after Darwin, less kindly of that huge enterprise, Vestey's Meatworks, a controversial subject which brought in a little yarn of tourists, then so very rare birds, in this case a mother and her little girl travelling through the Territory. "Oh, mother, who owns all those cattle?"

"Vestey's, my dear."

They came to the rolling plains.

"Oh, mother, who owns all those big fields?"

"Vestey's, my dear."

They were driven round Darwin, then round the meatworks.

"Oh, mother, who owns all these big buildings?"

"Vestey's, my dear."

When going home they were put aboard a Blue Funnel boat.

"Oh, mother, who owns this lovely big boat?"

"Vestey's, my dear."

Several days later the child was gazing dreamily at the sea.

"Oh, mother, who owns all this water?"

"God does, my dear."

"Just as well He got in early," replied the child.

"I'll say," growled a cattleman who had missed out. "They've taken possession of damned near the whole territory, picked the eyes out of it. But did you hear of that little Sydney woman in Darwin who was so scared of snakes?"

"No," answered Sam. "Out with it!"

"Oh, she wanted a window put in the little house away down the back yard with a lamp in it.

" 'You know,' she complained, 'it's so dark these nights you never know when I may walk down there and meet a snake in the grass.' The only one I saw was a two-legged one!' observed her lady friend."

"She needn't have gone all the way to Darwin to find a snake in the grass," said a stockman, winking. And the crowd grinned at a rusty-whiskered old museum piece dreamily puffing his pipe on the veranda edge, a blackfellow's dog gazing adoringly up at him as if he were the only Old Joe in the world.

It was only last week, here on this veranda, that a lady traveller had complained bitterly of the heat.

"Toss orf yer duds, mum," invited old Joe, "an' take a cooler on my bunk."

The offer had come from Joe's good heart. His was the coolest bunk in the pub. He had had absolutely no designs. He was comically puzzled at what "all the sniggerin' " was about.

From cattle and the taking up of the great stations the yarning naturally gravitated to minerals, with talk of gold from Brock's Creek to Union Town to Pine Creek, of the "Chinee rabbit warrens" from Gandy's Hill for unknown miles. Incidentally, there were fantastic happenings deep down in among those black warrens, a little humour, but mostly a river of sweat enlivened by glittering treasure and hysterical joy, jealousy and hatred and tragedy, sometimes bitter tragedy within the pressures and suffocation and. darknesses deep down there. Enclosed spaces in darkness can be very, very terrible. But that wild northern story could fill books on its own. The boys yarned of tantalite and Hang Row's Wheel of Fortune pouring wealth at the lucky Chinee in the loneliness of West Arm along the western coast, of tin, copper, and wolfram finds, too, in much more isolated areas. All hands there had passed by a scraggly-timbered little waterhole near the Overland Telegraph Line, facetiously named Rum Jungle. My silly sense of humour makes me grin, writing this, when I wonder what those boys would have thought could they have seen the modern Rum Jungle and Batchelor uranium townships of today—let alone those carloads of tourists! What pickings the old aboriginal has missed by fading out just when the atom bomb was bringing him such rich passing gifts of fortune from modern roads and airport and transport, from "civilization" and "white-man" war materials and tourist trade.

But the boys were yarning of the Australian Inland Mission and the wonderful work of the Sisters in the little bush nursing homes. Of course, the talk drifted on to the "old abo", always an interesting topic, our Stone Age man and his missus of yesterday. Especially so in those areas where native life merged with the white, and farther out still where it was just beginning to merge.

An especially interesting topic at this period, the hectic years of Nemarluk and "King" Wongo, of Moodorish and Tiger, Merara and Tuckiar and "Longlegs", Natchelma, Woolaware, Nakaya, Marawata, Chugulla, Wadawarry, Walung, Maru, Chin-amon, Burar, "Stockman Jimmy", Deven, Minnara, Mangul and Lin, and a score and more of others, all wild men quick with the spear, who had made or were still making life lively in the wild country west to the Fitzmaurice and in fact right on into the Kimberleys. And to the east, throughout the buffalo country and Arnhem Land right to the Gulf. Hectic years these for the constantly travelling police patrols, "clearing up" the capture and massacre of crews of the *Ouida*, of the *Myrtle*, *Olga*, and the *Raff*, the killing of the white man Bill Tetlow, of Stephens and Cook, of Traynor and Fagan and others, the fatal spearing of Constable McColl, the troubles breaking out over such a short time. The boys could have kept on till dawn and beyond had they fully known the stories of the patrol leaders, that tiny handful of mounted men whose names already were household words throughout the whole vast Territory. As it was, they got in some interesting yarns of exploits of well-known trackers, particularly the three years' duel in pursuit of that fighting chief and, to me, native hero, Nemarluk, and his enemy, no less every inch a man, that implacable tracker, Bul-Bul.

The stars had twinkled out, figures of men had grown wispy, the evening air dreamy. From somewhere out among the shadows a snatch of native song rose sweetly, blending with the slumbrous bush night. Soft thud of hooves, then squeak of saddlery. The jingle of a bit, a soft order to a blackboy in the night, and another buffalo-shooter stepped up on the veranda with a nod and greeting to Wood. Which of course brought the yarning on to the Buffalo Kings of earlier years, to the Melville Island Buffalo King, Robinson, and Paddy Cahill, and their adventurous lives among the blacks in the days when the Malay proas ravaged the coast. Of shooters Cooper and Flynn, the latter beloved by the wild men of those early years, as they so clearly showed when he died of snake-bite. Yarns of the days of Cook, Rees, Rodney, Spencer, old Bill Laurie, Hardy, and others past and present whose lives were so packed with adventure that far-sighted America would never have let them "die" could she have claimed them as her own.

"A few of the old hands are still living," said a grizzled shooter quietly, "but most are gone. Some died hard, some by fever, accident, drowning, shipwreck, blacks. A black never forgets—feller I know caught one thieving the last of his tucker. He grabbed him round the neck, held a revolver to his chest. The black seized him by the throat. He pulled the trigger.

"It must have been twelve months later when the police came for him. Wonderful how they hear things. A man can be right back of nowhere and not a soul within a hundred miles. And yet they hear things. He got half a lifetime in an Adelaide jail, some two thousand miles away in civilization. Then he came back. And the blacks killed him."

Nelson, a lively chap, the Territory's politician who could take all coming to him and yet answer in good humour, spun some good yarns against himself. Not long before, from Darwin, he had wired "Old Tom" he was coming down to "the Creek" for a political meeting. Old Tom, a great supporter of Nelson's, haled himself to horse and spurred far and wide to muster the crowd and "herd them to the creek". But the importance of his trust and the hot weather grew too much for him, and when the great day dawned he became inebriated, filled with the best intentions and liquor and overwhelming fellow-feelings. Old Tom was very big and monstrously fat, and when the Member arrived he shambled up to him with tears streaming down his happy cheeks and insisted on throwing his arms round him to kiss him in front of the delighted crowd.

"Now look, Tom," protested the struggling Member diplomatically, "I'll bath and shave and be over at the tennis-court in half an hour. Now be a good fellow—get busy and get the crowd over."

Half an hour later when the Member arrived at the meeting-place a supporter pointed out Old Tom snoring soundly by the edge of the court.

"There's your friend, aren't you going to wake him?"

"Heavens, no! Not under a thousand pounds!" replied Nelson most definitely.

The Member got into his subject and, warming up to it, was soon spouting very well, airily taking taxation in his stride.

"Now, ladies and gentlemen," he shouted, "why do they impose this taxation?"

"To give buggers like you a thousand a year!" roared Old Tom and rolled over to snore again.

Brock's Creek Railway Station, 1912.

XVII

SORROWS OF THE OPIUM TRADERS

An old Brock's Creek man, patiently puffing his pipe while awaiting his turn, spun a yarn of a Chinaman speared by the blacks in the days when the Princess Louise, the Union, Extended Union, and numerous other holes in the ground were bywords in gold. This Chinaman was a "runner", carrying smuggled "twang" (opium) from Port Darwin to his compatriots inland at the Creek by following along the Overland Telegraph Line—a lonely trudge of a hundred and forty-five miles, very risky in those times. The only thing on the dead Chinaman the wild men couldn't find use for was the opium. But they certainly could find a use for the tins, to cut up into knives and scrapers. So they smashed the tins open and poured a thousand pounds' worth of potential dreams, that sticky, treacly stuff called opium, down onto Mother Earth. It did not matter much to the Chinaman, anyway, for he had already given his life's blood out to her; it was still oozing from the spear-thrusts and already the meat-ants were hurrying to eat it.

The wild men tried to eat the opium, obstinately tried with many a grimace. Puzzled, but still certain it must be good "white-man tucker", they scooped it up from the earth and put it on a charcoal fire to cook it. Of course, those violent fumes from that big quantity of opium put the whole crowd to sleep, even to their hungrily sniffing dogs. An old bull buffalo, wandering through the timber, stopped to stretch a neck and get a whiff of these strong, strange fumes, and they brought him stamping and snorting in amongst the living corpses to investigate, which of course woke them up in a dazed hurry. Half a ton of wild bull buffalo with a six-foot spread of horns snorting round with an inquiring disposition is not to be sneezed at.

"They lit out for the wide open spaces in all directions," concluded the old Brock's Creek yarn-spinner, "the dogs at their heels, leaving the old buffalo pawing the gravel and sniffing up that opium all to himself. Goodness knows what dreams that thousand quids' worth of twang gave the old bull."

"Easy to guess!" said an old Customs hand with wary, crows-foot eyes. "What would *you* think? Anyway, the funniest thing I've known in the opium-smuggling line was a heavy thud which sadly befell old Ah Tit. A Darwin character was Ah Tit, foxy as a cart-full of monkeys. Suspicious, too, so artful he wouldn't trust his own shadow. We'll say it was the old *Ti Yuan* steamed into Darwin, and Ah Tit hurried down to the wharf to buy a parcel of twang from the crew. They knew the grinning old sinner only too well, reckoned he was the trickiest bargainer out of all the Chinese hells, he wouldn't pay a brass farthing more than he was forced to for the best twang out of China. Anyway, he used to do very well out of it, the slinky-eyed cunning old devil. We never caught him—not until the base ingratitude, the horrible betrayal of his own countrymen broke his heart. His nerve, rather— old Ah Tit never had a heart. Anyway, he bought this parcel, hid the twang under his dirty blouse and, grinning like a Cheshire cat, came invitingly down the gangway right into our arms. Stood there grinning, the monkey faced old devil, grinning at us the invitation, 'Search me!'

" '*You'll* keep!' snapped my mate. 'We'll catch you one time for sure! Now get to hell off this wharf before I help you along with a boot in the pants.'

"Well, the old sinner got that twang safely back to his shack, pottered innocently among his vegetables until certain the coast was clear, then sneaked inside to examine the stuff and gloat over the profit he would make.

"Those tins were full of treacle!

"That near-demented Chinaman grabbed the tins and came racing down the street and out onto the wharf where the Ti *Yuan* was just ready to move off, one last rope holding her stem. Ah Tit ran gasping to the wharf edge and started hurling up tins at the ship's crew, yelling, 'Ah li, you ave 'im all along bread all light! No more spread treacle longa bread! Sell me bloody treacle, no more twang! Bloody robbers you! Take 'nother tin, you dirty t'ief, you — — —!' as he hurled tin after tin, screaming out a frenzied stream of Chinee curses as the steamer sheered off with two cheeky toots from her whistle—to this day I don't know whether by design or not. Anyway, a policeman grabbed Ah Tit's arm as he was throwing the last tin, but as there proved to be only treacle in it the police had nothing on him, except a big laugh. When Ah Tit in woebegone fashion came trudging back up the street he turned into the pub to drown his sorrow.

" 'What's the matter with you, Ah Tit?' inquired the publican's missus. 'You look like last year's misery with bells on.'

"He slung his arms heavenward, screwed-up face all tragic misery.

" 'Me velly clever man, me!' howled Ah Tit. 'Fifty lovely poun'! Bloody fool me! I pay 'em fifty poun'! To bloody t'ief! I buy 'em that jam belonga sugar-cane.' "

"Sugar-cane's what treacle comes from, anyway," growled old Gaynor. "What was the Chink moanin' erbout, anyways? He could have used up that treacle on his damper. He'll want Christmas bells on 'is grave!"

Old man Gaynor, tough as the cajeput. When he was lying out in the blazing sun one day, recovering from a bender, the boys thoughtfully threw a heavy wagon tarpaulin over him to protect him. Some hours later he awoke, or tried to awake, for no matter how he opened his eyes he was still in darkness. He tried to get up, but was bowed down as by some overwhelming weight. Reconciling himself to another attack of the horrors, he began laboriously to crawl along. Under that tarpaulin he made very heavy weather of it, to the delighted yell of a blackfellow, which brought the boys strolling outside to see what the excited buck was yabbering about. I'm afraid they played a joke or two on the thoroughly mystified crawler under the blanket, who by now did not have the haziest idea of who he was, where he was, or just what was what. But he was developing most apprehensive imaginings. How was *he* to know, weighed down in under that hot, heavy darkness, that when he was brought to an abrupt halt, when he could not move an inch, try and heave how he would, it was merely because a foot had been planted fair upon that tarpaulin corner? When he crawled away again, on through that dark, heavy silence, when something abruptly stopped his crawl ahead it was simply because two of the grinning boys were holding a pole right in front of his head. Of course, he was soon exhausted. When they pulled off the tarpaulin he gazed up from bloodshot, wondering eyes, open mouth dragging in that welcome air. At last he was game enough to venture a remark. "'Struth! I've heard about purgatory, but I never thought I'd be turned into a flaming tortoise an' carry me house over me head!"

Some of the boy's jokes at times, out of sheer thoughtlessness, could easily have ended in tragedy, which would just about have broken their hearts—if they had any. For instance, when they decided to "carve up" the Bull Tosser.

The Bull Tosser was the hairy-moustached old saddler, known throughout the Territory as the best saddler that ever was. And in those days it was the blacksmith and saddler and policeman, if any, who ruled the roost in every bush township. The only thing that had the Bull Tosser bested in saddlery was that he could never get a rinet long enough to counter-line a saddle.

Anyway, one torrid day when gold was booming round the Old Town the Bull Tosser, strange but true, was paralytic. It took quantity to get *him* that way. So the boys decided to have an operation. They carried him into the Dead House and chucked him on the earthen floor while they rigged up the "operation table". This was a couple of up-ended empty rum casks, over which they laid a broken-hinged old door. The Dead House of course was a somewhat familiar necessity in numerous far outback business places of those days, the little outhouse where you recovered from the horrors, or else———!

Anyway this gloomy iron shed was stifling this day, and with the door shut very gloomy, too. They saw they must have candles, and plenty, to "do the job proper feller". So they decided to dress up for the occasion, which meant white sheets thrown over themselves with eyehole and breathing holes cut in them. "Got ter look ther part," growled the "butcher".

And they looked pretty terrible, this vague idea of theirs of what an operating team would look like. The "butcher" was their term for their operating surgeon, he was a buck-toothed miner with the torso of a gorilla, only more hairy.

"Must have tools, too!" growled the butcher. "We can't open up 'is guts with our molars!"

"I wouldn't care to try!" declared his offsider distastefully, and bad-manneredly spat on the floor.

The "tools" consisted of a huge carving knife supplied by the grinning Chinee cook. As to the sheets—oh, well, when they had to pay the pub for those sheets later———!

Anyway, as preparations became shipshape they grew quite interested. They strewed a dozen candles in bottles round the shed, and lit up. Almost immediately, under that stifling iron, the candles began to fairly run away in molten fat. The operation staff undressed the patient, at which preparation he protested unavailingly in unconscious wrath. They lifted him, none too gently, to the operating table, upon hitting which he retaliated with a he-man belch and a lumbering, squelchy groan. From their exertions the operating staff paused to run a forearm across where their sweating brow would be, gathering round the table to stare down through the eyeholes of their "surgeon's gowns" at the patient. Sundry chuckles, exclamations of " 'Struth!" "It ain't a man! What *is* it?" came in muffled grunts of wonder from under the gowns. They had never seen the Bull Tosser naked before, to their muddled intelligence in this gloomy, suffocating heat it seemed as if they were looking upon their well-known friend and champion saddler for the first time. The Bull Tosser! Somehow now, for the first time, the name seemed to fit. Those gurgling, moaning snores of uneasy inebriation they were familiar with, but these labouring ribs, these scruffy looking patches of gingery hair, these knobs of bones, these stringy sinews, these brown and yellow skin splotches, these corny-looking protuberances attached here and there, these old-time scars, these shrivelled up "bits and pieces"!

" 'Struth!" came a sepulchral whisper of sheer wonder. "Ain't he a awful picture?"

"Who the hell woulda thought we look like this?" came another rumble.

" 'Course we don't!" came an indignant grunt. 'This is only the Bull Tosser!"

"Shut up!" hissed the chief surgeon. "We got to git to work. You'll wake the———patient."

"Well, git to work then!" came a muffled voice aggrievedly. "*You* wanted to be butcher and you ain't even marked 'im out yet!"

To this perfectly scientific piece of medical wisdom there came immediate muffled grunts of assent. The chief surgeon, professionally hurt, at this allusion to his inadequacy, screwed round his hooded head. The only thing he could see were candles dripping melted fat. He reached over and dipped a big finger into a candle, he would have dipped his right hand, too, but it was handicapped through grasping his scalpel, the carving knife. However, he daubed a line of hot grease along the patient's stomach, he dipped again and yet again and again. Just a faint shiver of the patient's stomach skin and splashes of hardening candle grease showed that the markings were "taking". Pleased with success, his big finger scooped all the guts from a fast-melting candle and ran the hot finger from the patient's navel right down to— — —

"Hey, there!" protested a voice. "Be careful! When you run the knife down his guts right to there it might slip. Go easy with them markings!"

"Wouldn't matter if it *did* slip," grunted the butcher. "'E wouldn't miss it."

" 'Ow do you know?" said the protester indignantly. "It ain't you is bein' operated, on!"

However, pleased with his job and determined to brook no more amateur interference, the surgeon took a business-like grip on the knife.

"Hey! 'Arf a mo!" growled a voice disgustedly.

"You ain't given 'im a antiseptic yet."

Taken aback by this second oversight of professional etiquette the surgeon glared round again. And yet again all he could see were fast guttering candles, now half melted down—nothing else at all to give him a line on "antiseptics". He stepped out and, gathering half a dozen of the lighted candles in his big paws; stepped back to the operating table, tipped them up and liberally splattered the patient's stomach with molten grease.

The patient's eyes slowly, wonderingly opened, opened wider, opened alarmingly wider, his mouth followed suit, wider still in his taughtening face, as in some depthless subconsciousness there was bom a feeling that he was staring up at a line of ghosts leering down upon him. In that silent stillness he felt his belly on fire and agonizedly melting away, all was a motionless void in which awful eyes were peering down, he caught the gleam of a huge knife— — —!

With a death-chilling scream the patient flew up off the operating table. It overturned on the doctors as he threw himself at the wall which in reply sent a hollow crash of iron down through the sleepy township. With another awful scream the patient hurled himself at the wall again, with "doctors" rolling at his feet entangled in one another's sheets in darkness and now in nearly as much panic as the patient himself. Again he hurled himself into the gloomy shades with another thunderous crash, and luckily hit the door, which spilled him out into the glorious sunlight, in half a dozen somersaults. The patient hardly hit the earth until, picking himself up with a piercing scream, he was flying down the dusty road. A tethered horse took one glance, pulled back on his bridle and broke it, and bolted down the road. Half a dozen black gins stood there petrified as the apparition bounded by them, then with one inhuman yell they vanished into the timber. A loaded camel train coming lumbering into the town...

It was then that the little iron township thought a cyclone had hit it.

But that was merely one still-remembered afternoon in the life of Pine Creek.

However, they were yarning about the "Living Snail", old man Gaynor carrying his tarpaulin home on his back.

"That old bushwhacker Gaynor talks too much." A cattleman nudged his mate slyly. "Not like some political friends we know of!"

At which Nelson, always quick on the uptake, led the laugh.

The reference was to him and visiting political friends, or friendly enemies. Nelson, Stephens, and several other travelling notables had arranged to speak *courteously* in turns, none poaching on another's preserves. This point of honour having been amicably arranged, now came the question of time.

"Two minutes will do me!" declared Stephens.

"Go on!" protested Nelson. "We must give them their money's worth—they expect it. Most have come a long way to hear us, remember. We must put up a show."

"Two minutes will do *me*!" repeated Stephens firmly.

So Nelson opened the ball and spoke for three-quarters of an hour. Then Stephens in turn stood up and began to address a now highly critical audience.

"I believe in forty-eight hours a day and more production!" he shouted. Nelson tugged at his coat and hissed that he'd made a mistake. Stephens glared down beside him and, believing his fellow politician was putting one over him, shouted back to the crowd, "No! I'll stand by what I said! Forty-eight hours a day and more production!"

After the meeting, the politicians were walking back to the pub, careful of their steps as it was a pitch-dark night. Footsteps of two locals came crunching behind them, voices critically discussing the meeting.

"Well, what did you think of it?" asked one.

"Oh, I don't know!" grumbled his mate. "That fat bastard would *talk* you to death, the other no-hoper would *work* you to death!"

The Territory "Puff-puff" arrives at Darwin Railway Station, about 1932.

XVIII

"SOOL THE WOLVES ONTO 'EM!"

Breakfast to the accompaniment of the aviary of the bush in piercing whistle and call and chuckle, some among these noisy feathered "hoarders" demanding *their* breakfasts from the very veranda. Then comes a ringing yell: "All aboard! Shake a leg! All-a-boar-rd!"

So we pick up our swags or suitcases, stroll across from the pub to the station, and, still yarning, "hop aboard", to the whistles of the noisy engine, energetic clanking of wheels, shouted farewells, and messages. *"Yak-ai! Mar-Muk!"* yell the aboriginal stockmen to the laughing, yelling, waving tribesmen and their shrill-voiced women aboard, and we are off again. Happy-go-lucky travelling in the Territory "Puff-puff" in those cheery days—now, too, I suppose.

The next "pull-up" of consequence was the Katherine, a whole two hundred miles inland from Darwin. Flat, lightly timbered country, tall grass brown and dry. The township a straggly little line of some twenty-five houses of iron, with Mrs Kate Bernhard's Sportsman's Arms and O'Shea's Railway Hotel nearly as prominent as Sergeant Woods stepping forward to greet his right-hand man, Constable Jack Mahony. The sarge a mighty man was he, jolly good company, too, and a double surprise for any naughty city "blow-in". For, besides being gifted with a native shrewdness, he was a champion wrestler. A score of bushies awaiting the train, a buxom housewife with her mouth full of pegs hanging clothes out on the line and scolding while kicking back at a playful puppy trying to undress her by tugging away at the hem of her skirt. A dozen men holding up the veranda posts fronting each pub lumbering erect to take a mean start to the "Clang! Clang! Clang!" of the "eat-up" bell which rang out across the grassland as the train pulled up.

We all piled out, of course, and strolled across. When the time came to stroll back I knew most of us would he letting out a hole or two in our belts. What interested me was a brave little one-horse battery standing up as if it owned the place. That battery spelt "gold", "tin" or "wolfram". In this case the spelling was "gold", for Tim O'Shea was crazy about mining and had a little gold show about seventeen miles out. Strange though it may seem, the show had been producing a little gold for some years past. The battery was for crushing the stone. I wondered whether the pub or the "show" was the better mine.

The O'Shea family were known far and wide, which really means far and wide in such vast spaces as the Territory. Mum and Dad O'Shea had reared a big family of jolly girls, all Territory bred. Thoroughly capable, too, of course, they have to be out there.

As we came stamping up onto the veranda and into the little old bar I had the silly thought of a cattle stampede. It's wonderful what a trainload of thirsty, hungry men can do to liven a place up. The good-humoured laughter, the noisy jokes, the rumble of their "hooves" along the veranda set the cockroaches galloping for cover. Of course, already draping the bar there had to be several sour-faced old grumps, you meet them now and then. This one in particular had grown hair on his teeth. He glared round from watery eyes.

"Huh!" he grunted after we'd strolled in. "Furriners! Ther time youse could put a ten-pound note on Tim O'Shea's bar in ther Katherine, plank a stone on it agin' the wind, say ter it, 'Wait here till I come back!'—*them* times is gorn. So is the ten-pound note. Huh! Youse can't do it now-ow!" and he graciously spat on the bar-room floor.

Of course, Big Sam the mailman seized the chance of a joke.

'You're dead right, dad," boomed Sam. 'The Territory is going to the dogs. What with motor trucks and aeroplanes and them flash women! Why, I was in this very bar only a month ago enjoying a gargle with a mate of mine when I asks, 'What are you looking around for?'

" 'I dropped my ring,' he said.

" 'Struth!" explained Sam to the bar. 'That ring didn't hit the ground—that city slicker drinkin' beside my mate should have been a fowl the way he could pick up things!"

However, it appeared the Territory men really were getting too soft now, ever since a *lady* ethnologist had trekked all the way up inland to "study the natives". As an instance, the boys were now objecting to beer-cases for coffins, whereas to be planted in a box instead of a moth-eaten blanket was once frowned upon as being sissy. Not so long back, just outside the Katherine, a man was reported drowned.

"Make him a box!" growled the sergeant.

The coffin was just made when the drowned man turned up, had a look at his box, then hit the roof because it was made of beer-cases.

"It's not daisies they'll be wanting on their grave next," grumbled the sergeant. "It'll be violets powdered with star-dust."

And some of them would deserve it. Mrs Fogarty, for instance, with that quiet smile that had weathered untold hardships, and nearly a lifetime of loneliness. She is a little sunburnt bushwoman blessed with a cheery smile and that sort of "never-give-up" personality, used to living in very lonely places where she would never see another white woman. She was long since used to the blacks, of course, but had seen the bloody law of club and spear fought out right at the hut door so very often that she could never trust them. She, with a daughter of sixteen, a lively girl going to be as good and efficient a woman as her mother, were just now travelling through. Her husband was at present brumby-running at Todmorden station, which then was the farthest-out station to the west. A wild stallion had recently bitten half the calf of his leg off. A few years earlier her son, a lad of ten, had also had an accident to his leg. They drove him through both Kimberleys right to Broome and put him aboard the *Centaur* for Perth and hospital, two thousand miles and a bit more all told, the overland trip, and very rough miles at that. Nowadays, the chain of Australian Inland Mission hospitals with their Flying Doctor Service do away with what would be similar long-drawn-out tragedies.

With the engine blowing its very final "Hop aboard quick-feller or I'll damn well leave you blast!" the last score of stragglers came gossiping across from the township, their gesticulating hands the subject of laughing jokes from the abo passengers piled waiting in their open truck. The white man's hair would stand on end at times if he could understand the aborigines' summing-up of him. Maybe it's just as well that few of us ever bother to understand "the lingo".

For lunch, that little personality train growled to a condescending stop at Mataranka, four or five houses under the trees. Mounted Constable Johnson was on duty with a ready joke for the train crew. And, of course, there was "the pub", a low-built place of iron, suffocatingly hot on that summer day. But a most inviting, pretty little oasis within that gloomy oven was a veranda gorgeous with ferns and palms in water-cooled abundance, protectively walled off from the scorching outside world with wire netting. This was the pride of the quaint little old lady who kept the hotel. I hope that brave little fernery, and its brave little attendant, are still there.

Flat country all the way now to Birdum, the end of the line, and it looked it, though maybe sundown made it appear lonelier than usual. Birdum was half a dozen tiny houses smothered in a vast area of flat bushland, our camping place a rather pretty whitewashed iron hotel with green lattice-work. Inside a cheery atmosphere—naturally so, when it was presided over by Johanna Kearnan, daughter of old Tim O'Shea. Only one slightly jarring note, though, from one of the half-dozen whiskery old locals draping the tiny bar. This was when Sam put down his glass for a refill with a tremulous sigh and remarked, "Ah! This thirst-quencher is a good 'un!"

"Who the hell wants a thirst-quencher?" growled old Charlie Long aggrievedly. And his mates nodded support.

Here I saw my first road train; it seemed a huge sign of progress to our admiring eyes. Proudly Captain Roscoe and the men in charge assured us that those huge trucks had already lowered transport cost by halves wherever they had operated, a mighty advance in the opening up of that vast, isolated area.

Road trains of today could have loaded our "monster" fifteen-tonner upon it, added a few trucks of cattle and a motor-truck or two for good measure, and rolled merrily on its way. Goodness knows what the road trains of tomorrow will lift.

That evening there was that rarity of the Territory at the pub, a thimbleful of white women. Of course, we gathered round, except a score of old diehards who smoked on the veranda edge under the stars, in low tones darkly prophesying, "Women an' these dam motor-trucks is goin' to ruin the Territory! A man will soon have to push further out!"

However, there's bound to be some blokes who'll grumble when they find angels in heaven.

One visitor we greeted most heartily was Mrs Ray, typical of the few scattered women leading such lonesome lives away out on the great stations. This one, Mainoru, was one of the loneliest in the continent before Ray took over. Jack Mahony told with laughing grimness of a visit to that station, when he and Police Constable Johnson, on patrol, were tracking native killers who for weeks had led them and their horses an exhaustive chase. One weary afternoon they rode up to the lonely homestead and were greeted by a host of snarling dogs rushing out at them, followed by a "mob" of naked black gins with an excited yabbering and yelling that set the snarling dogs to attacking the packhorses and mules. These promptly bolted, despite the swift riding and furious shouting of the trackers. This turned the dogs into a pack of wolves, some of which rushed snapping at Mahony's horse's heels. His horse started bucking as Johnson's horse began plunging wildly, with dogs now snapping at its heels also. The packhorses had bolted in a frenzy to scatter through the bush, despite the galloping efforts of the trackers to wheel and hold them. No wonder the horses went mad; they were being attacked by a bloodthirsty mob of howling wolves, which now had split up into two mobs, one in full cry after the vanishing pack animals and trackers' horses, the other ravening round the frantically plunging, kicking hooves of the two mounted men.

Mahony was forced to whip out his revolver and shoot those dogs away from his now almost uncontrollably maddened horse, the shots and yelping changed the yells of the gins to a screaming tirade as they leapt into the air, waving their arms as they howled threats to the riders now battling for their very lives. For if either had been thrown from his maddened horse he would have been hurled into the midst of a wolf-pack urged on by screaming women, their howls changing to piercing yells of abusive anguish as the dog pack was beaten off by bullets. The arrival of *that* patrol to Mainoru homestead was quite startling.

The half-caste who then was in charge of the place was away to the Roper River with the station pack-team for stores, no telling when he would return. Probably weeks, maybe a month or two.

Mahony and Johnson kicked the gins and dogs and their scraggy possessions out of the homestead in an endeavour to make it somewhat fit for civilized occupation—this to now wailing protests from gins and dogs.

If a man could only have carried one of those modern little movie and sound cameras of these days he would have taken quite an interesting, action-packed, piercingly noisy scene. For, of course, the wild cockatoos always gossiping in the trees round the homestead had joined in from the very start with a screeching gusto high above the screeching of the gins and piccaninnies, the snarls of the dog packs and the howls when the whips went cracking, the plunging, then bucking, then bolting of the packhorses and mules, the shouted orders, threats, curses of the mounted men desperately struggling to remain in the saddle, finally the sharp crack of revolver shots, the sudden change of "tempo" in now anguished howl of dogs, wails of gins and children, with cockatoos flying and screeching over the homestead and the whole mix-up—helped, of course, by the crowing of a couple of roosters and the few scraggly fowls that the dogs had not yet killed. And what the black trackers yelled to the abusive women when at last they had mustered and returned with the frightened pack animals—well, there'd be no need to censor it, it was all in their own lingo, anyway. Oh yes, an exciting little picture with plenty of noise, plenty of action.

"Too flaming much for *my* liking," said Mahony feelingly. "To this day I shiver when I think of what those dogs would have done to me had my horse succeeded in throwing me amongst them!"

XIX

AS TIME PASSES

But since Ray had taken Mainoru over that homestead had become a very different place. Pretty, too. It stands on a low hill commanding a far-flung vista of flat country, and Mrs Ray can see the signal-smoke fires of the station team returning from the Roper River with stores when they still are four days' travel away. As to "white gold", Mainoru spring is priceless, for it flows all the year round right past the homestead, gradually growing into a pretty little stream. Distantly towards the Arnhem Land coast flows the Roper River, up which a very occasional boat comes with stores far as the Roper Bar, Nature's rock wall across the river.

Ray had got a bit of a start on some years earlier, when Maranboy tinfield was found. He pegged out a claim and struck quite a nice little patch of tin. Then he and Andy Rose took up Mainoru.

The station lies a hundred miles out from the isolated Maranboy tinfield, on the Arnhem Land border. Mrs Ray had been out there for five years at the time of our meeting at Birdum. A cheery, strongly built, motherly type of woman. Women with her job in life must call upon all the personality they possess at times; things can happen which demand quick initiative and action, others compel them to keep a strong hold on themselves. A sudden spurt of development, though, had brought her a neighbour to live only seventy-five miles away.

'Which means we're right in the suburbs now," she laughed. 'We'll be saying good day to a weekly mailman next."

She had lived at Mainoru for three years, busy with station work, before she saw another white woman. She and her husband used to look forward to the arrival of a police patrol, one every six months as a rule, just to make sure that they were still in the land of the living. She laughed as she told of one wild night when mounted men Sheridan and Johnson came riding along with bowed heads against a howling wind as a storm roared down over the bush. From the veranda she watched the men and horses coming, ploughing doggedly on under rolling thunder as sheet rain blotted them from view. With frightening speed this "big blow", its howling punctuated by the crashing of uprooted trees, blew into a really frightful storm. Against it the badly buffeted patrol, with protective arms ready to ward off flying branches, came slowly battling their way up to that lovely big tree fronting the homestead. Round the butt of this handy tree horsemen used to hitch their horses. In a lightning crash the tree flashed into a sheet of splintered flame. Men and horses were brushed aside as if by some mighty hand, while two aborigines who had sought shelter under the tree were blown away as if from a cannon. For a moment, dazed within that blinding shock, she thought the homestead had been blown to smithereens.

Both husband and wife loved the land, enjoying the smell of the good earth and the wonder that it means. They planted cotton as an experiment one time, and Mrs Ray took a delight in the thousand beautiful plants that were soon springing up as from some magic touch. On one quiet afternoon she counted the seeds in a pod. 'There were five hundred!" she declared triumphantly.

When her husband was away mustering she was sometimes five months all alone, except for the natives. These always slept round the house and "looked after her". She and her husband never had any trouble with the blacks, in fact they both liked them, even though they did spear the cattle now and then.

This was a really big meeting at Birdum in this quiet Territory night.

Sheila O'Shea, with her pleasant laugh, was here at "the Council", too. Like her dad's place at the Katherine, this pub was built for quick and easy transport if necessary, of iron, mostly on a cement flooring. Thus the whole thing could be knocked down quickly and easily and transported elsewhere, which is a very handy type of a building, should a new mineral field break out some hundreds of miles away out in the bush.

Here was a large cement floor. Upon it, the rooms were mere walls, shells of iron sheeting, with a six-inch vacancy under every wall, and an opening of from four feet to six feet between the top of the wall and the roof. Thus air circulated throughout the building during the hot season. Of course, every sound, every noise, every snore, every sigh was audible from all the rooms. Men talking and yarning, chucking their boots on the floor, probably drinking, with an occasional swear-word or joking yarn, women's voices and the secrets they are discussing, quite distinct. But who cares, out where the bullwaddie grows? You just yawn, enjoy a last pipe, then roll over and go to sleep.

And what sleep!

Next morning we slung our swags aboard the mail-truck. From Birdum to the Alice, four hundred miles, in jolly good company. Sam Irvine the skipper, Harold Nelson the Federal Member, the one and only politician in the whole Territory ("and one too bloody many, so I've been told," remarked Nelson cheerily). With us, too, were W. and E. T. King, and P. A. Giles, son of Alfred Giles, explorer and pioneer with John Ross and pilot to construction gangs in the building of the Overland Telegraph Line. This line, the famous one, runs right up through South Australia to Darwin, a living, ever-working monument to the sons of that scantily populated State, South Australia. Giles was going to Adelaide for a holiday, so he'd be continually reminded of his father and those hardy teams of men by two thousand miles of line going straight on, seemingly ever on, through the scanty timber and giant anthills on, on, on—the track the usual bush dry-weather track now over level country. The long military road had not been built then, of course.

"Be careful!" Nelson warned our driver as I climbed aboard. "You've got an important load aboard."

"My Gawd!" groaned Sam as we started off. "A politician, a government official or two, a prospector turned author, and an overweight mail-truck driver! Must be a wonderful country to keep us all."

"I'll say so," agreed Nelson cheerily. "No wonder my constituents say the country is going to the dogs."

'That's so,' agreed Sam definitely as we drove off. "Reminds me of a mob one trip back at Brock's Creek, not five bob among the lot! All growling at being out of work, growling at the country."

"What's wrong with the country?" protested old Andy. "This country has put many a man on his feet."

"You should talk!" growled Slim Billy. "You've not made a quid in years. How do you mean this country has put many a man on his feet?"

"Well," explained Andy, "I came into this country with twelve packhorses. And now I'm walking out of it!"

Territorians of those few years back would remember that Andy was a great friend of that even better-known character, Maurice Brunton, author of *The Boomerang Cheque*.

"He's a great old supporter of mine is Andy," chuckled Nelson. "Only recently I've found out there's just one man in all this Territory he doesn't like. 'Do you remember old Tim the Fiddler?' I asked him the other day.

" 'Remember him,' groaned Andy. 'I've been trying twenty years to *forget* him!' "

"They can put things in a few words in this country," said Sam as the truck dodged a ten-foot ant-bed, "when they want to. There's a cook on a cattle-station just ahead loves this country, simply refuses to leave it, neither does his coin, must be the best 'stay right here' cook in all the Territory. Toiling there a while back was One-eared Mick. Mick was the reverse. No sooner does Mick knock up a cheque than you can't see him for dust racing to the city lights to spend the cheque, swearing he'll never, never return. He returned to the station after a bender recently.

" 'Oh! And so *you're* back!' grumped the cook.

" 'Yeh! I am,' replied Mick.

" 'Well, a rolling stone gathers no moss.'

" 'Yah!' sneered Mick. 'An' stagnant water stinks!' "

"It's wonderful what language can do," mused Nelson, "handled by those fortunate enough to know how to use it. A crowd of us were doing a tour of the western country a while back. A big car, heavily overloaded with our goods and chattels, and tremendously so with 'quality'—for we had Sir Archdale Parkhill, Minister for the Interior, aboard, with Mr J. A. Carrodus, Secretary of the Department and other important personages"—Nelson winked aside at me—"who were on tour right down through the Territory to the Alice and would receive numerous deputations, thus obtaining much valuable information respecting the people and conditions prevailing." Coughing discreetly, the first Federal Member for the Territory proceeded, "Meanwhile, neither the cockatoos nor the kangaroos out there had even seen a 'sir' before."

"I suppose they sat back on their moth-eaten tails and bowed," suggested Sam morosely.

"They did," agreed Nelson, "and Sir Archdale was quite appreciative. Especially when the cockatoos, clustered on the tops of the tallest trees, raised their golden crests and shrieked, 'Hearty welcome, Sir Archdale, hearty welcome!' They'd been well tutored by the locals."

"Yeah?" said Sam derisively. "And what did the pink galahs do then?"

"Not what the pigeons do from the roof of the City Post Office," replied Nelson. "We train 'em better up here in the Territory. Anyway, our car jibbed at a big steep rise. By some kindly whim of the wise old Fate that watches over all politicians, a teamster accompanied by a mob of natives happened to be camped by a muddy waterhole right at that outlandish spot."

'There would be," said Sam disgustedly. "If you political blokes were bushed out in the desert it would rain manna from heaven!"

"Of course!" agreed Nelson loftily. 'The country must keep its parliamentary system and personnel intact at all costs. However, as I was remarking, there the teamster was. He nearly swallowed his whiskers when with a flourish I introduced 'Sir Archdale Parkhill, Minister for the Interior'."

"He thought you were pulling his leg," grunted Sam.

"Why?" demanded Nelson.

"Park Hill. Weren't you parked by a hill?"

"Ah!" sighed Nelson. "How these Territorians can make play with words! Anyway, Will you give us a hand uphill?' I asked the teamster.

"'Yeah!' he almost whispered.

"The presence of a real live Minister of the Crown, a 'sir' to boot, seemed to have turned him dumb. Anyway, he yelled out to his motley crowd of natives and they had the team hitched to the car in a brace of shakes. Those disdainful animals simply walked away with the car, the cunning abos, men, women and children, pushing and yabbering behind as if they were doing it all themselves. Never tell me the Australian aboriginal has no brains. These fellows and their missuses had sized up this party as being the biggest prospect in tobacco and hand-outs they'd handled since Moses was a lad. Of course, for those parts, we really were an impressive entourage."

"Yeah," agreed Sam, "so I'd imagine. *Two* politicians together when the country groans under the weight of one! Well, I'm waiting to hear what the teamster said, or was he still just struck dumb?"

"He said nothing at all," replied Nelson loftily, "until we got to almost the top of the rise. By then the team were really feeling the pressure and needed a spell for the last heave-up.

"Put a stone behind the wheel," called back the teamster quietly to a native. Nothing happened.

"Chock up!" called back the teamster again. "Quick-feller! Chock up!" But the aboriginals, busy at shamming to be pushing with all their might, did not appear to hear him.

Then that quiet teamster stood back from the team, gazing down towards the car and those apparently pushing behind. You could hear his opening roar a mile away.

"You———black———! Put a———stone under that———wheel!"

Of course, they all dropped their paws from the car and scuttled aside to grab a stone, which enabled the car to roll back a yard or two, believe me. The teamster didn't cease roaring when once he opened his mouth, in fact it was one continuous roar even after the natives had come back running with a score of stones to block the wheels. Parkhill just stood there gazing in an awed admiration.

"What a sar'-major he would have made!" he murmured regretfully at last. "What a wonderful prize the Australian Army has missed!"

"Do you know," remarked Sam, "we've come ten miles while you've been getting that car up that hit of a sandhill?"

"But I'm only a politician," protested Nelson, "not a teamster, let alone a mail-driver. I'm only a learner in the use of words."

"Were *all* amateurs at times," agreed Sam loftily, "compared to some of these grizzled old niggers. A coupla years back, maybe a hit more, a young fellow came up from down south searching for his uncle. The family hadn't heard from uncle for some years past and were anxious lest something had happened to him. The lad wandered from station to station. But no one cared to tell him about it, we don't boast much up here in the Territory. Finally the young fellow came to an outback station where the cook at last took pity on him. "Oh, you go down there to the black's camp and ask old Jacky where your uncle is. Just show him a stick of Nigger Twist tobacco, and he'll tell you.'

"The lad hurried down to the camp. A bleary-eyed old cut-throat squatting in the ashes was pointed out to him as Old Jacky. The lad showed this relic a stick of tobacco and inquired, 'You been savvy that old George Lincoln?'

" 'You-ai,' agreed the native.

" 'Where you been see him last?'

" 'Me no more been see him! Me *eat* him!' growled Jacky."

Innumerable yarns helped pass the miles, the hours and anthills and lancewood and bloodwood and telegraph poles away. Young Giles was a bit on the quiet side, a listener like me, as were our other fellow-travellers. Sam and the genial Nelson, from their years of experience, could yarn for hours on end of this country. Vast though it was, Nelson had met practically every man and the very few women in it, while Sam at least knew them all by repute if not personally. The population has trebled and more now, of course.

Ernestine Hill, author of The Great Australian Loneliness, had been in the Territory since 1924, and met Idriess on this trip.

XX

THE LADY ETHNOLOGIST

"We're at the parting of the ways," said Nelson. 'The motor-car and aeroplane have come, your friends such as old Cannibal Jacky are speeding to their last cooking fires, the Bindi-eye Walkers of our day are vanishing."

"Bindi-eye Walker? Who was he?" someone asked.

"A tough old Camooweal pioneer of my Queensland days," Nelson replied. He refused to grow into these modern ways, and took a grim delight in the shortcomings of the motor-car along the awful tracks out there. One day recently, chased by a swarm of flies he drove into Camooweal with the very ripe leg of a horse dangling from the sulky.

'S truth, Bindi-eye! What the hell is *this* for?' protested the citizenry.

" 'Becos,' growled Bindi, 'a man can't travel this bloody country these days without spare parts.'

"After many years," proceeded Nelson, "I got a message from the boys telling me that they'd persuaded old Bindi to hop into the train and come down to the city for a holiday. I told Reardon, who always had a lot of time for the old bushies.

"'Well, we'll have to give him a party,' declared Reardon enthusiastically. 'Any pioneer who comes from the sunset side of Camooweal down into this city of Brisbane must be right royally entertained by the citizenry.'

"So we escorted him to Lennon's and the plush carpets for an introductory drink. You needn't grin! Even in the majesty of that hotel of hotels, even in the company of Australia's Most Distinguished Sons, old Bindi-eye from Bindabuloo was equal to the occasion—though his eyes *were* sticking out like pickled onions at that attractive barmaid. As Reardon did the gallantries that knowledgeable girl fairly dazzled old Bindi-eye with her thousand-dollar smile.

" Yours, Mr Reardon?' she said.

" 'Oh, I'll have a martini with an olive in it,' replied Reardon cheerily. I had to hide a grin at old Bindi-eye's amazed expression as he watched the olive go into the drink.

" 'And yours, Mr Nelson?'

" 'I'll have a Manhattan with a cherry, thanks.' And old Bindi-eye's leathery visage was a treat as he watched that barmaid's scarlet-polished fingers neatly spear that scarlet cherry.

" 'And yours, Mr Walker?' she said, smiling sweetly.

" 'Oh,' growled Bindi, 'I'll have a beer with a flamin' mango in it.'

"We introduced him to the modern girls.

" 'I suppose you think it awful to see girls smoking, Mr Walker?' said one little pretty.

" 'Oh no,' growled old Bindi, 'all the gins smoke up my way.' "

It's not only history that repeats itself. As Nelson was yarning of old Bindi-eye Walker I was thinking of a similar old character well known in the Kimberleys. He also was urged to go to the city, Perth in this case, and "see life". He was also taken in hand by the boys, and entertained by their ladies. And was smilingly asked the same question, and growled the same reply.

"There's a good many 'Bindi-eyes' in this country," mused Sam as we hummed along to Newcastle Waters. "See those hog ruts across in the spinifex there? Held me up for three days during the last rain. But these old Bindi-eye characters are rattling good coves—do anything to lend a man a hand. Of course, you politicians prefer travelling with the silvertails."

"Yes," replied Nelson, "though *you've* seen a blackfellow riding beside me many a time. I've even been known to shake a mit and quaff a beer with the wharfies at Darwin. I presume your lordly wit is referring to my recent fellow-traveller, Sir George Pearce. Very austere, a definite sobersides, but a warm human personality for all that. In Darwin I'd bothered him a lot, and you locals well know that when I bother a man for anything for the good of *this* country I darn near bother him to death. Anyway, I'd kept on telling Sir George that Canberra certainly should do something to Vestey's even if it was only to insist that they build better huts for the men. Later, as you know, Sir George and I were travelling across the Barkly Tableland to Lake Nash. And across this good country, of course, the homesteads of the great stations could almost be called palatial. We camped at one with every convenience, baths, reading rooms—everything except the dancing girls. And you could hear *them* corroboreeing away out in the moonlight.

"I was sitting out on the veranda with Smallhorn, the manager, admiring the beautiful old tree close outside. It is of huge thickness, rising straight as a gun-barrel before its mighty branches spread out against the sky. That giant old tree is white as the driven snow—for, alas, it was ringbarked forty years ago. Sir George came strolling along the veranda and I noted a certain glint in his eye.

" 'Well, Nelson,' he demanded, 'are you satisfied with *this* station?'

" 'Yes, Sir George, they've done the thing properly here.'

" 'Even to that tree!' Smallhorn pointed. 'And well they appreciate it!'

" 'Who appreciate it?' inquired Sir George.

" 'The cockatoos.'

" The cockatoos?'

" 'Yes. We built that tree for the cockatoos to roost on.'

"Sir George stared a moment, frowned at that now tell-tale whiteness, then rose from his chair.

" "You are trying to make fun of me,' he said severely, and stalked away."

"With that type of humour," declared Sam disgustedly, "I can easily understand the gentleman giving you the bird."

"Tut-tut!" said the political man. "Methinks I've heard of a ladybird giving you similar!"

Which brought a grin from our fellow-travellers, for the long drawn out duel between the "ladybird" and Sam the mail-driver was pretty well known along the whole length of the Overland Telegraph Line.

She was an ethnologist "studying the natives", and from Adelaide she was going north right out to the wild places. The South Australian Commissioner for Railways gave orders that, so far as the Northern Line and his authority extended, she was to be well looked after. And, of course, she was. A white woman travelling out there was a curiosity to all hands, but a white woman studying the natives was something right out of the box. So the construction gangs toiling along that lonesome sunburnt track willingly and good-humouredly "looked after her". There were whole teams of these buck navvies to manhandle her cases, anyway. It would be a very different problem when she reached the last camp on the end of the construction, which was Oodnadatta, a sun-splashed speck away out in the northern wilds by the Flinders Range. From there, only one man would take charge of any passengers travelling farther north to the Alice or beyond, one man driving a motor-truck very different to the modern motor of today, a driver who must battle his own way while travelling over a bridgeless, notoriously sandy-creeked, dusty track for a thousand isolated miles. And thus it was at the end of the construction that the mailman picked her up, a "great hulking brute" he was, he reminded her of something right out of the primitive as he just stood and stared at this woman's numerous hefty cases and boxes and bags stacked there, awaiting his loving care, on the red hot earth.

Sam Irvine passed his big arm across his dust-caked brow and grunted "Whoufff!" to the delighted grins of the railway navvies. These wise men and their mates knew these cases; they had carried them for her across dry creeks, panted and sweated with them up and over the sandhills in between the relays of construction line. Lugging those heavy cases over that rough ground had proved heavy work even for old-time navvies. Resignedly, but with a deep sense of injury, Sam turned to his truck to attempt the almost impossible job of turning it into a young railway wagon. With good-humoured chuckles the navvies helped him stack the cases while the Lady

Ethnologist looked unconcernedly on. At last Sam politely grunted, with a nod towards the truck, "All aboard, lady!"

And they were away, she gracefully waving her farewell greetings to the bowyanged navvies, Sam inwardly boiling at their grinning, shouted farewells, rich in hidden meaning which the lady could not understand and Sam could not explain or reply to. Anyway, they battled on in that long trip of seemingly endless miles, of heat and dust, of bog and dry, sandy creeks in which the car of those years, at times even with chains, sank and bogged in a helpless churning up of sand. Thankful indeed was Sam at such times if he had aboard some stockman passenger to give him a hand to dig the truck out, and help handle those oft-cursed cases. For again and yet again they had to be unloaded to lighten the truck until it was dug out, then reloaded when it had been coaxed onto firm ground again. Long trips through the vast stretches of the Centre then meant a constant anxiety over breakdowns and the possible failure of precious water, of days under the sun and nights under those brilliant, lonesome stars—such quiet, lonely nights.

Sam, of course, looked after her all he could—'like a bloody wet-nurse at a christening," he growled.

Anyway, tired and often anxious after twelve hours at the wheel, he thought of her comfort first and always when at last pulling up for the night. It was her camp that was set up first, as comfortably as the ground, weather, and conditions permitted. Then he would light the campfire, put on the billy, and prepare her "eats". But as time passed he was just about getting fed up with her complaints and grumbles. So that when one bright day she primly remarked, "Now what would you say if I told you that the men on the southern railways said it was a pleasure to carry these cases for me?"

"I'd say they were bloody liars!" growled Sam.

One day he was forced, through a long dry stage, to pull into camp after dark. With considerable pains he picked an open space for her, clearing the ground in the darkness so that no snakes or other crawlers, imaginary or otherwise, could incommode her. He spread out her swag, stood up, and growled, "Now look here, are you sure this place will do? You've been belly-aching a lot over the camps lately."

"This will do!" she replied, gazing severely round in the dark.

Next morning she woke up, yawned, and rolled over to find herself staring straight at three graves.

Lonely fellow-sleepers who had fallen by the wayside, of thirst and fever.

Poor Sam! He was to be an unenthusiastic cavalier to the Lady Ethnologist on a number of trips as she was passed on from mission or cattle-station back to the one so-called road by the Overland Telegraph Line, she and her cases, for Sam the mailman to pick up and carry on a further stage as she continued her investigations of the Australian aboriginal.

"It's *me* should be investigated!" growled Sam. "She measures their heads—by the time she's done with me she'll find nothing in my head to measure!"

Anyway, she and Sam got to know one another quite well.

Although they always travelled in a spirit of watchful neutrality tinged with a certain grimness on occasion, I've a sneaking idea each grew to feel at times that, after all, the other seemed almost human—though each would just about have indignantly choked in haste to deny such an outrageous charge. However, on one trip young Jock Nelson, son of the politician, was travelling down to Attack Creek, where recently he had taken up a block of country. He was travelling with the overland mail in Sam's cheery company when all of a sudden Sam groaned aloud, passing a weary paw over his forehead. For at the homestead just on ahead, sitting all prim and tidy with her boxes piled on the shady veranda, was the Lady Ethnologist awaiting the arrival of the mail.

"My Gawd!" groaned Sam as the mud-caked truck groaned to a halt. "Look what's there—the last rose of summer! You'll have to look after her, mind! Remember now, I'm only the truck-driver."

"I'll try," promised the young fellow uncertainly.

And thus the Lady Ethnologist was taken aboard yet again. With a resigned thankfulness Sam introduced the bashful young Nelson as the cavalier. Manfully Jock tried to entertain her, pointing out objects of beauty and interest as hour by hour the truck hummed along over the red dust by the everlasting Overland Telegraph Line, on over those fields of spinifex, those clumps of mulga, those serried anthills, that whitewood and needlewood and widjerdee bush, that grim heat-haze. After a particularly trying day they pulled into camp at last. Blessing the sunset, thankfully young Jock jumped down, helped the Lady Ethnologist down, then got busy breaking branches of shrubs to spread them out so they would form a thick cushion for her blankets and she would be comfortable for the night. Meanwhile Sam was busy putting on the billy and spreading out the tucker.

In the face of all this cheerful activity the Lady Ethnologist stood glaring round in a stony silence louder than a shout. Then, without even catching Sam's eye, she spoke quite loudly out into the sunset silence.

"What a dirty, filthy camp!"

'What's wrong with the camp?" demanded Sam belligerently as he straightened up.

"Look at that!" She disgustedly pointed. "Look at that! And that! And that! And that! And———"

'Why, *that's* all right!" snorted Sam indignantly. 'There's nothing wrong with that. This is cattle country, and they haven't built lavatories for them yet."

The Lady Enthologist - Daisy Bates.

XXI

WE COME TO THE TENNANT'S

Of course this low type of humour brought a laugh from us, a quizzical frown from Sam.

"You know," he meditated in puzzled fashion as he squinted along the dusty track, "she was a tough old bird—she *had* to be. Nosing around those abo camps out there within dammit of the real wild man's country is no picnic for a woman. She had a lot to put up with, believe me. She took it all in her stride, and asked for more. A pretty determined old girl, and must have seen some bloody awful things happen out there—clubbed women and leg sinews burnt through and flies eating out the eyes of children and starving dogs is all in the day's battle out there. Yet when she gets back here into civilization with me she turns up her haughty flamin' nose at a few blobs of dried-up cattle-dung!"

"As any lady would do," remarked the politician virtuously, "should the mailman expect her to camp on it. Now did you hear...?"

And so on, as the sunlit hours went by, and by the campfire under the stars.

A long run across a shrubby plain, with sunset fiery on a low range of pinnacles and queerly shaped hills thrown straight across the track. This fast approaching barrier opens out and displays buildings in the loneliness, several long, low stone buildings glinting white under lengthening sunrays. Sam nodded towards them.

"We've got our civic pride out here in the Centre, same as you city aristocrats. We mightn't be able to afford marble pillars and flash paints"—what would he have said to our towering buildings of glass nowadays!—"but we can splash on a daub of whitewash if there happens to be a bit of limestone handy."

"We'll have you civilized out here yet," replied Nelson cheerfully. "Canberra has given instructions for the taming of the Inland Savage."

Sam, big hands on the wheel, glanced aside at the politician as a surprised scientist might survey some weird insect. Then, turning his head the other way, spat expressively away out into the spinifex.

'Thanks!" laughed Nelson. "All contributions understandably accepted. These big old trees lining the creek and that waterhole always catch my eye. What a country we'd have if all this mulga and spinifex and tough red earth were only dotted with creeks like this! And there's the boys, and brother

Jacky, too, and his missus and kids and dogs all strolling out to welcome us — why, there must be half a hundred of the Old Folk all told, a really fine deputation! What a mighty man you are, Sam, to be the rip-roaring representative of Her Majesty's Mail."

"Yeah!" agreed Sam as we pulled up and thankfully climbed down, "and the mail has always got through ever since Charley Todd and Giles's father there and their cobbers built this line. Not that politicians ever seem to have heard about the few battlers living and struggling along the Overland Telegraph Line to help keep it going — let alone the Territory."

Nelson gave a suitable reply to this complaint, a common one at that time, as we strolled into this bare, clean, Tennant's Creek Telegraph Station. Like each of these stations, about two hundred miles apart, along that lonely two thousand miles, it held a story in every stone, in every smoke-blackened beam.

Just two long, low buildings of whitewashed stone, iron-roofed, standing solidly one behind the other, a cooking skillion, a meat-house, half a dozen tiny shacks, all enclosed within a fence. The long line of big trees in the creek fronting the little buildings. The Overland Telegraph Line, two wires always running, ever north and south. Just outside the fence and far beyond it to southward, flat country grey under spinifex, stunted timber in the distance, with here and there above it the distant top of a low hill. A feeling of distance, and a vast, quiet loneliness. And now, only seven miles "farther on", this wee telegraph outpost had a young goldfield in its territory. And the telegraphist and linesman were very puzzled indeed as to what the outcome might be.

In those spinifex days the boys there, and we, never dreamt of the wealth that was to be dug and blasted and crushed from those harsh, sunburnt hills, of the busy town that was to spring up in this sun-drenched wilderness. But how quaint it would have been had a sun-tanned fairy hopped up upon a rock and piped, "Poor doubting humans! Why, the Peko alone, in the year nineteen sixty, after having cleaned up a fortune in gold, will be selling to Japan half a million in copper a year!"

The mere idea of a township sounded silly when, a few days later, we sat and smoked upon that woefully barren Peko hill and wondered if the harsh-looking country round about would ever come to anything. In the months fast coming many a man out there would sit upon a similar hill of fortune and puzzle himself into wondering where on earth he might scrape up an ounce or two of gold. For it appeared then to be the most unpromising gold country that ever was.

Welcoming us with plenty of news, now that "the rush" was on — it was a very mild rush then, but out here a dozen men were a "big mob" — were

George Ashton the telegraphist and Cock Martin the linesman. Martin, an ex-navy man away out here in the Central spinifex, was a great mimic, to the constant and unbounded glee of the local aborigines. These isolated Overland Telegraph linesmen, used to seeing travellers only once in a blue moon, had not yet got over that phenomenal increase of population seven miles farther along the track.

'They came fair out of the blue," explained Cock Martin, "all because a wire-whiskered old spinifex-hopper found a bit of gold. Half a dozen of them, then a dozen, twenty, fifty, now there's a hundred! Mad as March hares, scratching those iron-bound hills for gold!"

"We hear there's a hundred and seventeen people camped there now," said George Ashton. "Seventeen are women. Who would ever have thought it?"

"One hundred people and two Wild West Shows." Cock Martin grinned. 'We can hear the guns a-poppin' over the wires. An' here's silly me goes an' leaves the navy an' trudges all the way out here to dodge the wars!"

"There actually has been a spot or two of shooting," said Ashton. "Sort of playful, no one killed yet. But someone will be getting hurt if those silly fools don't take a tumble."

"Are police stationed there yet?" I inquired.

"No. There's one mounted man camped here, just down there by the waterhole where his horse can get a decent drink. For company he's got a black tracker and two big Alsatian dogs. We're seven miles away from the field. Then there's Muldoon, the warden stationed at Barrow Creek, a hundred and fifty miles down the track. But, besides Tennant's, he's responsible for a district big as an empire, keeps him busy patrolling all that. The nearest police station that counts is at the Alice—three hundred and twenty miles south from here."

"Quite a lot could happen before they could get into action."

"I'll say! Quite a little war could get started. Which wouldn't matter, except that a non-combatant or two could get hurt. Anyway, the boys are agitating for police to be stationed on the field before someone does get shot. The hoys say it's a real wild west show at times. I never thought I'd live to see guns drawn on an Australian goldfield, let alone in this wilderness."

"What started it all?"

"Oh, a few young fellows from the south drifted into camp on the scent of gold. This place is three hundred and twenty miles north of the Alice, and the Alice a near thousand miles north of Adelaide. In such isolation the young fellows find themselves living what to them is a wild life, free from all restriction. Then again, they weren't born to the old bush code of mateship. A few of them feel that to be real he-men they must talk guns. And accidents can happen when a young fellow struts around with a forty-four swaying at his hip. Of course, there's only a handful of them."

"Pity there wasn't a battalion or two," sighed Cock Martin, "then we'd mount a naval gun down by the waterhole and I'd be the Freshwater Admiral in defence of Tennant's Creek."

"You could put up a good show," declared Sam. "You could sign on a good hundred boomerangs to the strength."

Down by the waterhole were camped a little crowd of Warramungas, the local tribe, "big-feller" men now, for in lordly fashion they were explaining white-feller ways to a visiting group of the Warramulla tribe. It was the Warramunga warriors who attacked Stuart, that tough explorer John McDouall Stuart and his tiny band on his first attempt—three attempts were necessary—to cross the continent from the south right up through the centre to the northern seaboard. A mighty feat indeed, two thousand miles across unexplored country peopled by numerous hostile tribes, two thousand miles to return. In those four thousand miles there was no hope of help should tragedy happen. On his first attempt Stuart had with him two men and thirteen horses. At a creek ever since known as Attack Creek, about fifty miles north of Tennant's Creek, the Warramunga warriors in two yelling lines raced to attack these strange white beings that were invading their Sacred Tribal Lands. Stuart was forced to fight, and quickly. Then blazed another terror for the Warramungas, terrible "thunder-sticks" that could kill a man at such a great distance, sticks that spat flame and smoke and thunder and against which spears and waddy were powerless.

Stuart admired their attack, stating, "We had to take steady aim to make an impression."

Stuart, his party and horses just about worn out, had to return back to Adelaide, whence he recovered to determinedly organize another expedition.

The Warramunga tribe, until the last two years, had known no white men except the lonely telegraph operators and linesmen, so far apart, the travelling mailmen, stockmen at a distant homestead or two, and, very occasionally, drovers of a passing mob of cattle. But now, with a camp of a hundred men digging for a yellow stone, they were learning that great puzzle all about "white-feller ways" with surprising smartness, and right now in lordly, superior fashion were retailing this valuable knowledge to their shaggy-browed visitors. These, freshly in from the wild lands westward, were squatting along the creek bank frowningly scratching their itchy hides while trying to absorb the strange doings and habits of these silly white men who worked in a lather of sweat under the hot sun looking for a useless yellow stone. The Stone Age man appealed to me in his primitive state. The world must progress as it rolls on through time and space—if there are such things as time and space—but I could not help hoping that these wild visitors, who now could not speak one word of English, would not carry to their wild tribesmen the urge to come a-visiting the Warramungas, and be introduced to the "white-feller man".

Therein lay disease, which spelled tragedy for the wild men. For, almost certainly the hardiest humans in the world, they fall prey to the "simplest" of our diseases. Our common cold in them swiftly turns into raging pneumonia. An influenza epidemic means the wiping out of whole tribes.

This was the extreme southern limit of the huge area of the Warramulla tribal grounds. Their country was west and nor'-west of Tennant's Creek. I'd heard about them almost as far to the nor'-west as Wave Hill station.

But we could not wait to help, in one way or another, the destiny of the Warramulla.

The mail-truck hummed over the last seven miles of spinifex and red earth. And now, rising from a brown-grey flat, a brand-new iron roof gleams above the grey mulga like silver in the sunset.

"The pub," said Sam.

"Stone the crows! Fancy a pub out here!"

"I'll let you know we're civilized," growled Sam sternly. "At least, getting on that way."

With a quickening of interest I saw the gleam of several other new roofs, half a dozen shacks, a few tents. Fronting the pub was the "street", merely the Overland Telegraph Line running down the centre of a broad path of dust churned up by motor and horse through the spinifex. At irregular intervals on either side of the "street" stood, or rather leant, a wobbly iron shack. There were others made of hessian and saplings, and tents reinforced by mulga branches. The butcher's shop run by young Nelson, the boarding-house where you don't board but "only tucker", the bakery, several embryo "stores", and half a dozen rough camps made up the settlement, with a few scattered beehives of dull grey-green—gigantic things, these.

"I'll bet you've never seen the like of those before," said Sam. "They're spinifex camps."

Of course. Only scraggly timber here, mere sticks, no such thing here as timber large enough to supply bark for huts. Throughout most of the Centre, excepting the often beautiful trees decorating some precious waterhole, the timber is very scraggy. Thus these "beehives", which were a framework of mulga saplings covered over with the thick, tough clumps of spinifex grass. Quite cosy shelters they turned out to be, too. Here and there some grey-clad figures were standing by the billy at the sunset fire, others came strolling out as the truck lumbered up to this brand-new pub beside the everlasting Telegraph Line. And wasn't I curious! The little place even seemed to be built of cement. Cement, away out here!

Some shallow board troughing told the story. These were moulds into which wet cement was poured to form small, flat blocks. And thus, the building material puzzle had been solved. A very small "frontier" type of hotel, of course, but with its cement bricks and iron roof, and even a little walled-in veranda of iron and netting against the flies, it looked inexpressibly modern out here in this primitive spinifex wilderness. A glimpse of a red ironite floor and the "puff-puff-puff" of a little engine somewhere round the back—later I learnt it was providing electricity—further amazed me with modernity.

"Think you're dreaming?" Sam grinned as we climbed down from the truck.

"It *is* hard to believe," I said. "What on earth is that 'puff-puff-puff?'"

"Oh, that's the Dead Heart coming to life."

As we stepped up onto the veranda a score of drunks and half-drunks rose, hitched up their strides, and came following us in, some with noisy, hoarse-voiced greetings which I knew would get Sam's back up. Some were brazen beer-bums who came butting in between us for their drink; two of them flung their arms round Sam's neck in a howling joviality. Sam gave a heave, threw out his big arms, and the two fools were flying back through the door to reel in a crash on the veranda. The deck thus cleared for action, Sam glared round like an angry bull. But not one of the he-men accepted the challenge. The crowing of a triumphant rooster outside sounded quite noisy in the sudden silence. Sam nodded us towards the bar—a modern bar. It was shaped like a horseshoe and "armour-plated" against intrusion with strong wire-netting. No chance of taking the bar-tender unawares when entrenched behind his "island fortress".

XXII

THAT ARMOUR-PLATED BAR

A little cove with a grin, what we could see of him, stood waiting in behind there to serve us a welcome, but what proved a disappointing, drink—hot beer. Above him a large notice spoke or rather seemed to shout:

NO TICK.

Here inside, also, was an air of surprising newness.

"Had a good trip, Sam?"

"Yes, Joe. Good weather. Good company."

"Good. No man could ask for more."

The genial little man behind that bar was Joe Kilgariff; he and his wife were two of the live-wires of the Centre. Having built up a successful business at the Alice, Joe was alert and in action at the first call of gold in that wilderness to the north. Without hesitation he took the chance. Whether he had lost it was impossible to say yet, for so far little gold had been won. But he was now established and ready for it, if it should be won.

He was eventually to "clean up big" for his enterprise. "Tennant's" was the only really new goldfield I'd seen in a trip of eleven thousand miles. To make it still more difficult for the working miner, it was a reefing field. For no alluvial had yet been found, and alluvial gold is so much more easily won. It only needs pick, shovel, dish, elbow-grease, and luck—plenty of luck. Much more difficult and costly to discover and to work is the gold of a reefing field, mixed within the solid rock. It takes an experienced miner with a little money behind him to hang on in such a case, especially when the mineralized belt is in such isolation. And the Tennant's was, and I believe to an extent still is, the most tricky field in Australia. To seek for gold at Tennant's at that time, even for the experienced miner, was like going to school to learn all over again. Geologists were to be tricked again and again by the unusual conditions of this field. No wonder that before its peculiarities were really understood the seeking of its gold had made a ladder of broken hearts reaching to high heaven.

But gold in quantity was deeply hidden there, to be traced at last.

Even Joe's dreams came nowhere near the magical transformation that was to spring up out of this sun-saturated harshness, the actual beginning, in fact, of the real development of the Centre. If little old Joe, protected by his armoured bar, could then have visualized a "Tennant's" hotel of today!

Sipping that hot beer, I gazed at that armour of heavy wire netting. From about twelve inches above the bar it stretched up to the roof. Thus you shoved your money in under the wire, and Joe pushed the beer across the bar out under the wire to you.

"Admiring my armour-plate?" Old Joe winked.

"What on earth is it for?"

He shrugged, with a glance at the now milling little crowd around. One impatient would-be he-man was thumping the bar with the butt of a gun.

So obvious. No hand could snatch out across the bar should gold or a wad of notes lie there. Also, in a brawl, no one could leap over the bar to take piratical charge, that tough netting was solidly built in to the bar and walls.

"Bullets?" I wondered.

"He's only got to duck down," growled Sam.

Startled at this instant reading of my thoughts, I looked into the grinning face of the overland mail-driver.

"He can duck down anywhere inside," Sam went on. "The bar is so built that he's covered from any angle. When the storm blows over he just pops up and whistles for the abo house-boys to carry out the corpses. Otherwise there is very little wreckage to be cleared up. Joe is a brainy as well as a busy bee. He's had it all thought out well beforehand."

"I suppose he's got guns down there, if necessary," said Giles.

"You bet. In under the bar, at a strategic spot, lies handy a blunderbuss that could blow daylight through a camel. But Joe is a man of peace."

And Joe's wrinkled face in behind the "armour-plate" wore a placid, understanding smile. It was all jolly interesting to me.

A bell rang, and we strolled into the dining room. I wish I had a photo of it today. Two cheery girls were employed, a cook and a waitress. Out in this sunlit ocean of spinifex and red dust, two smiling girls! Whoever would have thought it? As I mused thus, two stern looking "he-men" came stamping into the dining-room, a broad belt weighted with cartridges hung round each waist, a young cannon in open holster dangled down the right leg. Both stood, a bit bow-legged apparently, thumbs hitched loosely in belt, coldly surveying the diners.

Then I giggled, it all looked so silly to me. I glanced across at Sam to laugh, but he frowned back as his big mouth opened to take in fodder. At the same time someone's boot tapped me on the shin.

Just as well, probably. For if one of those "he-men" had strolled across the floor and tapped me on the head with the butt of that heavy gun there wouldn't have been anything I could have done about it, while if my mates had stood up to interfere then the other fellow would have started blazing away.

And that's what the decent miners were worried about—that sooner or later someone would call the bluff of these would-be gunmen, or otherwise put them in the position of having to open fire or be laughed at. So far, several among them had taken a potshot or two among themselves—not that the miners cared a damn about that, so long as no one else got hurt.

However, I would be disappointed before I left the Tennant's, because there was a strong feeling to turn the pub into "a man's pub". Which meant that the two girls would lose their jobs, probably the only jobs for them on the field at the time. One of those girls with her people had trekked all the way across country from Mount Isa, across Queensland and Centralia, the same track as taken by the drover of goats, a truly desperate track at that time.

They deserved luck, those quiet women, following, helping their men out into the heat and the dust and the distant silences, where a petrol tin is treasured as a valuable bucket, where muddy water is priceless, where their carpet is the red floor of Mother Earth, where the death of the old wagon horse is a terrible tragedy, where snakes glide in from the spinifex across the clean-swept space round the campfire. And the nearest doctor is at the Alice over three hundred miles away.

When we strolled out to the veranda some thirty miners had congregated to meet the popular driver of the overland mail and his live-wire passenger, Nelson. The political man was in sudden demand now, in view of this gold find and what its successful development could mean in this roadless, near waterless Centralian wilderness calling as never before for water, transport, police, development.

Giles and I left them at it, and went for a stroll. Which seemed silly, for there was nowhere to walk to, except to follow our noses across a thousand miles of spinifex—if we wished.

"I wonder," mused Giles as we stepped down on the red dust, "if this track to the Alice will ever become a real road. How excited, how pleased the dad would have been!"

And I knew he hoped his father's dream would come true—which it long since has, of course. The Alice nestles down in its ricky range three hundred and twenty miles farther south, but right here the dusty wheel-tracks meandering between the camps would become a main street. We moved on under a vast, now cool sky in which stars hung as if hitched up in some eternal quietness, still and unwinking. In the darkness here on earth a dim light shone here and there from an odd shanty, giving the appearance of some first faint attempt at a street. A typical camp, both here and back in the hills, consisted of a simple shed of saplings, roofed and walled with thick tufts of spinifex. Inside would be a table of boards, being bits of boxes, or merely half a dozen sticks from the surrounding bush spread between sapling forks driven into the ground. There would be empty petrol cases for chairs if the owner were lucky, otherwise a sapling supported by forks as a seat. Then there were shacks representing a store and a butcher's shop, with here and there straggling along the wheel-ruts a few "buildings" of mulga poles and hessian, and mulga and spinifex sheds. Thus a street is born.

As we walked along the road-ruts this impression grew as we passed widely spaced huts made partly of iron. Those few precious sheets of iron had been carted three hundred and twenty miles from the Alice, and before that had come from Adelaide, or Port Augusta, a thousand miles farther south still.

"It has meant a lot of effort and expense, carting that iron here," murmured Giles hopefully. 'The men who have gone to all that effort must believe this discovery will really turn out to be a goldfield!"

"Yes," I answered doubtfully. For this seemed unlikely-looking gold country to me. Besides, it was waterless, or appeared practically so on the surface. And the cost of material and supplies and transport to this isolation! The auriferous stone here, if any, would have to be rich indeed to prove payable.

Portions of it *would* prove to be rich. However, it was the development of inland motor transport which was to help so greatly. Marvellous how the internal-combustion engine has done away with distance, and time, and the slavery of hauling heavy loads.

Trying to follow the hazy outline of ruts and clumps of spinifex in this star-splashed darkness, we both fell into a gutter. I swore heartily and feelingly as we picked ourselves up. I'm an irritable cuss at times.

'That's a good sign," said Giles mildly as we picked ourselves up. "We fell into the first attempt at a gutter within a thousand or more miles. It really looks as if this Tennant's Creek might become a town."

'Yes," I grumbled, "and there *might* be street-lamps along here. And the stars *might* fall."

But Giles only smiled as he tried to brush that fine, clinging red dust from his pants.

We walked on. A few dark figures could be dimly glimpsed in the huts. Music of some sort, perhaps this newfangled wireless, was blaring from an electrically lit hut. Heavens! Fancy a little electric-light machine away out here! And another at the pub! And there was *another* gramophone blaring from away across the flat in the darkness. We walked across this tussocky flat towards a dim light filtering out through a framework of boughs. Several groups of men were squatting on their heels outside in the darkness yarning. A big fellow in a dusty singlet appeared out of the dark and called us "sir", which nearly caused me to fall backwards head over heels. To be called "sir" on a newly discovered Australian goldfield!

'Warm night!" boomed the voice.

'Yeah!" I answered. 'Where's the ginger-beer shop?"

"Right here! Come right in." He wheeled and took us inside.

Stone the crows! It was true. A ginger-beer shop—*ginger*!—out here in this wild and woolly land in this wild and woolly gold-rush. That a pub with real beer had already magically sprung up was amazing enough, but a ginger-beer shop! With hairy-chested, dusty toilers in pants and flannel drinking, and enjoying, it.

This go-ahead "shop" was a lattice-work of newly cut saplings built to the back of a hut or iron-backed building of some sort. Within the lattice was a long, rough table, *very* rough. Some kegs were standing up on boxes, pint pots on the table. A score of men were lounging in there in shirts and singlets, young fellows among them with newly growing beard, all with pots of ginger-beer to hand, all gravely talking gold. How quaint this tiny place, the goldfields atmosphere of a hundred years ago ready to spring to life again! But ginger beer already in this brazen hot isolation when the first signs of gold had only just been found and by no means proved as a permanent field!

The ginger beer tasted good indeed, and a jolly sight cooler than the beer in the pub. Only sixpence a pot, too—we marvelled at such cheapness where in the first place the precious water cost cartage in miles.

Other miners came crowding in; in this thirsty land the "ginger-beer man" and his assistant in Jacky Howe singlet were doing a roaring trade.

XXIII

TO DONALD MACKAY

We strolled out again and in the main "street" stumbled over a drunk asleep. If a car or truck happened along———! Horse or camel, of course, would just take one whiff of the corpse's breath, then pass out.

"Just as well there's no crime here," mused Giles as we set a course back for the pub light. "The one policeman lives in a tent seven miles away."

"There's been several shooting cases, so they say."

'Yes, I'd overlooked that for the moment. It's easy enough to keep little incidents like that quiet on an isolated place like this." "All in the family, like."

'Yes, so long as there is no fatal case. Which appears almost inevitable, according to the more responsible miners."

Prophetic words.

An entry in my diary simply states:

> *3rd Sept.* Beautiful sleep, cool night after lights out and the numerous insects were beaten. The drunks all drifted away when not a soul was left likely to buy a beer. This morning, everything visible out through the netting is bush and the pub backyard with all the new evidences of hurried building, the shack further across, and a dozen weather-stained motor vehicles of all descriptions parked all ways, men sleepily arising from their blankets. The motor truck has, or is doing away with the horses and buckboards. Good job, too—the poor horses would have suffered terribly in these great distances and heat and waterless tracks.

That morning I said "So long" to my goodly travelling mates; they hoarded the truck bound for the Alice, whence they would take a train to Adelaide, while I was determined to have a look round this most unusual-looking gold country. Young Jock Nelson, son of the political dad, would pick me up in a day or two and we'd go all round the field in his meat truck. He had a place about fifty miles north on Attack Creek, running a few head of cattle. Meanwhile I was watching little old Joe Kilgariff in action with his beloved wireless set, the fantastic invention that apparently denied space and distance and time in the far-out places. For Jack Noble had come hurrying in from the heat-hazes to the west because his mate was taken suddenly ill and was in need of urgent medical advice. Which Joe, his face wrinkled with seriousness, his gnarled fingers gently probing at mysterious gadgets on his beloved little machine, was endeavouring to obtain through the air from Adelaide. And he got it, too, his hunched up little body queerly reminiscent of a merry wallaby, his face all crinkling in delight as at last he made "contact", and cracklings and spitfire noises came in reply. We, who were straining eyes and ears in the listening, how delighted and amazed we were! For this was real magic.

An amateur was answering him from Adelaide.

"These amateurs are great." Joe rubbed his hands enthusiastically. "They'll do anything they can to help, go to no end of trouble by land or sea. They'll stand by their machines day and night to try to help in an emergency."

We all knew that Joe would do, and had done, the same. Anyway, in this case the amateur quickly got him in touch with a doctor. Jack Noble described the symptoms and the doctor sent his advice, which enabled the patient to survive the crisis until the boys could get him down to the "repair shop", over a thousand miles southward.

The baby wireless of those days, though a miracle, was of course nothing to the efficient machines of today. Yet what a mighty job they did, as witness the pedal wireless of the Australian Inland Mission, and the part played in the search for lost aviators of the 1930s, in police rescue work, and in helping various expeditions.

Jack Noble's mate was yet but another of the isolated ones to thank wireless for his life.

Little old Joe Kilgariff fairly loved that wireless, and would talk wireless for as long as anyone would care to listen. And because I was actually taking a few notes he proceeded to "talk me blind". Just on the off-chance that the wireless of those brave days may give the "modern" man a smile, here's Joe's wireless—if my amateurish notes be correct: "Receiving B batteries for power supply, can be carried anywhere in truck. Range very effective at times from Tennant's to Adelaide."

Back at the Alice, Joe had his "real big plant" at the Stuart Arms Hotel, which was in Mrs Kilgariff's charge while he was at the Tennant's. The plant was "semi-commercial", that already well known pioneer station VKZ, doing constant work. These are my notes about it: "3 stage crystal control transmitter. 150 watts. Final stage got 2/75 two-stroke valve—whatever that means. Powerful transmitter, Comet professional crystal model transmitter as used in U.S.A. The transmission power supply obtained from high tension generation driven by kerosene engine. Charge all batteries with Delco battery."

His wireless came in very handy indeed for the Lasseter Expedition, for the rush to the Granites, and subsequent troubles there, and for Donald

Mackay's mapping expeditions from Central Australia to the Western Australian coast.

The Mackay Aerial Survey Expedition was now on the 1933 survey. He had led an expedition well out into the west in 1926. But this series was a tremendous job of surveying and mapping. The first was in 1930. Yet another would be organized in 1935. The final expedition would be in 1937.

Donald Mackay, of Port Hacking and Wallendbeen in New South Wales, had set himself an enormous task indeed—to map thoroughly nearly one million square miles of practically unexplored country, the most fraught with danger in all Australia, from Ilbilba, just west of the Alice, to Roy Hill station, not far inland from the Western Australian coast, using his own time and resources, for patriotic reasons, and to help develop the country.

This great enterprise cost him a fortune. Even then he could not have carried on with the final expedition had it not been for the big increase in the price of wool, the long awaited rise which finally put the pastoral industry on its feet.

The organizing for each expedition included the setting up of bases in arid country far from help, and arranging for camel and motor teams, transport, supplies, personnel—and all hands had of necessity to be *good* personnel—and the purchase, management, and use of various little aeroplanes of the day. Of these, I suppose the best known being used in this area at the time were a Percival Gull and a Lovebird. On occasion, a Monospar and Puss Moth were used, too. Aviators of the magic machines of today would admire the men who staked their lives and reputations in such little craft over such distances and arid country. One mapping trip while I was somewhere about the Alice was made by three men travelling six hundred and ten miles across desert and near-desert country in just under six hours in a tiny plane with a wingspan of only thirty-six feet, on a petrol consumption of thirty-two gallons, and one gallon of oil. Such a feat may not seem much in these days of the Comet and Sputnik, but in those times, not so many years ago (1933), we were only emerging from the horse and buggy days. Incidentally, had anything happened to the plane those men would have crashed down into a sun-scorched, practically waterless, uninhabited wilderness.

But not quite uninhabited, to their surprise and the interest of us all on hearing the news. For three times during the crossing, at distances twenty and more miles away, big smoke-signals shot up into the still, sunlit air. Down below, the flying men saw huge patches of dark mulga set amongst the red sand and yellow spinifex, until they were flying over the terrifying sand-ridges of the Great Australian Desert. But even in the centre of this desolation there shot up a heavy signal smoke.

Wandering nomads of still Stone Age men and their families and half-tamed dogs were wandering down there where it was thought no human being could possibly live. And these were signalling; from just across the border to the coast of Western Australia they signalled the coming of this giant humming bird, sending the news across that six hundred miles much faster than it could fly. And as the pioneering aviators were doing a steady hundred miles an hour they thought they were speeding indeed, and were delighted with their "little bird".

What amazed the flying men even more than this startling evidence of humans in the wastes below was the fact that the tiny plane was seen from twenty and more miles away. Back in civilization they were still puzzled, wondering whether it was really the eagle eyes of the desert men that had made them aware of the plane, or whether their keen ears had caught this most unusual humming approaching from so far away and so high up, to drone past somewhere up there in the sky, its swiftly diminishing hum vanishing along the path of the setting sun.

This intrigued us also from the Alice to the Tennant's and beyond, all being keenly interested in the mapping of the wild lands away west out there, and in the wild men who could find water and make a living where it was believed there was nothing but sandhills.

Commander H. W. Bennett and Captain Neale were the aviators and map-makers who stuck with Donald Mackay through thick and thin. Both men had already made a name in navy and army and aviation; now they were known throughout the Centre and the Territory.

Maybe I have digressed too much on the Mackay expeditions, but with numerous others I liked old Donald; he was one of those lucky men almost everyone likes. Quietly spoken, steady-eyed, with a drawling voice, a kindly smile, and a ready helping hand to anyone in need. A lanky chap, he was well into his sixties at the time of these expeditions, but was still as tough as ironbark, as he had need to be.

A "Murrumbidgee boy", Donald Mackay had a long and adventurous life indeed, every now and again, by way of variety, taking a real exploring trip in his stride. He and Richardson, pedalling in opposite directions and passing one another midway, were the first two men to circle Australia on push-bikes. That was in 1899 or 1900—I don't suppose younger readers could realize what such a trip meant in those years. He led exploring trips in New Guinea, across Arnhem Land from the coast and in the Centre, by horse, camel, canoe, and now aeroplane plus motor vehicles. In between he worked at his pastoral interests. These seven years of mapping that country west of the Alice were his last adventure—here on earth, anyway.

He was to complete a mighty job for Australia, yet probably you have never even heard of him. Time speeds on rapidly, of course, but Mackay's job was such that he will very probably be increasingly remembered in years to come. Since those expeditions Frank Clune has written a book about him which he has entitled *Last of the Australian* Explorers, and I believe it a fair tide. That book, record of a grand Australian, will be far more read in the swiftly coming future.

Well, now, we were yarning about Joe Kilgariff, the practical enthusiast busily experimenting with this newfangled wireless. And greatly appreciated was his work, and a valued aid indeed was he to the Mackay expeditions, keeping in constant touch through Station VKZ, owned, erected, and operated by Joe Kilgariff of Alice Springs, Central Australia—and this well-known station was a little shack at the back of his store.

Thus the energetic Joe, successful businessman, highly successful wireless man, no longer a youth but still wide awake and active in the very forefront of happenings destined at last to start real development in the Centre and North.

Mineral discoveries! Motor transport! Wireless! Aeroplanes!

What mighty progress has been made in all these fields since Joe so enthusiastically worked and described his "machine" but a few years back under the blazing Centralian skies. Joe, so proud of the range of his wireless, from Tennant's Creek to Adelaide, a full eleven hundred miles and a bit more. And now men are bouncing wireless waves back off the moon, and flying machines are buzzing out into space around the moon and sun. As I revise these pages, in April 1961, Russia has launched a man into space.

There were a dozen of us there lounging round the set as Joe and Jack Noble did their stuff. Came a warning "Sh!" as a miner jerked up his wrist with thumb and forefinger poked out, other fingers clenched. That sign, I quickly learnt, meant " 'Ware! Gunmen!" Striding up the track and near the pub now was the lean form of the drover of goats, his beloved rifle gripped in sinewy hand. Striding behind him, "blackfellow fashion", were two young individuals under ten-gallon hats, walking armouries. For a huge gun swung down each thigh, handle protruding from open holster; a heavy cartridge belt was buckled round each waist. They slouched on past the pub, a half snarling glance thrown across at us. Yet again I just gaped at the American Wild West of bygone years prowling across an Australian wilderness. It made a man momentarily wonder if he were not really in dreamland.

"I can't make out that drover fellow joining in with that crowd," mused Russell.

"He didn't exactly," replied one of the men. "He's camped down by the Afghan's battery where his job ended. He got mixed up in one of their brawls and had to take sides. Though he didn't ask for it."

"That's the danger—might happen to anyone of us!" declared miner. Which was true.

"Bloody fools!" growled McCoy. "All of them!"

"Yes," agreed McLeash gruffly. *"Dangerous* fools!"

Michael Terry and Stan O'Grady, Tennant Creek, 1933.

XXIV

IRONSTONE AND SPINIFEX

"What gave them the great idea?" I asked.

"The pictures!" replied Digger Lane. "They're mostly a handful of young fellows from the cities brought up on Wild West pictures. Been driven away from civilization by the depression. So when a gold find breaks out here in the Never Never they buy a ten-gallon hat, strap a .45 Colt to their shanks, and slouch up here to do their stuff. A thousand miles from anywhere, of course. And they're beginning to think they're going to run this show."

"Why don't you old hands club together and teach them differently?" I suggested.

"And be forced to start the shooting match," said McLeash, "when they called our bluff? What we didn't cop in lead from them we'd cop from the law when *it* came. Wouldn't they just love *that*!"

A point I'd been too dumb to think of. It was all new and interesting to me. The discovery of gold in this barren-looking country, which barely one prospector in a hundred would believe could carry the precious metal, was of keen interest in itself. So, too, was the fact that the find was a thousand miles inland in such an inhospitable belt of country, practically uninhabited and waterless, the one sign of man in that vast expanse being the Overland Telegraph Line running straight through the field, with one dusty track from south to north beside it, right up through the centre of the continent. So that every man who had taken that lonely track in all these years had trudged straight over the field. And they would not be dreaming of gold; they would be thinking only of hurrying on, of water, of feed for their horse or camel, a bit worried, too, lest there should he trouble from the blacks. In recent years the main worries of such occasional travellers would be of the track and breakdowns of this new, undeveloped form of transport, the motor-car. Ever since the Overland Telegraph Line was built 1870-2, almost every one of these bygone travellers must have ridden over this goldfield, then camped at the waterhole by the Tennant's Creek telegraph station, the only water on this stage. And now at long last the gold was found, or rather the promise of gold. And now spread over this sunlit quietness was suddenly a "great" population of over a hundred people, seventeen of them women! All of which was miraculous enough, but along strolled these gunmen! Only a handful, it's true, but no wonder each new arrival rubbed his eyes at sight of these and wondered if he were not dreaming in some Wild West Yankee picture-show.

Which had me tickled pink. In the Far North, from Cape York Peninsula through the Territory to the Kimberleys, stockmen and prospectors invariably carried a revolver at belt when alone in country where the natives were wild or semi-wild. But this was mainly for effect. If a man carried a weapon then with ordinary caution he was almost always safe. If he did not carry one he was a fool, a temptation to any travelling hand of warriors. However, those guns were only small revolvers, nothing like the "cannon" strapped down the legs of these coves here. Then again, there were no dangerous natives here to be worried about. Nor did the miners working out in the hills carry guns. It was quite amusing to me.

"It's not funny to us." Barney frowned. "We're fed up to the teeth at the very sight of these fellows. Keep out of the way of them, Jack, or you might not find them funny at all."

No doubt Barney O'Leary and his mates, and most of the miners on the field apparently, were both puzzled and worried at the antics of these would-be gunmen, though my silly style of humour could not see eye to eye with them. Barney and his particular mate, McLeash, were typical desert-area bushmen-miners. Tall men, powerfully built, hardy. Barney, thoughtful, a steady type, appeared to be younger than his fifty years and was surprisingly good-looking in a rugged way. His mate, McLeash was younger, the slow drawly bushman type, pleasant-faced, always ready for a laugh. Both were firm believers in the Granites, that queer hole of desolation westward to which there had been a rush, and from which there had been a rush back, along that desert track of bitter disappointment. Yet Barney and McLeash, both experienced desert men, in the face of dogmatic opposition and ridicule, swore that gold would he found there yet. Recent years have justified that prophecy. Gold was being found there even at the time of which I write, though no one at the Tennant's or the Alice knew it. The desert romance of the Granites came to light only a very few years ago.

To me, who had spent half a lifetime in mining, the men in this primitive mining camp seemed to be composed of two main groups, the old desert prospectors and country workers glad to take a chance farther inland at the whisper, "Gold!" Time and hard experience, bitter experience to most, had now taught these latter just about enough of far-back-country bush to give them a chance of making good.

At that time there were about two score and ten or so of the old diehard prospectors, sunburnt as Arabs, men whose steady eyes had seen the glow of a thousand campfires, men who would travel a thousand miles with, for company, the crunch of their camels' pads, the shuffle of the horses' hooves. These are the men who "follow the storms", men capable of turning west towards the border and the desert, following the green tracks of the wandering storm that fills the soaks and gnamma holes. Such men are scattered every here and there across the continent in the arid places, the very few who are "desert wise", and know how and when to get back in time before those tiny desert reservoirs dry up. Tennant's is not desert country, of course, but really arid lands lie not far away.

Quite soon, while going for a stroll, I realized that the gunmen's antics were not quite as funny as I'd thought. In the middle of. the track ahead two miners raised their voices in wordy argument and became quite heated.

From a shack beside the track a gunman strolled out, calmly pulled the "cannon" out of its holster, levelled it, and fired. The bullet raised a spurt of dust fair between the two arguing miners, then ricocheted whining across the flat. Both men sprang aside and around, staring backwards towards us in amazement, as I was staring. The gunman waved his gun barrel slowly, threateningly at the two men, and drawled loudly, "Git, you bastards! Won't let a bloody man sleep, won't you? Git!"

They "got", one to one side of the track, the other to the other, and away. The gunman slowly turned towards where I was standing in startled surprise, regarded me for a moment in what I suppose he believed was a cold fashion, spat disdainfully, thrust his gun back into its holster, and slouched back into his camp.

I felt like calling out, "And nuts to *you*!" but didn't.

Luckily I'd seen nothing to laugh at, and now realized the danger as seen by all the real miners on the field for some time past.

Seizing an opportunity, I drove out to the Great Western with some of the boys seeking that elusive yellow metal which has called to men since long before King Solomon's days. The show was some eighteen miles nor'-west of the Overland Telegraph station. We passed through flat country, well grassed, a pleasing sight in this harsh red land, with thick patches of stunted lancewood, its rough bark, often gnarled limbs, and dull, thin leaves protection against heat and drought, and surely a disguise for its usefulness. For it is excellent fodder for stock, as are the many insignificant-looking shrubs, ranging from a dull, dusty grey to a bright green, that grow plentifully here and there.

Clever, frugal Nature. If she could not here grow waving fields of green she grew drought-resistant things in which are concentrated good juices that mean life to animals. A low ridge of dark-grey granite relieved the monotony, and behind it gleamed other ridges capped with snow—the hot, hard, milk-white of quartz outcrops. One in every thousand of these might possibly point the way to a little hidden gold. Then more flat country under a blazing sun, with half a dozen of those spinifex camps that looked like giant beehives squatting sombrely on the red flats. Then the beauty of a few white ghost gums and vivid green shrubs by a dull-brown waterhole within a dull-brown depression. Whistle and chirp of little birds, don't-care-a-damn "Kark! Kaar-k! Kar-kk!" of cunning crows. At eighteen miles there arose the abrupt little rusty ironstone hills, some heavily capped with black ironstone, hungry-looking country indeed. And yet, among such hills, at a fifty-mile radius round the little pub and shacks which really were the start of a town, would here and there be found deposits of rich gold. And, in much later years, rich copper.

Who'd have thought it"?

Puzzled at gold being in such unlikely-looking country, I discovered yet again that there is always something to learn. So did sundry geologists, a few years later. For more than one highly trained man declared the field would never prove payable.

Here and there among the hills loomed a dull grey lump that might have been a near-black granite boulder, like a "big-feller" Devil's Marble—another spinifex camp, the hut, otherwise the home, of a miner.

I was to prove that they were quite serviceable, and pleasantly cool. A "big-feller" house erected for a number of men, or for one of the half-dozen families on the field, would he simply and conveniently built into a number of rooms, kitchen and tool-shed, and "garage" for car or truck. No messmate bark to he obtained here as building material, no paperbark, no timber of straight saplings. Just a few crooked mulga sticks, and unlimited spinifex. It is wonderful what men can do with simple materials when needs must. We forget that men, women, and children lived out their precious little lives with "simple" natural materials for long ages before the days of modern discoveries.

This big old hill of the Great Western was typical of the mines and environment in those first early years—if they could be called mines. Just a bit of a hole in the ground, in this case a far from completed tunnel driven into the hillside about fifty feet, with a fair amount of costeening (shallow trenches) across the black stone outcrop on top—what hard, sweaty, dusty, thirsty toil under that cloudless sky and brazen sun!

One hundred and thirty samples had averaged nine and a half pennyweight of gold to the ton. Though this was not payable under such conditions, it was a very promising indication of richer gold somewhere in the hill. But the little syndicate of working miners had no more money to carry on the work in the heartbreaking struggle to dig their way into richer ground, if any. Work must cease until they could make a bit more money for tucker, for water and mining supplies.

Such was the story of hill after hill. A reef must yield good stone, a couple of ounces or *so* at least to the ton, for it to be payable away out here, far from treatment plants. The payable reef had first to be found, then mined. Then the stone had to be carted to the Alice, three hundred miles, then taken by train nearly a thousand miles to Port Augusta and a treatment plant. Not only in money, but in time, this all had to be paid for. And the prospector and working miner seldom has that sort of ready money. Added to which, the barest cost of living in such isolation was a bit tough. Some of the battlers out there at this time were living on the smell of an oily rag. Which all goes to explain why men toiling out there in the early years sometimes found a fortune but would never get it, not having the money necessary to hang on and get it out of the rock.

Michael Terry examining rocks in gold pans, Tanami Desert, 1928.

XXV

THE BLIND MINER

Young Jock Nelson was an ideal travelling companion, for lie knew everybody, knew every show so far found on the field, knew all that was doing. Which was fine for me, for I wanted to meet everybody and see everything in the short time available. With Jock I roamed the entire circumference of the field, visited every camp, every claim, in his meat truck. Fifty miles each daily trip all round the compass, the "hub" being the pub and dozen shacks round which the future prosperous town would be built, bumping out into the sunlight, dodging the spinifex tufts out into a dreamy vastness which westward knew no township even for a thousand miles.

"I wonder if there ever will be a town here," mused young Nelson. "Doesn't seem possible, does it?"

"Not now," I replied, "but if there really is payable gold in 'them thar hills', then certainly a town will spring up. A town would spring up at the North Pole or the centre of the Sahara if they found gold there."

"Here's hoping!" Jock smiled. "A few good crushings have already been taken out of the Pinnacles and Peter Pan, small parcels, too, out of one or two other shows. But isolation and distance from a treatment plant eat up a terrible lot, even out of good stone. It will have to be rich to pay. But here's hoping."

'They'll soon erect a treatment plant right on the spot if you coves can find the stone.'

"Water?"

"Subterranean," I said at a wild guess. "You've already got evidence of it."

"We'll find the water, too, if it is there," he said determinedly with eyes to the west.

"You'll grow with the place," I suggested, "like Joe Kilgariff and any others who can start some little business and stick it out."

"I'll stick it out," he declared.

He did. But surely he never dreamt that in years fast coming you would be welcome to walk into the modern shops of the prosperous town of Tennant's Creek and buy anything from a needle to an anchor.

But now, throughout this vast, warm quietness was not the buzz of aeroplanes, only the faint buzz of insects.

On the due meat day we drove out to Mount Samuels, really only a rough, sun-blasted hill, but the highest "mount" here. Barney O'Leary and his mate McLeash, with Schmidt, welcomed us to their camp. With pick and shovel, hammer and drill, and what little gelignite they could afford, they were opening up a lode formation three hundred feet long and ten feet wide, and were ten feet deep. Fine gold showed here and there in the stone, a sight that had thrilled me since boyhood days. And would again, even now. Burnt the colour of their ironstone hills, Barney and his mate, as all others on the field, toiled at the tough rock under that hot sun with their brows running a rivulet of sweat. But at quite a number of camps there showed some sign of real gold in these beginnings of workings, and all hands toiled on in a stubborn hope. Nothing like the sight of gold to put new life and hope into a struggling man.

Barney and McLeash were old Granite hands, thus used to a waterless isolation and hardship greater ever than this. Quite a lot more so, in fact.

Out at the Hammer Jack, McCoy and Lane were plugging into the stone, with a shaft twelve feet down in jumbled country, and dolly samples going one ounce to the ton, which would have meant a fortune anywhere near civilization, if it could have been maintained. But under the conditions here, one ounce to the ton was no more than promising. Later on, though, their persistent picks would bite into a rich seam. Mrs McCoy was the mother looking after the camp. Those seventeen women then on the field all deserved that their menfolk should find gold, and certainly they deserved their full share of it.

All hands were hungry for meat here, and a yarn.

On again, among spinifex-covered ridges walling innumerable gullies. Bold, shaggy hills black-capped with ironstone, or a hot, dull-brown capping to harsh, abrupt ridges.

Hidden in the innumerable short valleys among these hills were the miners grey camps, looking cool but strange, these enormous beehives of spinifex tussocks; from the hilltops they suggested giant bearskins of some race of Cyclopean Grenadier Guards. It was in tough country like this that an equally tough old pair of diehards had fought out a sporting duel. More like a vendetta, it seemed, though the hoys seemed to think it a bit humorous, perhaps because it did not have too bloodthirsty an ending. The victim probably thought otherwise. The finale had taken place some months ago. These two antagonists were not "gunmen", they were simply miners who had crossed one another's paths in some fiercely hostile way. I've known precisely similar incidents happen on a number of isolated mining fields. Some smouldering dislike, distrust, imagined or intended slight, or mutual antagonism finally breaks out into gunfire in a blistering, isolated, or deadly monotonous environment.

Anyway, as the boys told the story to me, the combatants were an irascible little old fellow and a particularly tough hillman. In a bit of a brawl old Leather Sinews had no chance with the hillman, so he snarled, "I can't beat you with my mitts, you———! So I'm coming after you with a gun. Look after yourself!"

"Go your bloody hardest!" growled the hillman. And it was on.

Open warfare broke out in the hills around the Peter Pan. The antagonists took to walking to work and back to camp with rifle and gun, taking a potshot should one catch a glimpse of the other under cover of those rocky hills. This certainly broke the monotony and was highly diverting to the dozen men toiling in the hills round about—"toiling in that there line of fire". They talked it over, grinning, while the hilly was boiling. Anyway, there were several of these chance "hit-and-dodge" encounters until finally the old chap, proving the most cunning sniper, crept away round his adversary, then up behind him, and lathered his backside with buckshot.

They told me that the resultant haka sent every eaglehawk and crow for miles around scuttling to the skies.

So that everything would he tied up nice and official, the hoys picked what lead they could out of the victim's sit-me-down with a pen-knife, then sent in word to Muldoon the Warden that he'd better come out and straighten things out.

"Blast it!" growled Mul. "I hope I haven't got to bury a corpse. Not in this weather!"

On the way out to the battleground Cock Martin hailed him with, "Hullo, Mul, going out to the Peter Bang?"

Just by the way, when the heat and smoke and bad language blew away the combatants shook hands and called it a do. The quaintly assorted pair remained firm friends for years, until the little old fellow's death (he never lost his fiery temper) fairly recently. Also, they both, eventually struck gold. Which was far better, they both agreed, than lead!

It was the Peter Pan, then the Willadora, that struck really payable gold first, swiftly followed by a strike of sensationally rich stone at the Pinnacles.

"Fair set alight to the spinifex," said big old Carter. "Set the fossicker scratching in gullies that had never seen a white man before, and in such a place as this!"

With his mates, George Row and Anzac Russell, Carter was boiling us the billy by Shaw's Show after claiming their supply of beef. Young Nelson's enterprise was indeed a godsend to these widely scattered groups of men, three hundred miles away from the nearest butcher's shop.

On again, weaving through those sun-baked hills hard as the hobs of hell. Again and again and again I was puzzled at such barren-looking stone actually yielding gold. In twenty odd years of prospecting, and more of mining, I'd never seen the like. Neither had anyone else, until they actually struck the yellow streaks within it. Puffing like a grampus, the meat truck began climbing a prehistoric-looking rock, the likes of which made up the hills in these parts.

"The Rising Sun," said Jock.

"It would get plenty of sun, especially up on top."

"They all do." Jock smiled. "It would be funny, wouldn't it, if that was what put the gold into it?"

"Payable?"

"Yes. And looks as if it could turn out into a rattling good show. Fifty-three tons they knocked out of it, which when carted to Peterborough gave three hundred and nineteen ounces of good yellow gold."

"Good-oh! That would help them to keep going."

"Yes. Several smaller parcels have been as good. They have to be, worse luck—to stand the expense of transport a thousand miles and more, then the cost of treatment. That's what we're all worried about. Will other shows turn out as well, or will the field prove to have only half a dozen or so shows that are payable?"

"You can be pretty certain that if there are half a dozen good gold-producing shows in *any* locality out in the bush, then there must be more waiting to be found."

"I'm banking on it," said the young fellow grimly.

"Good on you! That's the spirit."

As the truck ground its protesting way up that bouldery track Nelson asked: "Know who found the Rising Sun?"

"No. A couple of tough old mountain devils, I suppose."

"A blind man found the Rising Sun."

"What?"

"Weaver, from the King River."

"Well, I'll be blessed! I heard at Wyndham he'd struck gold. How did he do it?"

"Well, when he arrived here with his family there were only half a dozen men on the field. With Jack Noble giving him a guiding hand, he drove straight up here and camped. Camped on top of the Rising Sun, a goldmine, a real goldmine. Camped where men with two good eyes had camped before, many a time. For this is where the boys from the Hatches Creek wolfram camp used always to camp when riding to the Tennant's. They camped right here, many and many a time, ever since they found wolfram away out there at Hatches Creek. The telegraph station at Tennant's Creek was their nearest touch with civilization. Now and again they'd come in there for their mail and to learn if all was still well with the world. For, out there, the end of the world could come and they wouldn't know about it. This spot was a handy camping-ground, both going and coming. But they never ever dreamt of looking for gold here. It was the Blind Miner who 'saw' the gold. In the morning he said to his sons, 'We might as well sink here as sink anywhere. Sink a shaft!' And they sank straight down on into the Rising Sun."

"Good luck to them!" I said fervently. "Somewhere or other I remember reading a story called 'And the Blind Shall See'."

Up on top was the activity of a family at work at the mine. And the largest, most compact, most comfortable spinifex home I'd yet seen.

XXVI

THE RISING SUN

Mrs Weaver and the children welcomed us heartily; there would be no escape here from the morning billy of tea, but here was also a most unexpected, heartily approved of luxury—scones on the bake! Right out here, where flour cost a fortune! That delicious smell came wafting through the spinifex rooms. This lively family home was built most comfortably, framework interlaced with spinifex into big and delightfully cool rooms and kitchen. Of course, gold had provided the wherewithal for luxuries such as scones, and sufficient water, and other simple comforts in living out here, where water was practically worth its weight in gold, and had to be bought and carted from the Tennant's Creek waterhole, seven miles away.

The blind miner was sitting there, busy too, his quiet face deeply thoughtful. Jack Noble, Schmidt, and Gregg, who held a few shares, with the lads were explaining to him the previous day's development of the young mine. In his mind he was seeing the progress, foot by foot, as they talked of sinking the shaft so many feet, the direction of the driving of a tunnel foot by foot into the hill, the possible value of a cross-cut to intersect a reef. Time, cost, success or result of failure, timber, cartage, labour, tools, gelignite, all had to be worked out efficiently and carefully.

Here, within this warren-like home, kept spotlessly clean by the womenfolk, lived several families. And here daily the blind miner sat in the cool gloom under the grass roof and recognized every voice, every step, every truck or car or horse that bumped or jolted past and on up the valley, recognized the protesting grunt of the camel as it came or went. From here the blind patriarch directed the young men who worked the Rising Sun.

The "whouf" of a camel's pad, then "Histha!" and the camel's gurgling grunts as cumbrously it lurched to sink down at the command. Then the heavy-booted, cheery entry of the travellers, their eyes wrinkling to the change of cool gloom from the glare of bright sunlight.

Poor Mrs Weaver, I thought, and her scones! But there were plenty. Seldom you catch a hush woman unprepared with tucker.

These were some of the very men who again and again had lit their campfire on this very spot when coming from the Hatches Creek wolfram camp to the Tennant's Creek telegraph station for mail.

"Camped right on top of a bonanza!" one said cheerfully as he accepted a pannikin of tea and a scone.

"The luck of the game!" a companion laughed. "Here we were punching along the camels, mile by mile, day after day, thinking of nothing but water and wolfram. And again and again we and others camped right here and baked our damper on a hill of gold."

"Yes"—his mate grinned ruefully—"and with the rising sun we'd be in a hurry to saddle our camels and ride away."

"We were blind."

The blind man smiled.

The Rising Sun was not yet, of course, proved to be a "hill of gold". But, with that fierce optimism that burns in the hearts of men working a new goldfield, it was now firmly believed to be, for it had proved there certainly was gold there, proved by several crushings of stone. As Jock Nelson had told me, the first parcels had yielded good returns and gave every encouragement for carrying on—with the heartfelt wish that other miners also would quickly strike payable stone. For the more gold found, the more men would come, and the quicker this apparently barren country would be proved and developed into a real mining field, and thus transport and everything else would cheapen.

This eventually happened, but only after some years of heartbreak and an ocean of sweat for many. But that is the story of nearly all "way out" mining fields.

Right now, there were only a handful of men and women scattered over this spinifex flat enflanked by its ironstone hills. And a little muddy water, lukewarm, precious as gold. And sunlight. And red earth which, where unaccustomed wheels churned it, became red, red dust.

As time droned on the Rising Sun would prove to be truly a "hill of gold". And men from the cities would come hurrying in aeroplanes, and offer the Blind Miner gold for his "golden hill".

What must have been the feelings of the blind man, sitting quietly there with his quiet face, his slow smile and his pipe, just sitting there, head slightly bowed towards the earthen floor with hand on his pipe, listening there to the eager entreaties of the city men trying to thrust upon him a fortune for his mine!

Alas! Though fortune comes to some, tragedy comes to many, too; it seems inseparable from life.

Kathleen Weaver, a pleasant lass of sixteen, helping the mother with tea and scones to fill our hungry maws, made the morning seem bright with her smile. From far north-west in the East Kimberley she had helped with the horses and cattle and the rough frontier homestead before her dad went blind, through an accident while mustering nearly wild cattle in rough country. She'd come with the family on the long trek from the East Kimberley in the two-ton truck through practically trackless country to Newcastle Waters, then south to this Tennant's Creek at Jack Noble's first whisper of, "Gold!"

And now they'd "struck it". And it looked as if dad and mum and the brothers and sisters would all be rich. It would not matter quite so much now that dad was blind. To the Blind Miner's family, life was wonderful.

Just three years later Kathleen was killed in an aeroplane accident.

But we could not sit there all day yarning while Mrs Weaver cooked scones for our hungry appetites. Climb up into the truck again, crawl cautiously down the golden hill to where, a few miles farther on, was the iron-brown dump of the Golden Forties. And men brown as the ironstone greeted the meat truck with dusty red smiles and cheery jokes. For after months of solid toil, living on the smell of an oiled rag plus a little salted beef and damper, they had just struck what appeared to be payable stone. If the dusty notes before me—which I wrote on the spot 'way back in '33—be correct, McLeod and Troy were working this show with Renfrey, who was on quarter-share. We wished them luck.

Another day and on to the Peko. Brilliant sunlight was reflected from the hot red ironstone of this hungry-looking hill, sparsely clothed with its spiky, dull-grey spinifex, a petrified relic from harsh, primitive days of ages past. Who on earth would dream of brightness, of life, of gold within this barren rock?

A few shallow holes here and there were punched into the red rock of the hill. The Peko was to break men's hearts, as well as their backs. But a year and a day would come when, to everyone's astonishment, rich gold would be struck there—at depth. None of us dreamed that on this desolate spot fine bungalows with electricity and refrigeration would he erected for two hundred and sixty or more employees. This hole would pay rich dividends indeed in time to come, as would other holes now being punched so toilsomely down into the tough, red rock. Finally, at still greater depth, the Peko would turn into copper, perhaps the richest copper-mine at present known in Australia, for that fabulous Mount Isa, far to the nor'-east in North Queensland, is of copper, silver, zinc, and other minerals.

On then to the Pinnacles mine, a rough camp, but well supplied, and a cheery one. For rich stone had early been struck here; already a number of crushings had been followed by rich returns. There was no worry about the storekeeper's bills here.

"It's not gold we're worrying about," said Killicoat as we strolled to the galley for a billy of tea, "it's water! There's gold in 'them thar hills', but not enough surface water to fill the beak of a thirsty crow."

A sentiment glumly agreed to by his mates, McKillop and King. Water is more precious by far than gold.

A rumble of explosive dully booming among the hills told us we were approaching the Lone Star. Most of the boys slaved into the rock with pick and shovel, hammer and gad. Hammer-and-drill toil was a luxury, for explosives were very expensive after transport a thousand miles out here and could only be afforded by the half-dozen shows that had struck gold, or appeared likely to. And there looked to be a good chance of this happy event in the Lone Star, as Jim Maloney and Schmidt and big George Bolan assured us. After superhuman labour they'd driven a tunnel one hundred and fifty-two feet into that tough rock and cut an ironstone reef which they believed, by dolly-pot test, went one ounce to the ton. They had a good many tons of surface stone at grass showing even better prospects. So all hands in this rock-bound camp were toiling on the hopeful side.

One of the prospectors of the El Dorado was Clarry Standley, noted for his ill luck. A trier for years on numerous fields, still he kept doggedly on, certain that a day would dawn when he would surely strike it rich. So he did, but did not know it. Desperately hard up, he and his mate sold out the El Dorado for a few pounds, less than twenty was the figure I heard. Of course, the place was not developed then, the only trace of gold in this El Dorado was a fairish prospect from the dolly-pot. But the mates could not live on air, they had to find negotiable gold or clear out.

Standley went prospecting for wolfram. A couple of years later he would find himself six hundred miles to the north, in Darwin hospital, awaiting an operation for appendicitis. In the cheeriest mood he told friends of a big, "a real big" find he'd located in untried country, away out there, down somewhere in the Centre. As soon as he came out of the repair shop he was going to hurry back to the bush with a big load of tucker, peg out the show, and then hurry in to Tennant's to report his finding of a new wolfram field. His luck had changed at last.

Peritonitis set in. He died.

Of course, life has plenty of ups and downs anywhere; it's only the lucky ones for whom it flows smoothly on to fortune. But on mining fields the ups and downs seem particularly noticeable, and at the Tennant's they certainly were so, for even twenty-five years after discovery the mineral and geological conditions were still a bit of a puzzle, not fully understood.

Anyway, if Clarry Standley and his mates, if all of the early prospectors, had been able to hold on even to shares of their claims until they were fully developed———! Standley then need not have been starved out to go seeking wolfram and die of ill luck. For in the years to come the El Dorado would produce three million and more in gold—I don't know the full figure. But this, of course, could not happen until capital put money and machinery and expensive time into development at depth. This phase of development of the whole field would happen to most of the shows before they would develop into mines. The prospectors would sell out for a few thousand, except for the few who could hold out with their shares. Most of them would thankfully wash the red dust from their bodies, then hey for the city!—to wash it out of their lungs.

At the time these notes were being written Jack Noble had just found his Noble's Knob, and was belting into it with pick and shovel, hammer and drill, in a lather of sweat, living on the smell of an oiled rag. Jack would hang on as long as he could, ever in hope as the field seemed to take a bit of a boost on ahead, clinging on desperately when "things turned dead". Then, in the years that were to come, he would sell out thankfully for a few thousand when capital came seeping into the field. After long, hard years of "outs" Jack's overworked body would demand its chance of a spell. Most thankfully he would take the long trek to Adelaide, delightful and extremely interesting among Australian cities. He would hit the high spots—while the money lasted.

With development, Noble's Knob, too, became called the "Hill of Gold". Over five million pounds' worth of gold came out of it.

Yes, life can be full of ups and downs. All the same, lots of these chaps in all walks of life who battle on to finally hit the high spots have at least done things and earned their hit of fun.

Having nothing better to do one day, I went off for a stroll and came face to face with a scowling young fellow swinging a .44 at his hip. We passed by, each minding his own business. It was curious, though, to be walking out amongst the Australian spinifex under a cloudless sky and meet this rejuvenation of the American Wild West of an earlier generation. It reminded me sharply of one day in the Kimberleys when I stepped out onto a native pad face to face with a startled young warrior dressed in rancid goanna fat and pipeclay, his sinewy black hand clutching a handful of wickedly barbed spears. There, too, each went on his way, strictly minding his own business.

But such a meeting was natural out there, over the range in Wild Aboland. But here, a heavy belt of cartridges and a .44 swinging at the hip looked ominously out of place, making it difficult to realize that here was really an ordinary happy-go-lucky Australian mining camp. I knew there was only a handful of these chaps in this large area, with the dinkum miners keeping sternly aloof, yet it was rather startling to meet one of them suddenly.

Down near their camps it was ordinary enough to see a man strolling along, then stopping suddenly to wheel round and blaze away at an anthill, firing from the hip. Any stray kangaroo that hopped across the flat these times had the hop of its life—and kept hopping. This wheeling round to blaze at anthills was practice to become "quick on the draw". Some among them *were* quick, too, they must be given that credit.

Came a morning when Jock Nelson was to drive out to his place at Attack Creek, some fifty or so miles north, for a fresh supply of beef. It was a brilliant Sunday morning, 30th September 1934, when we sat down to breakfast at the pub. Hot news was served up.

It appeared that in the small hours there had been trouble down near the Afghan's little battery. One camp had "rushed" another. There had been a beating-up, and guns had been "pulled".

"No corpses yet," said the vendor of news, "but it looks as if they'll be starting that private cemetery of theirs they've been skiting about for so long. Mighty quick, too!"

Prophetic words!

We strolled out to prepare the truck, stopping on the pub veranda for a final cigarette. For the boys were coming in from their claims and congregating on the pub veranda and round the butcher's shop and the store for the usual Sunday-morning yarn. Over a radius of nearly two hundred miles of country the boys generally downed tools on Saturday evening and came in on Sunday to "town" for stores and mail, if any, and to hear the news, for all hands were eager to hear news of any strike of good stone. So the boys were just beginning to drift along, earlier and more in numbers than usual. Were they urged by premonition? It did look just as if the stage were set.

Before Jock Nelson and I left in the car sixty men were gathered round the pub and two little shacks. And sixty men were a full half of the population of the field. The report of the trouble down by Fazil Deene's camp at dawn had spread like wildfire, but surely not in such a farflung radius as that. Having got the car ready for the road, Jock and I rolled yet another cigarette with Barney O'Leary and McLeash and the boys lounging on the pub veranda. According to the latest arrivals, it now appeared that this dawn argument had arisen over a rifle that one man had given to another, a half-caste, to sell for him some months before, and for which he was now demanding payment. In a dispute over this the previous day the half-caste had turned away with the challenge, "I don't want to fight now. But if you come down to the camp in the *morning* you'll get all you're bloodywell looking for."

And that was that!

And now was now!

XXVII

THE GUNS

That particular camp was the one three miles down the track from the pub by the Afghan's battery, where O'Brien, the drover of the goats, was camped, with the half-caste and several others. He had been drawn into the brawl. So explained the latest arrivals, now telling us how the "pay-back" had come that morning at dawn. A car-load of men, friends of the original owner of the rifle, rushed the camp and gave the half-caste the father of a hiding. He awoke as the blankets were snatched off him, then was fighting in a lather of curses, flailing fists, and kicking legs. His mates were held back from helping him by gun threat.

"I reckon there'll be a return visit," grimly declared the purveyor of the very latest news.

"Sure!" declared his mate. "And there'll be skin and hair and guts flying!"

How very, very true!

I could not believe it, it was merely a camp brawl. All hands from pub veranda and butcher's shack and store were by now covertly watching the camp beside the pub, for this was the headquarters of the dawn raiders. Outside the tent a man was unconcernedly cleaning his car. No sign whatever that he was aware of all those quiet glances. A beautiful morning, deathly still, a man quietly cleaning his car.

Young Nelson threw away his cigarette butt, stood up and stretched.

"Moving off?" suggested Barney.

'Yes," said Nelson, smiling, "it's pleasant here and I'd like another smoke. But we'd better be moving. Come along, Jack."

Our dust was still in sight trailing the northern track when the drama was played out. We heard the story when we returned.

O'Brien, with the half-caste and his friends, came driving up the road from the Afghan's battery. Just passing the pub, they pulled up opposite their enemy's camp. Casually the man cleaning his car, straightened up, glanced across at the men tumbling out of the truck, then went quietly on with his work.

The new arrivals stamped into the bar and ordered a drink or two, which they spiced with sundry grim threats. Then they strode along the veranda and down across to the man by the car. The sound of angry voices on the still morning air brought more onlookers from shacks and tents to watch, from a safe distance, the group now gathered round the car, arguing heatedly. Their accusations and abuse grew more violent, and suddenly there were guns in their hands. O'Brien leapt for the truck and grabbed his rifle.

"*Bang!*"

O'Brien reeled at the impact of a slug in his stomach, then jumped behind the truck, fiddling with the rifle.

"*Bang!*"—and he staggered back at the thump of another heavy slug in the stomach. He whipped up the rifle, but—"*Bang!*"—and this time the drover of goats staggered out onto the road, convulsively dropping his rifle. Clutching his stomach, he fell into the dust. So the bullets started whistling at such close quarters the lookers-on scrambled for cover; some became jammed in the pub door. But Barney O'Leary and McLeash and their mates jumped up and rushed the combatants and disarmed them, while from round the corners of shacks heads stretched upon elongated necks cautiously eyed off the scrimmage.

The smoke and the dust now having cleared away, Barney O'Leary took possession of the guns, which he would later hand over to the police.

O'Brien was badly hurt; there was little they could do for him. The drover of goats showed great fortitude, particularly as from the first, he seemed to know he was done.

"I've had it!" he gasped. "There's not much you can do for me 'cept keep the flies away. And give me a smoke!"

O'Leary jumped into a car and raced for the telegraph station at the Creek seven miles north and telegraphed Doctor McCann at the Alice, three hundred and twenty miles south. At the telegraph station was camped the one lone policeman, Constable Cameron. He made haste for the field—too late, of course, to be of any help to the drover of goats.

All hands rolled up for a Sunday-afternoon meeting, strongly urging police protection for the field, and the disarming of all gun-carriers. The miners scattered all over the field were both angry and hurt by the shooting. All seemed deeply moved, even when Jock Nelson and I returned from Attack Creek.

"If we don't get a police post here quick and lively we'll have to pack a gun on each hip."

"To hell with them!" swore others. "Shooting went out with the Wild West days!"

"Did it?" was the retort. 'Then what did you see only a couple of hours ago?"

The drover of goats saw it through to the bitter end. They made him as comfortable as they could, carrying him into the shade of a shack where they laid him on a rough bunk, fanning away the tormenting flies.

'Thanks, boys," he breathed relievedly. "Now give me cigarettes. Bring me a bucket of water and let me drink all I want. You can't do any good for me—neither can the doctor, even if he could get here soon, which he can't. I've seen too many of them die across on the other side not to know that."

He battled against great pain; his intolerable thirst, usual with stomach wounds, he tried to drown with pannikin after pannikin of water, which he couldn't hold: it all ran out of him through the bullet holes.

The Government Medical Officer at Alice Springs, Doctor McCann, drove day and night at reckless speed after receiving the Tennant's Creek wire. Futile, though, to hope to beat the Angel of Death hovering over the drover of goats.

The morning had passed into a quiet, hot afternoon when Constable Cameron came into the shack where O'Brien lay and looked down on the now obviously dying man.

"Can I do anything for you?" he asked.

"No," replied O'Brien. "I'm finished now. There's only one thing I'd like now. And that's a gun to shoot that bastard and take him with me!" But he did not seem to speak with malice.

Later on, he turned to a man sitting quietly there. 'Well, Macdonald, they can say what they like about you, but you're a white man. You've sat by me all day. 'Shearing's done, my race is run...' Bring him in. I'm dying. It's no good squealing, nothing I can do will alter anything, it's no good going to the grave with a grudge."

Time dreamed on. Cool night came, those countless stars of the Centralian sky came out in pin-points of gold twinkling in blue satin. Far down here on earth all was very silent. With the first cold streak of dawn came a sound, a hurrying sound fast approaching—a futile speed now to the dying man. As Doctor McCann stepped from the car and peered inside the dimly lit shack a man who had been sitting beside O'Brien stood up, with a nod, to walk outside. Looking down at the dying man, he drawled, "Well, so long—good luck."

"Good luck." O'Brien nodded.

As the man went out the doctor inquired, 'Who is that?"

"Oh, that's the bastard who shot me," replied O'Brien. 'Well, doc, how long have I to go?"

One glance and the doctor knew.

"You're pretty bad."

"Oh, well! Two hours?"

The doctor nodded.

It was later on that the dying man murmured, "Well, the time is coming close now." And asked again for his former enemy.

"Well," said O'Brien, when the man came in, "I'm going now. If it does you any good, I tell you you're not the man who shot me. Well, I'm going now, lads. And with an easy conscience. I never squealed."

Captured kangaroo, no shot, Central Australia 1928.

XXVIII

GOLD!

Jock Nelson and I sped away in a puff of red dust, vaguely aware of gunshots astern. Out under the blazing shy, past the lonely telegraph station with now the only sign of man the whispering poles of the Overland Telegraph Line above faded tracks ever heading north. Bold, black-capped ridges, stubby ironstone bluffs under a blazing sky, grey spinifex like tufted hair gripped to the pate of the brick-red earth. Dry gullies shadowing down into winding flats scantily grey under mulga and needlewood. Startling visibility for many miles over harsh, wild country that suddenly mists into ghostly purplish hazes. That overwhelming silence of the Centre. I leant back in the truck to feel that listening silence, to inhale the burnt earth and twisted shrub, to glance at the speck of an eagle in the sky, then at the shimmering horizon—to see emerging the gigantic neck of a camel and rider as they came floating through the air in some distant mirage.

Level country then, the scantiest of timber, but shrubs and spinifex everywhere. We could now see a long way over the spinifex and shrubs to other openings and other spinifex and shrubby flats that seemed to go for ever on like the two thin wires of the Overland Telegraph Line. Then a wall of trees, which rapidly fanned out into the scanty timber lining a big dry old creek-bank. Masses of hot, loose washstones in coarse sand, a shallow pool of water up above the crossing. Cheery sign of a camp, two men standing up to welcome us. This was Jock Nelson's Attack Creek station, with its headquarters by Attack Creek. Just here was where McDouall Stuart, with his two staunch men Bill Kekwich and Ben Head and a baker's dozen of perishing horses, had been attacked by the Warramunga warriors.

Here at Attack Creek Jock would load up with a fresh batch of beef. Meanwhile I greeted "Woody" Woodruffe, the persistent little tiger who had such a lot to do with the opening up of this newly discovered Tennant's Creek goldfield. In charge here was Harry Phillips, one of those kindly old chaps you meet so often in the far-out places.

Woody was "recuperating".

"Too many years in the spinifex, Jack," he said, smiling, "then comes the find of real gold—gold! Gold! Gold! Then off to Adelaide and the bright lights—and weren't they bright! And the girls and the horses and the wine! Far too rich for a spinifex groper like me, Jack. So I just flew back here to the spinifex to recover. Me! Fly! When I've been used to a country where a man will ride a hundred and thirty miles to deliver an urgent letter to a neighbour and think nothing of it. Whereas if down in the city my neighbour's letter is dropped into my post-box I hand it back to the postman. And the noise, Jack! I'm used to a wilderness and sand and spinifex and the whispering wires. And a silence big as the sky. Not a solitary thing to see but crows. And you're just as sick of the sight of your mate as he is of you. When you think Christmas must be coming if one day you catch sight of the dust of a mob of cattle drifting down from the Territory. And yet I fly back to all this in an aeroplane, and couldn't make it fast enough!"

Jock Nelson grinned amiably at little Woody's puzzled visage.

"You've enjoyed variety in your young life, Woody, anyway."

"I'll say," agreed Woody. "Half a lifetime in Abo Land with witchety grubs and goanna and the mulga. Then gold—and Adelaide. And can't they lay it on in Adelaide!" Woody sighed.

"The change proved a bit rich?" Jock smiled.

"Yes," sighed Woody. "The system couldn't take it. But I'll be back there again to get the spinifex resin off my chest."

He probably would, for real gold would soon be found. But Woody would never find another Peter Pan.

Woody, quiet little chap, enjoyed a campfire yarn, and he had plenty of good stories. But they were generally of the loneliness. And most were a hit grim. He had been a linesman and then a telegraph operator at the Tennant's Creek station before the gold discovery. And it was mostly in the "gold days" I was interested.

"I used to think and think, Jack," he explained, "by the campfire. Goodness knows we had the time, and the environment to think in. Anywhere along the line. But I had so little to think with. Anything to read, Jack, we would just 'eat' over and over again. Naturally, when you'd only see the mailman jogging along once every six weeks or so. Anyway, when that yarn came out about Lasseter I chewed and chewed over it. I didn't know whether he'd found gold or not, of course. But it gave me something to think about. For even out here, once in a blue moon, a prospector would come wandering along. Gruff old blokes. Hard as their ironstone hills, and just about as communicative. Naturally so, I suppose. No one to talk to but their camel or horse or myall natives. But several had found traces of gold here and there, one old one swore there'd be a goldfield found some day hereabouts. As I knew his 'hereabouts' could mean anywhere between three hundred miles south to the Alice, or three hundred miles north from here, his information wasn't much help. And his 'some day' could mean 'now', 'some day', 'never'. There was no such thing as time in this country then. Anyway, I wouldn't know gold if I saw it.

"At last I wrote to Adelaide for a prospecting book. And I stewed over that, believe me. And started crushing bits of stone in a jam-tin and washing it in a frying-pan down at the waterhole. The abos camped down at the creek were immensely interested, thought I'd gone mad, squatted round me watching with grins on their frying-pans like the horse-laughs on a camel. Believe me, I strained my poor old eyes looking for that gold. I carried bags of those stones for miles and miles to water until I didn't have as much sweat left in me as would fill the beak of a crow. With never a fly-speck to show for it. I learnt then, Jack, what a delightful sight that despised fly-speck of gold really is—when you're lucky enough to get it in the dish. Yet all the same, the more I struggled with those rocks and dreamt about it, the more certain I grew that there really was 'gold in them thar hills'!"—and we laughed with Woody.

"Anyway," he went on, "I couldn't be out all day and every day, I had my job to attend to. And, besides, the gold-bearing hills are near seven mile from here, which means another seven to trudge back. I found that this prospecting is a full-time job, whereas I had to put in my shift at the station. So it cost me a few sticks of tobacco to get the natives on the job. When a little crowd of them came in to the waterhole I'd give them a bag and a stick or two of bacca and tell them to go out into the hills and bring me in the heaviest, funniest-looking stones they could see. Just didn't they think me mad!

"But for that tobacco," he went on, "they brought me in what seemed to be tons and tone of stone—in what was my spare time from the wires, I grew corns on my hands a camel would have envied, pounding the samples in that home-made dolly-pot, which soon wore out. So did my heart, too, an' damn' near my pocket, keeping the tobacco up to the abos, the grinning capitalists. All that tobacco had to be packed along by the mailman every few weeks and these skinflints of abos wouldn't carry a stone without it." Which only brought a grin from old Harry and young Nelson, for it was well known that Woody had a very soft spot for the knowing old abo.

"Ah well, Jack," resumed Woody, "I'd just about done my dash when a miracle happened—a double miracle, for I'm blessed if he didn't have his wife with him. Just fancy, a white woman out *here]*" And Woody whistled, still amazed at the very thought. "He was a real prospector, Harry Udall, he blew in from out of the blue. Seemed to have come from Arltunga way, working his way up through the Centre prospecting any likely-looking country. Anyway, he camped among those hungry-looking ironstone hills. And one day his wife—she was a heroine if ever there was one—was attracted by a pothole someone had sunk—God knows who—and she picked up a lump of stone that had been thrown up out of it. She turned that stone over and over in her hands. It was heavy, it interested her, her interest grew as slowly she turned it over and over. She couldn't be certain, but at times, with the sun glinting on it, she could almost swear she could see a pin-point or two of gold dully gleaming in it here and there. It might be new-chum's gold, of course, might be anything, might be nothing.

"She took it to her husband. He dollied it.

"It was rich in gold!

"Of course, he cleaned out the old prospecting shaft and began searching for where that stone came from. Took him some time to find it, though he really had only to sink the shaft a few feet further. Whatever weather-beaten poor old bandicoot had first sunk that pothole, all on his lonesome out there, had knocked off right atop of a fortune. It's happened before, so prospectors tell me. But there's more of an excuse out here, it's such cussedly difficult stone here, difficult to believe any of it could possibly carry gold. It's beaten some good men here already.[4]

"Anyway, Harry Udall and his missus—found it. Results of dolly-pot samples looked real good. And were the four or five of us, between the old telegraph station here and the old-new prospecting shaft seven miles out there in those hills excited! I'll say we were!

"Then came the real big test. By mailman Udall sent a parcel away north to the Mining Warden at Darwin to be assayed. Norman Bell, the Chief Warden—you know him, Jack. Anyway, we hung on those wires. It takes time, of course, or it did take time then, doing things like that from an outlandish place right out here. In time the result came back—a highly payable assay result.

"Well, of course, Harry, aided by his wife, who was as good a man as he, belted into that rock. It took them quite some time to strike the really payable body of stone. They belted into it then hauled it up by a windlass Harry had made himself out of a few bush sticks. You can bet I was interested as a crow at the killing yard watching things, what time I could ride away from the station. So there lay a few tons of dirty-looking old browny-black rock on the surface by the dump. And that had gold in it. Or so Harry believed. I couldn't. And now—to get that gold out of it!" Woody paused, grinning at me across the campfire.

"You see, Jack, I'd found out by now that even if you *do* find gold in a stone, you've got to get that gold *out* of the stone!" He lit up again, smiling at his memories in the firelight.

"Anyway," he resumed, "this wizard man, Udall, fashioned machinery right out here in Wild Man's Land. I'll admit he had an old motor-car engine

---

[4] In the coming years, it was to beat many more.

to start with. He rigged it up on supports to do the work of a stamper. He cut down a tree and made the butt into a stamper, and shod it with a lump of old iron. Made his screen and plates and pulleys and Goodness knows what. Rigged it up so its own vibration wouldn't shake it to pieces. He plastered, or painted, in that cunning way the experienced man knows, a film of quicksilver on the little copper plate, shovelled some stone into the hopper he'd made, then set her going. Whack-oh!"

Woody's enthusiasm brought sympathetic grins to our faces.

"You could hear that baby battery 'clang-clang-clang' all over the hills," said Woody. "The euros and wallabies sat back on their tails and wondered what in the name of all the Sacred Goannas was happening now, the abos scratched their beards and wondered what in blazes the mad white man would do next!

"But it worked!" There was triumph in Woody's voice. "He crushed that stone and extracted the gold, smelted it from that dirty little greyish-yellow looking lump of amalgam—it took him a fortnight of know-how and sweat and patience to do it. And there was the beautiful little lump of gleaming gold—a few shiny yellow ounces—finally extracted by all that work from some tons of hard rock. Alluvial miners now here from other fields have often growled what a hell of a lot of Australia there is in an ounce of gold. Well, long before they arrived here I knew what a hell of a lot of *rock* is mixed with an ounce of reef gold. And yet that stone was really rich—we know now, of course, by assay, that it really went six ounces to the ton, six ounces of gold in every great big ton of dirty old ironstone rock! But very sweet, very sweet indeed!" We grinned at Woody's reminiscent enjoyment. "Something else, too," he said. "These know-how prospectors have got more in their heads and hands than you'd dream of. We know, of course, that in the surface, anyway, of the Great Northern it is a bit patchy in places with bismuth, and this makes the stone refractory to treat. But a little thing like that only put Udall on his mettle."

"Good boy!" laughed young Nelson. 'Why, I don't believe the old man could better that talky-talky."

"Well, now, that's some compliment, believe me," said Woody, "for I've heard your old man talk. And how! Anyway, the Udalls knew they could now 'eat' out of their mine, as we called it now. They'd proved there was enough gold in the rock to give them a living while Harry toiled like blazes to strike the fortune we felt certain was somewhere deep in that mine. It was, too, but it took them another twelve months' battling before they really got on their feet. And that's how the Great Northern was found."

And Woody, with a very satisfied gesture, paused to light up. Living his memories, he had become quite animated. And it seemed to me, sitting there quietly waiting by the campfire in that dreamy Centralian silence, that starlight was playing gently upon his little old lined face.

Boring for water, Northern Territory 1933.

XXIX

WOODY AND THE PETER PAN

"Anyway," puffed Woody, "through all these mighty happenings I was keeping on going, as full of hope as a butcher's pup is of meat. But it seemed as if I'd have to crush every stone in the hills and then never find gold. But one day—wow! I fell back on my own tail with excitement. A real tail of gold in the pan! A real, lovely, yellow, floury tail of gold! I harried those bucks till they were nearly running to the hills—and how green those rusty old hills suddenly looked. I got them on the run to show me where they found that stone. The same stone, or what appeared to be the same, lay there all right, about two miles south of Udall's show. I dollied a sample of stone, and blessed if it didn't show traces of gold! Real, good, gleaming gold, and what seemed to me must surely be *payable* traces of it, too.

"At sight of my excitement at those tiny yellow grains of yellow 'mustard' the bucks really thought I *had* gone mad. But I still hadn't found the reef. Not that I could tell anyway. When I could scrounge the time I'd hurry away out there from the station and do a bit of amateur loaming around where I'd found the stone. I'd heard the few old roughnecks who'd camped at the waterhole growling about 'loaming'. And blessed if the loam didn't show a tail of gold, too! Restless nights for me then, believe me, dreaming I was digging up gold by the ton, just shovelling in bag after hag full of gold. But what was I to do? I knew nothing about prospecting, or mining either. Where *was* that gold—if it was really there? I didn't know enough about the game to find out. Besides, I had my job to do.

"Anyway, just about this time Jack Noble blew along—you met him away across in Derby, Jack, when he returned there to get some of his friends to try their luck out here. Anyway, I grubstaked Jack and he set about the job properly, loaming and trenching by experience. Eventually he struck the cap of the reef, but not the reef itself. It proved tricky to find, believe me. But finding the cap proved we were on the right track, and that was another big step ahead. Old Bill Garnet had come along by this time. For years past—he seemed old as these very hills—he's been fossicking a line of country for what must be a thousand miles. Disappears for a year or two, sometimes more, but always reappears again. And from a mineral point of view, anyway, he knows this hard country as few others do. And from time to time, he'd had a bit of a try at this very locality, for years believing there was gold here somewhere. Anyway, he reappeared here just at the right time, for

Jack had the gold-fever bad and wanted a claim of his own. So he set out to find it—Noble's Knob! Well, old Garnet grunted approvingly when Jack showed him a sample from the capping on my ground, and agreed to come in with me and try to find the reef for a quarter share. He'd have to do the mining, of course, while I kept the home fires burning from my job at the telegraph station. Old Garnet finally cut the reef. And all together we'd found it, the reef of the Peter Pan."

"And good luck to you!" we three declared. For the Peter Pan was now—well, the Peter Pan!

Woody was very proud of his little "never-say-die" share in finally locating the Peter Pan, which really had been the practical start of the field. Work on the Great Northern had been held up when rich and easily worked surface stone blazed out from the Peter Pan, bringing the first sign of a "rush", sixteen leases quickly (for those parts) pegged and applied for along the Peter Pan line of reefs.

After a few rich crushings had been sent to Peterborough, Woody had developed itchy feet, sold out his share of the mine, and, so I gathered, shaken the red dust of the Centre off his feet for good, retiring to far away Adelaide to "do the Grand".

He had done the Grand right enough, as the lucky ones do, but of course they generally return to the Centre.

And here was Woody back again, looking somewhat the worse for wear but obviously relieved to be back in the red dust and his Land of Hope again. As soon as he'd recuperated, he assured us as he put the billy on again, he would seek another Peter Pan.

Alas, those Peter Pans are so very, very hard to find.

Increasingly now, as rich pockets of stone would be found, men would sell out their interest to speculators for a few thousand, in various cases little dreaming of the wealth they were leaving behind. For it would be a number of years yet before men learnt the "working" of this country. Only time and development, of course, would prove "the Tennant's" a rich goldfield.

"Have you met old Bill Garnet, Jack?" asked Woody.

"No."

"He's one of the well-known old characters of these parts, tough as the mulga. Travels mostly with a donkey and buggy. Since the motor has come and Tennant's broke out he gets flash when he makes a strike, lives on the best the Alice can supply, and buys a motor-car while his luck lasts. If his luck keeps in he gets real flash and pays the natives by cheque. The funniest thing you could ever watch. That leathery old face of his screwed up like a sun-scorched walnut the crows have brought home, the tip of his tongue licking his lips as laboriously he scrawls his name. The old Stone Age abo gazing on, standing on one foot, scratching his hide wherever he can reach it through the ashes and goanna fat. Garnet hands out the cheque with a great flourish, the abo takes it in his dirty paw, wondering what's going to happen next, while Bill strides away like a haughty tycoon, leaving him holding that hit of paper.

"They bring it to me, of course—for years now in these parts old Wallaby Holtze or me is the man who knows everything'. You ought to see the expression on their faces when I've tried to explain that that scrap of paper really means money—if they can get it to a bank. I've had the funniest times. A bit scared once or twice, though, I thought they were going to club the old fossicker. He simply waves them away as if he was a lord when he hands them that scrap of paper, simply will not condescend to explain to the heathen, they can take it or leave it, but they must not dare to question that mighty piece of paper. A very different man to when he's the old spinifex wombat sitting over a native fire chewing the tail of a goanna!" Woody had got quite wound up, but we were content to listen.

"A while back old Bill was right down on his luck," he resumed. "Everything went against him, he owed 'everything', and was even feeling a bit sick.

" 'The dust blows right through me whiskers,' he moaned. 'I've got so poor me hair is failin' out, even me old donk sniffs like he's disowned me—he's smelled me many a time, God knows! I'm the faded flower, I'll *never* bloom again!'

"But he did. Old Ted Hayes of Love's Creek station put him onto a show some twenty-five miles east of Barrow Creek. Ted, while hunting for stray cattle, had ridden across it years ago, but only cattle interested Ted, he never did anything with the show. The natives found it again for old Bill—he called it the 'Homeward Bound'. He opened it up a bit, sold it for a thousand or two, so his luck 'broke good', and he swore his whiskers began to grow again. Grew more when he struck a bit of gold at Kurranulli, away out at Whistleduck Creek between Bonney Well and Hatches Creek.

"Anyway, Old Bill could always sniff gold—just as he did when he saw my dolly-pot prospects, got to work, and finally cut the reef of the Peter Pan. What a crazy day *that* was! It was the first show registered, and rich, too. We didn't have to wait so long to prove it as most of the other battlers did. And here I am again. Difficult to believe, with all that's happened since, that we struck gold barely two years ago. The Peter Pan, the Willadora, the Pinnacles. They made Tennant's Creek."

"And now it looks as if it is going to turn out into a real goldfield," said young Nelson eagerly. "I hope so."

"Sure it will!" Harry smiled. "The place hasn't even been scratched, and yet look at the good shows already located under these difficulties of isolation and transport. There must be hundreds of good shows hidden away in these old hills just waiting to be found. They'll be found—now that the boys are finding out a bit of how to look for them."

"Yes, and it's taken and is taking a bit of finding out," said Woody feelingly. "The real prospectors tell me this field is the most tricky they have ever known."

"No wonder that every man who has passed this way has ridden over the golden stone," drawled old Harry.

"No wonder," said young Nelson, "seeing how well it's hidden. But all those gangs that erected the Overland Telegraph Line—all that worked on the Tennant's Creek section, anyway—worked over the field, and had to camp at the Tennant's Creek waterhole for water."

"And before them," said old Harry, "McDouall Stuart himself. And he camped right here, too."

"Blessed if I ever thought of that!" said Nelson. "So he did. And it's right here at this very camp that the Warramungas attacked him. The old explorer rode right across a goldfield—and how many times? He was forced to return twice, he and his men rode three times at least across gold when travelling north, three times when travelling south. If he'd only known!"

"Yes. If during those desperate trips he or his men had struck gold, what feverish excitement it would have brought to the tiny population of the day!"

Woody liked company, yet was so used to the lonely places. The packhorse mail used to jog along then once every six weeks, and Jack McCarthy's horse-team, straining slowly along with the rations came once every twelve months. Woody had been stationed six years at Daly Waters without seeing a white woman, then one well-remembered day, out of a misty haze, Mrs Rodgers with her husband came driving along, buggy and horses monstrous apparitions looming up out of the mirage.

In that country, in certain areas over dry stages in a bad season, horses and bullocks, too, would have to plug along seventy-five miles between a drink of water. Mrs Rodgers then was one of the very few white women— you could count them on the fingers of your hands—north of the Alice or south of Pine Creek. Happily she and her husband made good eventually when the country began to look up.

Poor Woody Woodruffe, easy-going, kindly, could not hold fortune when fortune came. His last letter to me was that he was trekking west seeking another golden dream.

He gasped out his life in a desert shooting affray in which both men died.

XXX

A STUDY OF BALLISTICS

Back at the Tennant's, Nelson and I strolled into the little dining-room for breakfast. The morning was already warm, and half a dozen men were sitting there in shirtsleeves at the bare board tables. We had heard that a man had been arrested for O'Brien's murder, so we were not surprised to find the policeman and his prisoner there, too. During breakfast they were deeply engaged in a discussion on ballistics, a topic on which the accused man seemed to be putting it all over the policeman, discussing high-velocity bullets, what happens on impact, what happens if the nickel tears off, the wearing and clogging effects of high-velocity powder on a revolver and rifle barrel, and so on. He explained that a chemical reaction takes place on explosion which in the course of time will pit the steel lining of the barrel, and he most certainly seemed to know what he was talking about.

He and the policeman used to stroll round together, sleep on the pub veranda opposite one another — since there was no lock-up there was nothing else to do until the law got a move on. He was eventually acquitted.

Trouble simmered on the field for a while, but the arrival of police to be stationed there finally put a damper on those ambitious to start a private cemetery — to the content and benefit of the gradually growing field.

However, these things happen even in the best regulated families, whether at home, on a mining field, or within a nation.

I took the road again to the Alice. Heavy skies, red earth, red anthills. The truck buzzes along through the waving, now yellowing stalks of the drab grey spinifex. Past lancewood, stunted ironwood, and the startling white trunks of the stunted ghost-gums. The haze makes the sky appear so low that to the south-east it seems to rest upon a long string of hills, so far away that the line of the range-top shows as grey as the thin grey leaves of the lancewood-trees. We pause at Kelly's Well long enough to read "Travelling stock not to stay more than 4 hours". Soon we pass the little white border peg on the side of the track with the broad arrow cut into it on top, and a B on that side of it facing the track. A tiny peg indeed to mark the border between two vast areas, North and Central Australia. How different that drab grey track, that thirsty, harsh red track, to the now great, macadamized ribbon of the Stuart Highway! But, of course, it took a war to do *that*.

Bonney Well. The shimmering line of the Devil's Marbles, the sunrays refracted from the steel hard, grey-black boulders rising up in a sort of miniature valley among hills, as if left there by children of the giants in some forgotten game when the world was young.

I've read, and heard, of the Devil's Marbles as being a freak of Nature. But this seemingly weird habit of granitic rock cannot be a freak, it must have been caused by some law of Nature operating under special local environmental conditions. For the same phenomenon occurs just here and there far apart upon the continent, for instance, the Black Mountain, outside Cooktown. The Devil's Marbles are a line of bare boulders about two miles long; in places one is balanced upon another. The black mountain is a hill of granite boulders piled one upon another, not a shovelful of earth between them. Similar strange granitic curiosities occur elsewhere throughout the continent. What upset the Mother Rock that in vanished ages, just now and then, her wayward "offspring" behaved like this?

Anyway, soon after we had rumbled down through the Devil's Marbles there appeared, merging with its harsh surroundings, a sombre, solid stone building obviously built for defence as well as utility. This frontier outpost was the Barrow Creek repeater Overland Telegraph station, with its stone deeply marked 1872, set firmly there down among its rough hills. A high stone fence was built protectively partly round it, and behind it, overshadowing the compact little building, rose the bare, rocky hill from which on one breathless morning the blacks spied down upon the station, to await their time, then creep down and launch their surprise attack. A sudden, screaming, murderous mel6e *that* was. Fronting the station were several well-kept graves of the telegraph men killed. A big sandy creek lined with gums, a big mob of goats, too, and, great surprise, an odd sheep among the goats, all in good nick. Handy indeed, that mob of goats, three hundred miles or so from a butcher's shop and milk-run. Nothing else in this place except the great sky and flat-topped hills all round. Ah! Yes, there is, but surely not—yes, a fact! A few hundred yards ahead an amazing sight, a brand-new pub and store!

Joe Kilgariff's, of course. Built of those handily made cement bricks. And there is the "puff-puff" of his little electric-light plant. And, of course, he's installed a "young" radio plant, too—modernity in the wilderness with a vengeance. This good-humoured, bustling little Joe is a true enthusiast for this modern trend. And Mr Clarke and his smiling wife manage this mushroom business, while becoming used now to the amazed surprise of travellers to the Tennant's. A chap who'd been a telegraph linesman drawled, "Barely seven years ago we only saw the pack-mail every two or three months, the new motor mail every six weeks. Now it comes once a month. Five years ago there was no such thing as traffic, then the country began to open up a bit. Then came Tennant's—and now we've got this!" and he nodded towards the little pub.

I wondered when and where this lively little man, Joe Kilgariff, would stop. To make this new business pay, he'd have passing traffic to the new goldfield, of course, but no one knew how long that field would last. Could he really smell out mineral in these harsh, waterless, lonesome hills round here, too?

Looking round, I believed then (and believe yet) that it might come. For as a prospector I thought the "make-up" of this country seemed very favourable for tin, wolfram, scheelite, and even gold. Probably other metals also

However...

Here was stationed Muldoon of the Mounteds, well liked throughout all the Territory, but growing telltale furrows across his brow. For from here he had to manage that distant and turbulent Tennant's Creek as Mining Warden—promotion, of course, but carrying in this isolation such fast accumulating responsibilities and difficulties.

Mrs Muldoon was one of the pioneering women, and like all of them could laugh at her memories.

"Our honeymoon?" she laughed. "Well, we camped that night on the Finke. No water."

That "no water"—I could visualize it so easily. A young city girl, whom her husband must take fifteen hundred miles north to Newcastle Waters, his police station. At the most she might meet half a dozen white women on the way—if lucky indeed. Wild blacks, a few pioneer cattle-stations far apart, fifteen hundred miles of loneliness. The big old Finke, a dry river except when rarely in raging flood for three or four days, after which it would be merely a water-hole here and there, that so precious water long miles apart. But now—honeymoon trip—dry!

And when the Finke is dry it *is* dry.

Travelling through that heat, tired and itchy from fine powdery dust, she longed for a bath, gazed wearily round at this great parched bed of gravel and sand which was the "river". A thousand miles of dogged travelling had now taught her tired bones there was no chance of a bath here.

"I want a wash."

"If you have a wash," warned Muldoon, "you can't have a cup of tea!"

"Well, then, can I have a drink of water?"

From that precious water-bag most carefully he poured her out a small pannikin full. Lingeringly she drank nearly half, then sneaked behind a handy bush and surreptitiously washed herself with the remainder.

"I made every drop count," she said. "I had to. And," she added triumphantly, "when the billy boiled I had my cup of tea, too!"

It is only when we need water badly that we realize it is worth far, far more than its weight in gold.

"There was I," she said, "all dusty and tired and thirsty under the stars on the Finke on a Saturday night, and if I'd been in Adelaide you know where I would have been—at the Palais!"

It would be a long time before she would see the Palais again. She could laugh at it now, they all do, though maybe there is a sigh in the laugh. Our pioneer women of the Far Out, from the earliest days, have been wonderful.

Son and heir, young Eric Muldoon, about knee high to a pack-saddle, came strolling in.

"What have the natives done with the wallaby they speared, Eric?" inquired his mother.

"I don't know," replied Eric, "it wasn't there when I saw them last," and he settled down to the important job of a cup of tea.

Travelling in the Territory, 1933.

XXXI

THE ALICE BRIDES OF YESTERYEAR

All aboard again and south for Burt's Plain. And glad were the thirsty, dusty travellers of those few short years ago to see arising from the plain the bold outline of the MacDonnell Ranges.

The Alice of 1933-4 was just beginning to sit up and take notice of itself. Only seven years previously it was nothing but a score of lonesome shacks built on a dry creek hidden among lonely gorges within the heart of the continent. And now — — —!

A dry creek in which big gums grew thickly, giving perfect evidence of the cool, fresh water below. The wee township, completely ringed by brown, rocky hills, grey-foliaged trees stubbornly growing out from the hillsides here and there. Seen from those harsh hills, the neatly laid-out little township looked quite pretty, its white roofs sharply contrasting with the sombre hills. The new houses were nearly all little modern bungalows of cement bricks, dull green or grey. We made for Kilgariff's Stuart Arms Hotel, and on the way I admired the Alice Springs Hotel, a nice little modern place, right out here in the Centre, where so very few years ago were only those shacks, a telegraph station, a little pub, and an inland mounted-police station. Then my eye was drawn to the two stores, Wallace Fogarty's and Kilgariff's, near a pretty little railway station. The end of the line, of course. What a great day it had been for the Alice when at long last the little railway from "way down south" came creeping right up to its heart!

Everything was very quiet, and only a few people were to be seen about. But I noticed that the large open flat was just about filled with little houses. If the township were to spread much further it would have to creep out among the hills themselves. And who would ever have thought that the Alice would spread to that!

So, with Carrington as Government Resident, J. C. Lovegrove as Sergeant and Mining Warden for the Arltunga and Winnecke goldfield seventy miles east, for the Harts Range mica fields and for a huge area of country north, and with Frank McCann as resident doctor, the Alice had grown really impressive, believe me.

Even so, none of us then dreamt of the Alice of today. May she grow even more in the future!

We pulled up at the Stuart Arms Hotel and entered into the cool quietness thereof, though we did disturb a blackfellow's dog. And to think when I open the paper in Sydney this morning the first news I see is, "Fire at Alice Springs—Modern Addition to Stuart Arms Hotel, costing £100,000, burnt out". Ye gods, what a fortune a hundred thousand seemed in the early 1930s!

About seven years earlier Mrs Kilgariff had come battling up from Oodnadatta to start the new life with the ever vigorous Joe, so badly bitten with that bug to constantly "push on, push on"!

Leaving the southern city, a young wife with young children, she was anxiously dubious as to what life was to be like in those great sunlit distances stretching ever ahead, seemingly without end. The mail-driver was a big, rough man they called "Sam", the passengers were the usual tough-looking characters, smoking those smelly pipes and now and then making some drawling remark to one another, with a well-timed spit over the side, as if casually watching to see the little puff of dust it hit up. Just the men, and the crows and the sky, and the hum of the truck, and herself and the children, and a "couldn't-care-less" black-gin squatting in the back. And the days travelled by. Late one dusty day they were crossing the usual dry creek on the Tragic Mile, and her aching bones were longing for sundown, for then at last they would camp. As they churned down into the sand Sam, the driver, yelled *"Quatcha!"* ("Water!") and the black-gin leapt down from the truck to squat there and start scratching a soak-hole in the dry creek sands. The heavy car slowed down in the sand and the men leapt out and began to push, obviously expecting the woman passenger to leap out, too—of course the brutes never dreamt of pulling up. She did leap out, but so leisurely she landed on her dignity and nearly landed on her nose as the children yelled delightedly and followed her.

Sam, all hot and bothered at the wheel, struggling to force the car across this last creek of the day, yelled over his shoulder "Push, you bastards! Push!" Mrs Kilgariff just stood there and gave him, or rather his broad neck, her best stony stare, and stonily looked on at the bowed backs of the old hands pushing for all they were worth. Otherwise they would have had to dig the darned thing out of the sandy creek, for the motor car of those years was not the powerful machine of today. She just stood there glaring at the back of the great hulking brute who had dared to shout at her like that. Meanwhile, as slowly the men pushed the panting car farther and farther along through the sand, the black-gin, that couldn't-care-less child of Nature, kept scratching her head with one hand, scratching out gravel with the other, until a little brown water began to trickle between her dirty fingers into the soak-hole. She sat back with a grunt on her rump, lugged the stub of a burnt-out pipe from her clay-daubed hair, lit up, and gazed dreamily across the sandy creek at nothing in particular. Muddy water welled up and slowly seeped into the soak-hole, to the astonishment of the children, who with cries of wonder and delight pulled off their shoes and paddled in this magic waterhole. The sweating toilers, determinedly ploughing on well ahead, now finally manhandled the car across the creek-bed to the opposite bank, had a much needed blow as they lit up, then came straggling back across the creek, carrying a water-bag and billycans. As their voices in drawling conversation came plainly towards Mrs Kilgariff she frowned.

"Brutes!" she muttered.

Then, noticing the waterbag and suddenly realizing its significance, she clutched the children, hoarsely ordering them and their socks and tell-tale shoes back from the soak-hole, to the black-gin's puzzlement. The young woman dared not utter a word as cheerfully one of the "brutes" sat back on his heels and with tin pannikin began filling the water-bag and billycans from the dirty brown soak. She knew that the water-bag now contained their drinking water for the hot travelling tomorrow, and the billycans held the water for their tea tonight, but she dared not say a word. As they began trudging back to the car the campfire sprang alight beside it.

It was after the rough evening meal, when they'd spread their blankets round the campfire, that big Sam strolled out into the night bush for something or other. One of the boys—privately she thought he looked a cross between a baboon and a bushranger—looked across at her with a half-grin and asked, 'What did Sam call out to you, lady?"

"He cast aspersions on my parentage," replied young Mrs Kilgariff haughtily.

The inquirer looked puzzled, glanced at the others, spat out on the sand, but inquired no more.

You see, "aspersions" was a new one in the Centre then, and the boys wondered where in the blazes Sam had got the "asparagus". Privately they thought the woman passenger a bit queer, anyway. They let it go at that, there were plenty of queer things in that country. They were sure she was queer, though, a few months later, when a camel-team came plodding into the Alice loaded with all sorts of things, the most amazing of which was a bath!

For quite a long time after the young wife got settled in at the Alice with Joe and their soon expanding business she cherished the incident of the water. She used to see those men quite frequently, that big brute of a mail-driver every time he returned from his twelve-hundred-mile trip with the mails, and she did not forget what he had called out to her—well, it *sounded* like that to her, anyway. Gradually, though, she began to know the men better, and was surprised to feel that she was actually beginning to like them. Then one day, patiently awaiting a time when those who had been on the trip were all mustered together, she let the secret out. With a smile which betrayed no little degree of fiendish pleasure, she told them the children had washed their feet in the soak from which they'd filled the water-bags and billycan the evening they'd crossed "that big creek".

In answer Big Sam glared at her, looking just about fed up with human nature.

"It's what a man gets for bringing you ———s into the country!" he growled disgustedly.

It never occurred to her, of course, that the men knew perfectly well the only time the black-gin ever washed her hands was when she had to scratch out a soak. She just couldn't help it then.

Mrs Kilgariff was great company in telling yarns of those rough years, as indeed all the women are who did the pioneering with their men throughout the Centre and the Territory. The difficulty is they're so quiet about it, so used to hearing their men do the talking. It took me years of wandering throughout the continent to wake up to this.

It was only four years before our visit to the Alice that Mrs Kilgariff drove to the "gathering of the clans" one hundred and seventy miles north along the Overland Telegraph Line, at the Barrow Creek races. Plenty of sunshine, plenty of good spirits (on two legs, not only in the bottle), plenty of excited aborigines, horses, camels, and dogs, plenty to drink—all alcoholic! They, those he-goats called men, never dreamt that anyone could feel like, could despair for, a cup of tea! Of course, there were twenty case-hardened men to one woman, but even so the women did have mouths! Certainly the men had! They were so busy filling them you could hear them.

Did they ask her? No!

In thirsty desperation she walked up to one of the committee men, the one with a nose like a camel and the huge bare feet.

"Can I have some water for a wash and a cup of tea?" she asked with all due deference.

He stared, hardly sure whether he'd heard aright. She felt like boxing his ears.

"Got anything to put it in?" he grunted at last.

She fossicked around, but all she could find was an empty meat-tin. She knocked the ants out of it, then brought it to the committee man, expecting that he would find her at least a billycan. Instead, from a dusty water-bag he carefully poured about a spoonful of water into the greasy tin. She put it down and stood there, staring into it. Gradually it dawned within his big thick skull that something was amiss.

"Anything the matter?" he growled between drinks.

"I was just wishing I was a canary so that I could hop in!" she replied.

Mrs Kilgariff began to learn in earnest what the Centre was like when Joe started the pub at the Alice. The pub was an event, believe me, but of course it was not like the nice little modern hotels of today. At that time, when a man died anywhere out in the spinifex the boys invariably brought the corpse to the pub and started a beano before they "planted" him, as the uncouth brutes expressed it. Very soon Mrs Kilgariff realized she had to learn how to make a coffin—the boys called it "the box"—having visions of corpses being left on her hands too long. For Joe, constantly going "all out" from daylight to near daylight, had no time to make "boxes". Besides, he'd seen them simply rolled in their blanket when the time came for their last sleep and they never said a thing against it. So Mrs Kilgariff set to work and earned a reputation of making "bonzer boxes". She insisted upon using up hubby's worn-out pyjamas to make things nice, and she used to line the "box" with unbleached calico. She would work alone out there in the shed, with the hum of insects and the screech of birds in the big gums just outside along the Todd, with the sunlight and the dreamy day and a sigh for the passing of the lone sleeper.

Nobody ever seemed to worry much about tombstones or frills like that, just left them there, a freshly filled-in little mound on the hot, red earth.

At that time the aborigines used to hold their corroborees right up in the township, the wild ones coming along with their spears and woomeras, their naked bodies rubbed in stale goanna grease and ashes, their piccaninnies and dogs shrieking and barking in their train. Noisy nights with the 'Thump! Thump! Thump!" of warriors' big splay feet in the dance, the chant of wild songs, quite often, too, violent quarrelling, howls of men, shrieks of women down by the fires among the big creek trees. For a young woman from the civilized south this life took some getting used to. Much worse, though, was an incident in the big drought. The white population had lived on short supply of tinned meats for eight months when Bloomfield from Love's Creek station, with Ted Hayes, brought in a side of fresh beef. That handful of half-starved women in the Alice just gloated over that beautiful fresh beef, almost afraid to cook and eat it. They hung their share of the meat overnight outside in drip coolers. These were the refrigerators of those days, consisting of wire framework with wet bagging over it hung out on a tree branch in the night. The breeze, if any, with evaporation kept the meat cool, anyway kept it from actually walking away. But next morning, when Mrs Kilgariff came out with a voracious after-drought appetite, that precious beef was gone. Only the "visiting card" was there—the bag and the meat-safe torn to shreds where the blacks had thrown it down on the ground for their dogs to chew.

XXXII

THE STONE AGE STEPS INTO THE MODERN

Maybe you're a bit interested in the old aboriginal, last of the Stone Age men,[5] for I've got to dawdle for a while in the Alice, a pleasant while. And at a time which marked a very definite phase in the life of the aboriginal tribes, as in that of Terry, our problem child of the moment.

At this period, right throughout the north, many of the aboriginal tribes were going through a rapid and painfully puzzling period of transformation, owing to increasing contact with the whites and with the white man's ways. The motor-car and aeroplane played a big part in this—strange that the internal combustion engine should affect the destiny of Stone Age Man. But it has done so—and that of native peoples all over the world.

However, our particular hero just now in the Alice, hero or bad man, whichever way you prefer to look at it, was already, like plenty of others in their early teens, a very "modern" man, and would fight savagely if called otherwise. And he was determined to be yet more modern and to go one better, to be independent of the laws of white or black or any other colour— unfortunately, in the "Wild West" way—or in this case the 'Wild North" way—which, I suppose was the only way he understood.

Unfortunately so, because had his balance been tilted just a little the other way he could have done a great deal for his tribesmen. For he was undoubtedly clever, with plenty of initiative, and a quick thinker and mover. Handy with wits and hands, he was apparently tireless, but ruthless and determined.

He chose the hard way of proving himself. And it was fortunate that, when excited, he proved to be a poor rifle shot, otherwise he could have caused a great deal of damage, as did Pigeon and Captain in the West Kimberley, and Major and Banjo in the East. And others.

Terry was born among the precipitous ranges of the Arltunga goldfield, some seventy miles east along the MacDonnell Ranges from Alice Springs. A very different Alice then, in Terry's boyhood days, just a convenient camp for teams, mostly camel-teams bringing out stores to the lonely stations forming in the back country, and the very occasional small mobs of cattle plodding doggedly on that long, harsh track southward towards Adelaide, their last long trek. From the Alice, along a rough wagon track indeed, stores were

---

[5] True, he has some cousins in New Guinea. But most tribes there are somewhat more advanced in culture.

dragged eastward through Undoolya station to Love's Creek station, thence on to Claravale gold camp in the heart of the Arltunga Range. A dray track, rough as the hobs of hell, and a packhorse and camel track ran northward from Claravale Mining Camp through rugged ranges, creeping up along primitive gorges, along the winding beds of creeks that lead towards the Harts Range and out to the Jervois, where even in those years, in that isolation, a few men were mining for mica among the coarse granitic outcrops, the masses of dikes of felspars and quartz. All else is a wild tangle of rocky, mineralized ranges, gorges which are raging torrents in the wet, a chain of waterholes in the dry. "Nowhere else to go", to north or south, while eastward the end of the Arltunga Range drops straight down into a desert area which was, I suppose still is, No Man's Land. Men have perished of thirst, or never been heard of again, when trying to cross that desert strip into Queensland.

In such wild country then—and the few folk battling there were a hit on the wild side, too—young Terry was born. Terry was his "white-feller" name, which he earned very quickly and clung to, for from a toddler he developed an intense curiosity as to "white-feller" ways. And it was not long before he was "ratting" the lonely camps. He grew so expert he became too bold to take the broad hint of a bullet whistling about his ears when traps were set for the black phantom of the night. Several frighteningly narrow escapes, though, taught him a wary cunning that developed his agile mind, and saved him from falling into further traps.

To lose tucker by thieving in those lonely camps was a serious matter for the handful of isolated, scattered miners. They reacted angrily but ineffectively in efforts to catch this baffling culprit.

Not that this lively young blackboy was unpopular, far from it, with his quite good-looking young face, ever ready to smile, perfect teeth flashing in that friendly grin, big black eyes so bright and innocent and ever roaming, though you had to be a smart man indeed to notice this latter characteristic and interpret it. He was always willing to do an odd job or two about the camp or mine; in fact, he seemed to like such jobs. Trouble was, like most natives, he wouldn't stay on the job for long.

He didn't need to. All he wanted to learn he would see "quick-feller"— where the tucker and other desirable things were hidden.

But the miners never connected him with that "bloody Black Phantom!" Not until well after he'd completed his education at that great big "white-feller" camp, Alice Springs.

Like all his clan, while on walkabout young Terry would be here today, gone tomorrow. Up over the ranges and away, particularly to that mica camp. It would take a white man a couple of days to negotiate those creeks and gorges between the gold and mica camps. Terry would go as the crow would fly and be there in half a day. And no one would know, either, until he showed himself.

He used to love to watch, hidden among those rocky tors, some sweating miner using hammer and drill and gelignite. The clang of hammer on drill seemed to fascinate him. But the thunder of the explosion echoing among the gorges used to send him into the seventh heaven of delight. Later on, when the Italians came to work the mica, he got away with coils of fuse, some hundreds of caps, and it was believed, a full hundredweight of gelignite.

What on earth his dusky mind planned to do with all that sudden death goodness only knows. I asked one of his tribesman. This abo rolled his eyes heavenward, then threw up his arms, grunting like an angry camel. "Whouff!—Him blow bloody place sky-high!" he growled.

But whether this tame abo meant the jail, or the Alice, or the mines away out in the Arltunga he would not condescend to, or could not explain, but strolled away, looking as if he were afraid he'd said too much as it was.

Before he was sixteen, a fine strapping lad now, Terry had hied himself to the Alice, where he had a whale of a time. There were so many opportunities in this marvel of a place he did not know where to start. Really, the white man's world was very wonderful indeed.

They had built a little train-line from Oodnadatta to the Alice by then. Train day was a miracle day. There were these wondrous carts that ran without horses, though they often stopped and the white men used to curse and swear and toil, and had a hell of a job to get them going again. Terry would give a hand if asked to crank or push, he was so eager to learn. Once he'd learnt, though, they couldn't even shanghai him to put his shoulder to the wheel. Yes, it was wonderful at the white man's camp; occasionally he would even see one of those gleaming white-man birds flying through the sky.

Terry learnt very quickly.

He broke into a store, robbed it of seventy pounds' worth of goods.

To his astonishment, with surprising swiftness Terry found himself in jail. There, with a sulky respect, he began to study the "white pleece". He had never dreamed they were so efficient. He sorely missed his liberty; in fact, he found it a bit difficult to realize just what had happened to him. There was something he must learn here—quick feller!

They were very easy on them in jail, though, it was actually a home away from home. Terry did not know how well off he was.

'Flu broke out. The Resident Medical Officer ordered all abos into the Compound. And then Terry thought he really *was* in jail. Of course, it was only a precautionary measure to try to stop the 'flu spreading.

Around that Compound were big iron walls that would keep a white man in. But Terry, like a wallaby hop-climbing those precipitous gorge walls of his Arltunga hills, was used to cliff-climbing, as a sport when it was not a necessity, from boyhood.

At night Terry scaled that wall like a grinning monkey, silent as a shadow sliding down the opposite side. And then the Black Phantom was in the jailer's quarters, and then he was bending over the sleeping jailer, his slippery hand was in under the pillow, and within seconds those sinewy black fingers had closed on the jailer's keys.

How easy it was! He told afterwards how he grinned down at the sleeping official as he stood up with his fingers sliding round the keys so that they wouldn't clink. And he thought, "How easy it would be to kill him without making a sound!"

He did not act upon the thought, fortunately. Terry was a clever aboriginal, remarkably quick of learning when you remember he was barely sixteen and but a month or two before had been running wild in the bush.

The Black Phantom really earned his name. Noiseless as a shadow, he now not only slipped out of the jailer's quarters but was next back at the Compound walls. He could, of course, have vanished into the darkness of night, but no, he could "hardly stop from laughing" as he unlocked the main gate. Then he was inside, whispering. Half a dozen or so prisoners were game enough to follow him out. And then the Phantom was leading them through the sleeping township. It was a devil-may-care whim of Terry's that he led them past the police sergeant's residence. And as he did so, with another grin, he threw the big jail padlock over the sergeant's fence. "Better him lock him own self up!" he said, grinning back at his scared companions.

However, Terry had not been quite so smart as he thought he was. He had left that big Compound gate wide open, for all to escape who wished to, of course. But not long after the prisoners had gone a black-tracker came yawning back to quarters after saying good night to his girl-friend under the big old trees by the waterhole. The tracker passed by the Compound gate and casually noticed it was wide open. In an instant he was wide awake and running to raise the alarm.

The hurrying tracks from the gate were quite plain, the police followed them with torch and car. They caught up with them just at the Gap, but of course the escaped prisoners ran for the plentiful cover and got away, all except one man. He was so scared he doubled back in the dark, ran all the way back, managed to climb up and over into the Compound and, hurrying across to his blanket, rolled into it and curled up, sound asleep—of course.

Next day the police and trackers ran all to earth except Terry and his mate. These two were watching events from the hill-tops. The crags of his native Arltunga Range had already proved good friends to Terry. And now, to his unbounded delight, he was learning very rapidly that hill-tops could prove good friends to him here against the white man, against the dreaded "white pleece", and those soon hated trackers.

In this rugged country, where the bed gorges had so often to be used as roads, the rocky, often almost inaccessible hill-tops were both hide-outs and look-outs from which hunted men could spy down upon their enemies' movements and thus easily outwit them. What he learnt in these few days of liberty Terry was to turn to advantage on later occasions.

From hill-top to hill-top they watched until it seemed certain the police patrol were hurrying along the gorge to close the gap eighteen miles ahead, sure that the escaped men must be making for it. With derisive laughs Terry and his mate slithered away down into the gorge behind the police, rapidly crossed over, then doubled sharply back across to the Alice railway-line. Terry's cheery personality now got him and his cheeky mate hand-trolly lifts down south along the line from two working gangs, and got them tucker also.

Meanwhile the patrol, sensing they were outmanoeuvred, made all haste back along the gorge. The sharp-eyed trackers cut the tracks. It was a case for horses then. They rode two hundred and twenty-four miles in three days and overtook the confident Terry and his mate. Yet again he had been too smart, and he thought himself so civilized. Angrily he swore he would not be so cocksure next time.

It was wonderful how quickly he learnt. He did not realize, of course, that he had stepped out of the Stone Age, confidently expecting to learn all the tricks of the white man within a few months. He could not understand how many tricks there were to learn.

So Terry, to his sulky surprise, found himself back in the Compound. Found also, that he was watched more closely now. Things did not seem as easy as they had been before. But he continued to learn. He had already worked out a way of beating the speed and, more important, the endurance of that thing called a motor-car, a frightening thing when it was in pursuit of a man.

Keep to the very tops, travel on the tops of the roughest hills. Let that grunting thing gallop past away below, thus you don't exhaust yourself.

He was still grudgingly afraid of the "white pleece", though not so much physically, man to man, as of what a constantly moving patrol could do. And herein lay this great big fear—the black trackers! He did not realize it was the white man's mind that directed the trackers.

How he hated these men of his own people!

He had already reasoned out that there was only one thing that could heat them—fear of the rifle. He had never forgotten when, on some incautious occasion, he had found himself running for life with a bullet hissing past his ear. He still shivered at the memory of that frightening whine as a leaden slug hissed hotly past his swift retreat and, striking a rock ahead, ricocheted away with a blood-curdling screech.

Eagerly he sought to learn all about a rifle.

Our hardy young buck Terry, growing into an upstanding "heady" young man, a truculent good-looker, too, was now fast becoming dangerous.

The Arunta tribal camp near the Government well, just outside Alice Springs, 1924.

XXXIII

THE BLACK PHANTOM

Terry, freed from being an enforced guest of the powers that be, was more than once ordered back to the bush by the sergeant and told to stay there. In no uncertain terms he was assured of his reception should he return to the Alice seeking trouble again.

For he was now in that part-civilized stage of the bush aboriginal that in every State has often given the police and others a lot of trouble—a "cheeky-feller" boy who believed himself so civilized and clever that he could get away with anything. A pity, for it is an egotistical state which has prevented many an abo from turning out to be a good and useful man in his new environment. This stage of "development", or "degradation", depending on which way you look at it, was becoming general among aborigines throughout the entire North at this time—though when all's said and done it seems almost the same state of mind that has put untold numbers of white men into jails throughout the world.

On one occasion when Terry was kicked out of the Alice for his own and his tribal good there occurred a little tragicomedy, the counter-part of which has occasionally occurred in white homes also. For his father and uncle indignantly accused him of being the black sheep of the family, of bringing disgrace upon them all, of breaking his mother's, Long Topsy's, heart—as well as those of a string of aunties and nieces and nephews. And now they ordered this "bad feller" Terry back to the sergeant to be taken care of until such time as he should see the light—which was not bad, such sentiments coming from the wilds of the Arltunga hills.

However, Terry's eyes blazed at the threatening commands, he drew back with a snarl and yelled at his father and uncle just what he thought of them and what they could do about it In a moment the little camp was in an uproar. Father and uncle rushed him, but in the furious row that followed they were only just able to knock him, nearly panting their guts out, and they knew they would never be able to do it again. After a ding-dong scrap they overpowered him and marched him all those long, hard miles back to the Alice. He arrived sullen, in the devil's own temper, his swollen face covered in dried blood and clotted dust, a most unwelcome visitor to the Alice.

This little correction, the attempt to lead him on the straight and narrow path by his tribespeople again taught him a lot. From now on, he would not trust his own people.

From now on, when he found it wise for his health to slip swiftly and silently back to the bush, his people would be afraid of him. To turn and suddenly see him standing there, black eyes gleaming, mouth drawn back partly in a smile, but more in a snarl, body taut as if ready to pounce, sent a swift chill of fear through them. Lamely they would offer him food. Lithely he would step forward. Grinning, he would take what they had to offer—and more. Never again would any among them dare to lay hands upon him.

Swiftly Terry grew to be a young man, a powerful young brute all smiles and laughter and cunning and sudden, raging tempers. And still with an eager capacity for learning and absorbing things. But he could *not*, or rather would not, keep away from the Alice. In between long walkabouts back to the Arltunga and Harts ranges, to Winnecke's Depot and the Strangways, he would again and again, eagerly though now cautiously, return to the Alice.

That lonely little place was slowly, yet surely growing. That railway from Oodnadatta, of course, brought such wonderful things. Stores, and the Italian mica miners, and all sorts of fascinating "pickings" for a smart and ambitious lad like Terry.

The arrival of the unfortunate Italians, or at least several batches of them, was sheer delight to this playful Terry, this now dangerous Black Phantom of the night. The men from the Mediterranean, bewildered by this country during the long, take-it-easy train ride of nights and days, ever creeping on into the unknown, creeping deeper and deeper into the heart of a continent, nothing ahead, nothing to sunrise or sunset, no such thing as towns, just a telegraph line on skinny poles with a tiny train puffing on, on, on into hazy land, land, land.

It was quite comical, to us, after they'd been a year or two in the country, to listen to them describing their awed feelings on that first journey. Quite understandable, though, when we remember that in their own land they were used to cities, towns, villages, every few miles, let alone such commonplace things as roads and water-taps. They travelled on, voluble at times, at other times silent, for none of them had ever before gazed out of a train window to see the sundried carcass of a beast lying out there amongst the saltbush, the whitened skeleton of another beast under that thin old mulga-tree upon whose scraggly branches perched black crows, nor had they seen a long black snake wriggling away from the line to vanish into the spinifex.

When at last they arrived at the Alice and climbed from the train, gazing for the longed-for city they had expected to see————!

Still worse when eventually they were carted away out through those wild ranges and landed in the rugged wilderness of the Harts Range, even though that country is frighteningly beautiful in its own grim way. Imagine the feelings of the new-comers, dumped down in this wild immensity. Rough camps, rough work—but they took to this part very well—in the centre of a rocky fastness, where their only visitors were an odd cattleman and a prospector or two, and beetle-browed blackmen who gazed at them with no appearance of deference whatsoever.

Oh well, those mica miners did good work, and certainly earned their money. Mica had then suddenly come into prominence on the mineral market and Australia definitely wanted mica miners right there. An electrically-minded world was fairly shouting for this gifted mineral.

This meant nothing whatever to our Terry. These innocents abroad were manna from heaven to our uncultured Stone Age boy, whether in the Alice or away out in those lonesome ranges he went through them, or rather their suitcases, like a packet of salts.

Suitcases! For some quaint reason Terry went through every case he could lay hand on with far greater curiosity and delight than he would have gone through a swag.

But what must have been the feelings of those particular Italians who were his particular victims? To be thus "gone through" out in these prehistoric ranges in a manner only too familiar to them in their long-vanished cities? This one thing, anyway, which should have been so easy to understand they found bewilderingly difficult. If, at the time, they had known it was a grinning Stone Age man who had "milked them dry", it would have been adding insult to injury with a vengeance.

This was when he acquired the gelignite. Fortunately he did not use it immediately. Perhaps he was saving it up for some big scheme, perhaps he was cautious of using it without practice. Often he had quietly watched miners using it and had seen how dangerous it could be in ignorant or unwary hands. And he certainly did not wish to blow his own self up—he thought far too much of Terry.

Nor, very fortunately, was he a good rifle shot yet. He could handle a rifle and get by, for now and again he had managed to coax a miner to lend him a rifle to go shooting for meat. And, to his extreme delight, after a time he had succeeded in bringing down a euro or two. And at this time —just about two years before we came bowling along on this trip—he imagined he was a good shot. And all that he now most urgently desired was a rifle, and ammunition—the more the merrier.

He was to learn that shooting at a kangaroo or emu just nice and steady, with nothing on your mind, was tragically different to shooting at armed men who were swiftly shooting back while he was worried in a hot pursuit with enemies fast closing in all around. Under such circumstances it takes not only a good shot but a steady wrist and a cool "hell-or-nothing" command over the nerves to shoot back with a deadly accuracy while timing a split second in which to duck under cover or get right away. Which is why, in the world's history, there have actually been very few really successful gunmen. It is easy enough to "tote" a gun, but when it comes to using it you are far more likely to be forced to drop your gun or be shot yourself. But this is one of those little things in life that Terry, like many another man, would have to learn for himself.

Yes, there were pickings to be had by an agile lad around the Alice, and away out in the Arltungas, let alone by a certain unknown who had earned the nickname of the Black Phantom. For, though Terry was known to the police, they had not yet found out that he was the Phantom. A few of his own people guessed, but by now they dared not even whisper it round their own campfires. Yes, there were certainly pickings for a bright, smart young fellow game enough to seize the opportunity. And there came a case in point, a case that could easily have been the death, and a terrible death, of this cunning, arrogant young fellow from the wilds, had not his learning of civilization by now taught him to be always wary. Easily enough he "ratted" a case at the railway yards, took it from a truck, opened it, and wondered at the unfamiliar-looking bottles. With some difficulty he opened one and cautiously sniffed it, and it nearly blew the top of his head off. It most certainly did not smell like rum. He poured some out and was startled at the way the fiery acid ate into everything it touched. Alarmed at what could have happened to him had he gulped the contents down his throat and tender precious stomach, he broke every bottle in a growing fury at the mess that terrible acid made of things, what it would have made of him! He threw fragments of the heavy bottles far and wide, behaving like a maniac because splashes burnt his hands. Never before had he imagined that a liquid could burn—burn like hell! Like many a better man before him, he let his rage blind his caution. When the railway staff came to work next morning it looked as if a lunatic had been at work.

Next night, in a spirit of malice, he ratted the railway again. A police car suddenly flashed its light on the trucks, and in a split second he was lying motionless in the grass. Presently they drove away. Then he was back at the line and got away with two bags of flour. A hefty job. But he was a powerful brute now, and lithe as a panther with it, and knew just what he was doing. And under cover of night "Black Phantom" was a perfect name for him, particularly so when he was on a ticklish job, for he delighted then in working in his natural black nakedness. In black night he was simply invisible. Always, too, as is the aboriginal custom, his body was well greased with goanna fat or natural native oils. At night he could thus make himself invisible to a man standing only a few feet away, he could lie motionless at a man's very feet and not be seen, while if half a dozen men had grabbed him they could not have held him, not against his lightning-like swiftness, his agile strength fighting off the clawing hands that would have slipped everywhere from off his heavily oiled body and powerful limbs.

Yes, it was all so easy, but—he had not learnt to control his temper. That caused him to lose caution, and a time came when he did a bad job.

Next morning the police, who certainly had not been sleeping, and had been expecting something to happen, being warned by now somewhat slipshod, familiar signs, were there. And they sooled the black trackers onto his tracks. For in losing his temper he had left his tracks! Contemptuous Terry, fool Terry.

He had not even bothered to travel on into safety. They tracked him to a rocky hill just behind the township, and recovered one bag of flour. He had now become alert in time to escape sudden arrest and was watching them from another hill, where all by himself, with only the rocks and trees to listen, he was raging at *them*, all because of his own carelessness.

Some little time later an old Afghan teamster who had camped a few miles from the township came to the police station and complained bitterly that someone was stealing from his tiny mob of sheep. A very serious thing to an Afghan, for, because of religious requirements in the killing, he cannot get his meat as easily as we.

The police rode out and cut tracks. Yes, the grinning trackers told the mounted man, these were the same tracks as those of the man who had stolen from this last batch of store flour. Yes, maybe these could he tracks of the man who was wanted for such a lot of things. Happily they followed the tracks, it would be such fun to lay this elusive fellow by the heels.

Terry had been quite contemptuous of the Afghan, and was still in the sullen rage that had made him so careless. Easily and swiftly they tracked him right to the Afghan's yard, and there he was; he had just seized a sheep and was throttling it while bashing its head with a stone.

XXXIV

THE PURSUIT

And thus Terry saw the inside of jail again. And, as usual, while seeking an opportunity to escape he settled down to learn things. The first thing he had to learn was that there was lots more he had to learn. And lots more after that.

One thing he brooded over, glumly at first, then with a savage anger—his tracks!

They would always know them now, these trackers at the Alice, they would always know Terry's tracks. No matter where or when or how many years later, if any one of those trackers should come upon Terry's tracks he would simply point and grunt, "Terry's!"

Bitterly he resented that clumsy night's work, and the rage that had made him careless of leaving his tracks right to the Afghan's yard. They had followed the tracks, had caught him red-handed, thus proving the tracks were his. And now for ever he would be known by his tracks. So many a white wrongdoer has bitterly regretted leaving his finger-prints.

By now Terry had grown into a strapping man of twenty-five, an arrogant cuss with a cunning shrewdness to which was now added a burning ambition—to prove, as he assured his jail and town mates, and had boasted to "friends outside" right to the Arltunga hills, that he was as good as any man, white, brown, black, yellow, or brindle. And he found yet again that he was not quite as good as he thought when, right in the main street of the then tiny township, he rushed the jail warder and, seizing his rifle, sought violently to wrench it away. As it happened, the sergeant and a constable saw the incident from the station and, running to the aid of the struggling warder, overpowered the so nearly triumphant Terry. They threw him to the ground just in time, the cuffs clicked upon his wrists even before he could burst out into maniacal rage. To say he was surprised at the swift efficiency of that arrest would be to put it mildly.

Watched before as a bad boy, he was now marked as a dangerous man.

How this had happened, and a closely similar incident was presently to happen, was that the prisoners were not kept all the time in durance vile. For their own good and exercise they were marched round the township here and there wherever there was a job to be done, little outings which were greatly looked forward to.

However, there came the nineteenth of September, a bright morning (as it should be, heralding the day before my birthday). Warder Shannon had marched a few prisoners out to near the Springs to chop timber for firewood. The birds were singing, the Supreme Artist was painting the rocky gorges in those pulsing reds and yellows, blues and orange of the colourful Centre. It was going to be a beautiful day to be alive, if a bit on the warm side. The grizzled old warder contemplatively wiped his brow with a hairy forearm. Warder Shannon had now been thirty years toiling in the Centre and was looking forward to another thirty. Automatically wary, though suspicious of nothing whatsoever, Shannon stationed each man a little distance apart—they cannot rush you "in a mob" thus—and set them to work. Cheerfully enough the axe strokes echoed among the hills. Warder Shannon's approving eyes noticed that that tough native, Terry, was working cheerily. Still, he did not trust that smarty, know-all fellow, he must keep an eye on him.

Which he did, ever and anon in between keeping an eye on all the rest of them. Which is a ceaseless, wearisome job as time drags on, with insects humming in the air while a wonderful morning developed into breathless heat, an ominous silence. The warder did not notice Terry's covert glance, did not notice him straighten up with a glance at the sky and warily all around, sniffing the air as he did so. With an eager, satisfied grin at the warder's back he bent to his work again.

A dust-storm was brewing—fast!

It came first, strangely enough, with an icy chill as a puff of wind hissed past. Then, from the west a red haze was rapidly approaching. Soon its hot smother would blot out the sky.

A dust scurry arose as by magic from the earth and came scurrying along in little whirls of dancing "sandy devils". The warder glanced round, sniffed, frowned. A nasty storm was brewing, for sure. He'd do one more job, and then, if this storm blew up right this way he'd better muster his prisoners and march them back to jail.

He turned to cut down and trim a sapling to use as a lever to roll over a log, and did not notice that Terry then swiftly cut a sapling, too, but not as a lever, only a short length—like a club. This he kicked under the log he was chopping. With a mighty swing then he buried the axe-head in the log. The warder turned to a smart snap.

"What did you have to go and do that for, you clumsy galoot?" growled Shannon. "Go and snap a good axe-handle like that? Anyone would think you'd never handled an axe in your life before."

Growling morosely, the old warder picked up his sapling lever and shoved one end under a log to give an old myall prisoner a hand to roll it over. The warder would never thus have turned his back on Terry had Terry still held an axe in his hand. The warder put his shoulder under the lever and with the old blackfellow began straining to turn the log over, his rifle outstretched in his right hand behind his back. In a second Terry had snatched down for his club and with noiseless bounds was leaping on the warder. Suddenly he dropped his upraised club and snatched at the rifle instead, jerking it back out of the warder's hand, the sharp sight ripping hand and arm. Shannon jumped round as Terry sprang back with levelled rifle, then the old warder lowered his head and with a bull-like roar came straight at Terry's stomach. This immediate decisive battering-ram charge upset Terry's balance and he wheeled round and ran—fair into a swirling cloud of dust hissing down upon them. Impossible to catch him, of course. He wheeled round with half-levelled rifle and shouted, "Come and get me—I'll shoot any man that tries!" Then he turned and unconcernedly walked away into oncoming sheets of fine red dust.

The warden shouted his orders against the rising wind, mustered his startled prisoners from the police paddock, and marched them straight back to the police station.

Terry, who could be dangerous, now *was* dangerous. He had got away with his liberty and a .38 calibre rifle. But there were only six bullets in the magazine. Six lives, should the marksman prove a good shot. Mounted Constable Hamilton, with trackers—shrewd old Peter, George, and Fred— was quickly in pursuit. Peter, who was looked upon as being part of the Alice, tracked Terry to the rocky hills west of the township, where the telltale tracks were lost. Quickly he again picked up tracks, blotted out here and there by the windblown dust of the storm. Soon that whirling dust would blot out everything. Those tracks led up towards Mount Gillen, highest point near the Alice. And now Terry, helped by the drifting dust, kept them occupied, casually lured them over these hills, then doubled back and, swiftly circling the low hills directly round the township, watched in comfort from the northern hills for the remainder of the day. He stripped himself of clothes so as to feel a real man again. With a feeling of frustration they got the police car and tried to hedge him in by motor-car power, by horse and by human foot. From the vantage points of the hilltops round the township he played with them until a fierce red sunset blackened into storm-clouds. Hoping rain would not wash out any tracks Terry might make that night, the police were forced to give up in the darkness. They felt sure that under cover of darkness he would make his break-away for the wild bush.

Not he. He was not a frightened bush native, he was civilized and knew just as much as the police did. He knew, too, he needed more cartridges. Food also.

Late that evening he stole back into the township. He played the star role that he could play so well—the Black Phantom. He got himself a drink. Then, of all places, he glided into the trackers' quarters at the police station. The human bloodhounds were still away on the search. He went through those quarters and did damage and stole things he most desired. Fiercely he wished to set the place afire, but this would bring the whole township down upon him. Instead he stole some clothes; he could have done without these, but with a malicious grin he took them. The fact that these clothes belonged to the Government Resident's blackboy seems to have given him a little spicy pleasure. He vanished into the engineer's yard and raided the fowlyard of eggs. From somewhere he stole what he most keenly desired, a few handfuls of cartridges. He was bitterly disappointed to find only a few that would fit the .38. But soon afterwards, in the jailer's quarters, he found two full packets. With a satisfied grin he vanished through the township, taking his time eastward along valleys in the hills. Not a soul had seen him. And now he did not hurry. All was well, he did not feel as if he were being pursued, he felt this was merely the home call luring him away towards Arltunga and the White Range. He hardly bothered to disguise his tracks. They were fresh and plain, only enough rain had fallen to lay the dust.

Peter next morning cut his tracks at the canter.

Constable Hamilton and the trackers were after him by car and horse—Hamilton and tracker Peter in the cars, with trackers Ned and George riding a parallel valley trying to hem in the runaway between them. All day long—a rough track indeed, that wagon track, but the only one.

To the Todd, then over stony country to a shady waterhole at Emily Gap, only seven miles south-east of the Springs. Tracks here showed that Terry had knelt down and drunk as an animal drinks, an unhurried animal, not a hunted one. Then he had begun to climb the precipitous side of Mount John.

"Him bin look about," said Peter. "Then he bin make for Undoolya."

Frustrated in the hope of a swift capture, Hamilton stared up at that rocky height. Useless even to think of tracking up there, of course. The trackers would work another way. By deduction.

Undoolya station is on the track to Arltunga, Terry's country. Several of Terry's tribesmen worked at Undoolya station. Terry would make his way there, so Peter believed, demand shelter and tucker and news from his tribesmen, then push on when and should the pursuit come near the station. So, by horse and car, they would make for the station by different routes, keenly alert for verifying tracks at any locality where the runaway must come down to the low country. They must and would follow similar tactics again even where the cunning of Terry and nature of the country made tracking, if not impossible, then impossibly slow.

At sundown Hamilton stopped the car, in forlorn hope of some sign of the elusive man before dark beat them. Down there in the valleys it was growing cold and still and dark.

"Ssh!" hissed Peter and excitedly pointed.

Hamilton stiffened, thought he saw a shadow figure quietly arising from a sheltering hollow, a shadow that seemed to be dragging on a hat. Then it stood up; it seemed to be clad in coat and trousers. Hamilton and Peter, staring out through the dim light, thought it must be a tracker until suddenly it slipped behind a tree and levelled a rifle.

"That's him!" yelled Peter.

"Quick!" hissed Hamilton as he leapt out one side of the car and Peter the other, but their outflung hands both grabbed the one rifle.

"You stop!" yelled Peter.

"Hell I will!" came back a defiant shout. "I'll shoot policeman or white man or blackfellow or half-caste—I'll shoot any bastard who comes after me! I will shoot all you bastards!"

"Come out from cover and drop that rifle before you do any damage, you fool!" shouted Hamilton.

A stab of flame and the sharp smack of a bullet was the answer. Peter flung himself down and fired. Terry leapt back to the crack of Hamilton's rifle—and the shell stuck in the magazine. In almost a crying fury Hamilton tried and tried to jerk out that infernal shell as bullets from Terry's rifle whined into the earth around him. Several miles away, the other trackers reined in their horses to the sharp echoes of the rifle-shots reverberating along the gorge. Terry fired six shots rapidly, then Peter fired again at his shadow leaping away among the trees across the Gap to the rocky gorge-side.

Hamilton shouted a warning to stop, but the shadow vanished into the other shadows of evening. They jumped up and raced after it, until from behind a ledge of rock, flame stabbed out into the darkness and a bullet whistled by Hamilton's ear. He ducked and ran doggedly on, and now at last freed that wretched shell and jerked a fresh cartridge into the breech. He thought he saw a fleeing shadow, he whipped up his rifle and fired, but the figure vanished. Then again flame spat out from behind a rock, the bullet whistling so close that Hamilton swerved violently to cover before levelling the rifle and firing again, but the bullet whined away off rock.

It was now dark down there in the Gap, but away above they could see the hilltops lit up by the fading sunset, as always in such places.

Warning Peter to keep a sharp look-out, while standing well back under cover from the big rocks lest Terry climb away up and fire down from above, Hamilton ran back to the car and drove off in an attempt to quickly find and bring up trackers Ned and George. Peter felt very lonely crouching there in the cold gloom and peering up towards the black rocks while listening to the diminishing hum of the car. It was quite different being brave while the policeman was standing by, but another matter altogether when alone in the deepening darkness facing a desperate tribesman savagely shooting at him with the white man's weapon. Peter, the most experienced old tracker in the Centre, knew, of course, what a rifle could do. He shivered a bit as his eyes stared up at the rocks, feeling what a horrid thing it would be if a bullet spattered his brains all over the place.

Where *was* this devil of a Terry? And just what was he doing?

Terry was not idle; he was climbing those rocks, agile as any rock wallaby. He got cosily away up there where the sunset was and peered down into the gloom. And with sunset behind him, beating down into the Gap, he could distinctly see the crouching outline of Peter. Eagerly he tilted the rifle-barrel down, glaring along the sights. Had he not been so eager to kill his first man he would have hit him. He fired, and the hot breath of the bullet thudded so close by Peter that he seemed to leap skyward before falling back and rolling over the ground into darkness.

Terry was bitterly disappointed. He should have got his man, he had a clear shot with nothing to distract his attention. He had missed, and perhaps this brought a gloomy fatalistic feeling that he would always miss again. Certainly he now had a rifle, but this had proved he could not use it as well as he had thought he could.

Soon after daylight they were on his tracks; he was making towards Arltunga as they thought he would, but they soon lost the tracks. For now, thoroughly alarmed, Terry was keeping to the tops of those rocky ranges, only descending to flat or watercourse when a range spur would give out. Now and later they tried all they could to keep him from reaching the rockholes for water. Hamilton spread out his trackers over the miles. The country here ran in rugged lines of extremely rough ranges; one narrow gorge in between ran for ten miles. Hamilton had to follow it down and cross its creek seventeen times. Not too easy a job along a rocky, roadless gorge, this recrossing a dry creek, which was a mass of boulders, while negotiating a car—and cars in the 1930s were not as easy to handle as modern ones—with a maniacal blackfellow away up on the crags seeking a pot-shot down through the timber at the car. The trackers riding other gorges on horses could move easier and faster, and on occasion they did, when to a yell of "Terry!" each would swoop over his horse's neck and gallop for cover.

That first night, quite warm in a cave, Terry devoured his stolen eggs raw, no need to light a fire. He was not hurrying either. Hunched up there with his back to the cave wall, that precious rifle across his knees, he grinned into his native darkness. He felt good. He had led them a merry dance without exerting himself much. At sunset they had verynearly taken him by surprise—he must be still more wary in the future—but he had beaten them off, and now had nothing to worry about until morning. And he felt confident of the morning. He yawned.

But they came seeking his tracks with the dawn.

Erkita Corroboree, Alice Springs, 1896.

XXXV

HE WHO WALKS IN THE NIGHT

Terry slipped away just before dawn. Cold now, because of course he had lit no warming but tell-tale fire. With uneasy frown he was keeping a sharp look-out, remembering that he had engaged in a fair little battle with a policeman and a tracker and had not hit either—that was bad. And now he was hungry, and had no tucker. And those blasted trackers were now hidden at the waterholes ahead of him; he had easily guessed their tactics by watching their movements from the hilltops yesterday. And so they would keep him from his very own tribal country? Even prevent him from drinking at the watering places of his people! He has since told how he ground his teeth and wheeled round with rifle at the ready in a spasm of mad rage at this bitter thought.

However, he grinned sarcastically and trudged on. He was in no hurry; when he should be he'd move so fast and far they'd never see him. Meanwhile he would play with them, keep them moving day and night until they and their horses were exhausted. Then, one by one, he'd pick them off and shoot the lot of them. That was the plan he decided upon as he walked along over the rocky crests, instinctively keeping his feet to the rocks. There are abundant outcrops lining those ridges, goodness knows; the trackers would be baffled time and again trying to pick up his footprints. He stopped by a clump of acacia-trees in bloom. Reaching for the branches, he collected the blossoms in handfuls and threw them into his capacious maw. Strolling on, ever up there amongst the topmost rocks, the bushland scents sweet to his nostrils, the calls of bird-life companionly music, then down along a ridge, where he stopped again by a group of heavily flowered acacias. He ate handfuls more of the blossoms, then, squinting down, saw the burst of fine yellow powder amongst the roots. Squatting down, he tore at those roots he could break or snap off with his hands, quite careless that here at least the pursuing trackers would see at a glance he had certainly come this way and stopped for a feed. Honeycombed with tiny tunnels those roots were, as was the corroded bark, and filled with big fat witchety grubs. He ate them raw, not even bothering to snip off the head with his thumb and fingernail, just popped the big white fat delicacies into his mouth and swallowed. He picked a long sharp splinter, and where the grub in its tunnel was hard to get at he shoved in the splinter and probed about and hooked out the soft, fat body. Plenty of them. He raked out an appetizing handful or two also under the bark of a gum-tree. This is the "tribal" grub painted in bold relief in red and yellow ochre on the eastern wall of Emily Gap, that prized grub and totem symbol painted elsewhere, too, on quartzite rock, with hook in its tail and three stripes down its back, sign of the Utneraniger, men of the Aruntas. Terry frowned as he thought of this, and of the Lizard men, and of the Eritcha Tribe. Ah, but he had finished with all these primitive beliefs of his tribal boyhood, he was civilized. Uneasily he frowned, picked up his rifle, glanced down into the valley, and grew still as the rock beside which he crouched. Right away down there, riding past in the direction of Undoolya station, were two trackers, Ned and Wyndham Jack. His deepset eyes blazed as he frowned down at Wyndham Jack, looking small as a monkey on his horse. He did not like that tracker, Wyndham Jack.

The trackers were driving laden packhorses, supplies for the patrol riding on ahead to Undoolya station.

Which angered him. The patrol were not going to go hungry, while he had to battle for his tucker and fight them, too! This did not seem fair to his sense of justice. Well, let them hurry on ahead to cut him off from his tribal country—they just could not do it. He strolled on and suddenly grinned, gazing down at a flat, sunbathed rock. In the warmth upon that broad surface now gleamed brown and golden coils.

Undethekera and Utniar!

Two carpet snakes, "cousins". Seldom indeed that you find the two together. And both these "breeds" were edible. To him, these two reptiles in amiable companionship meant a sign of good luck.

Sheltered in among the rocks he coolly lit a fire, with very little smoke. Presently he had coals. He killed the snakes, coiled them upon the coals, and covered them with ashes. Then he climbed to the highest point and gazed back along the rocky ridge.

It was an hour or so later that he saw Peter, patiently seeking tracks wherever there might be a small patch of earth along the rocky crests. Slow work indeed, tracking over rocks.

Terry scraped away the ashes, picked up the near-cooked snakes, and walked casually on, not bothering to disguise his tracks, throwing aside a little skin, a fragment of backbone of roast snake here and there. Now and again he'd bend down and snatch up a tuft of coarse grass, wipe his hands on it, and throw it carelessly aside.

Not all the grass, that is, only half of each tuft. The other half he would carefully twist in his belt, until he had quite a lot of grass bound round his waist. The spur of this ridge was leading down into a patch of level country among the ranges. Terry knew that down there horses would be awaiting those particular trackers tracking him so slowly from away behind. He came to an acre-wide patch of bare rock. Walking now as if he actually were trying to leave no trace of track, he walked right across it to a break-away. Here the rock ended in a ledge. Below the rock were tumbled boulders, masses of them, leading down to that little patch of level country away below. Terry jumped easily down on to a boulder. And now acted swiftly.

Seizing grass from his waist, he twisted it expertly round a foot, then the remainder round the other foot. He was now wearing thick grass soles, actually a form of moccasin, with which it was practically impossible *to* leave even a faint impression of a track, except on soft earth.

And now he jumped, not to a boulder going down the spur, but to one well aside. And, turning directly to his left, he carried on from boulder to boulder until he was leaping down along the left side of the spur, and down this he swiftly climbed, gradually turning completely round.

Thus at the bottom of the spur he was away below, walking back the way he had come, while now Peter, up on top of the spur, was passing him, following his tracks until that break-away would give him a headache.

Thus Terry strolled back for miles the way he had come, while the ever searching patrols tracked him to puzzle after puzzle. Then they had wearily to spread out for miles, circling to try to cut his tracks again somewhere or other, sooner or later.

By day and night now, continually he would plan many a little trick like this, again and again with grim amusement watching the pursuers' frustrated attempts from an eyrie upon a range-top.

At night, though, he had to come down into the low country and sneak to a rockhole like a thirsty dingo. And he did not like this—not in his very own tribal country where the waters and the foods and all therein had been his and his ancestors from that immemorial dawn of the Dream-time.

And then it rained—when he was only two days out. He would be able to get water anywhere now, the police could not possibly watch every rockhole in this country of innumerable gorges and creeks. His own country would look after him, he could *feel* it through and through as the rain hissed down. Cosy in a cave, but hungry, he laughed aloud as, gazing down into the gorge below him, he saw two trackers jog-trotting by, huddled in their saddles, disliking their ride in the rain. These two human bloodhounds would be riding, he was certain, to his own country, Arltunga. There was a frontier police station, in charge of M. C. Murray, camped by Kangaroo Well. At this White Range camp Kangaroo Well supplied water for a handful of gold-miners, of natives who worked for them, and for the police horses and the numerous horses of teamsters who carted stone for the miners. That is, so long as the well had not fallen in. He grinned as he thought of having a drink at that well, they would never dream he would be game, for so many were camped there, there must be twenty men. While the rain hissed down he let his thoughts dwell upon those wells that served the mining camps, the Kangaroo, the Star of the North, the Wheel of Mundy, the Wheel of Fortune, the Claravale, all close by the White Range. They had served white men and black men and brown, and horses and camels and goats and wild animals of the bush, too; they had freely yielded their life-giving water to all. They would be watched by the police now, but he would drink of all these wells, and of new ones sunk in recent years.

The rain stopped, the sun blazed out. With a new determination he grasped the rifle and stepped out of the cave into the sweet, warming smell of the wetted bush. With a startled grunt a euro jumped to a rock a hundred yards away and sat back, prick-eared, a solid chunk of an animal, its reddish coat gleaming in the newly washed sunshine.

Terry whipped up his rifle and fired, and the euro lurched back with its last gasp—a dead shot that, for the euro is a tough animal to kill. Terry bounded forward in the seventh heaven of delight. He could use the rifle after all, he had *not* lost the secret of the kill. He did not care one razoo that now the very hills had ears—how that rifle shot rolled and rolled away! Let them all come! He would take them all on!

Yet once again he would learn that shooting a standing animal is a very different thing from killing another man who is firing back.

Terry took his time. He knew now they would be away ahead, laying ambushes for him at Arltunga, along the White Range, even to the Harts Range. What did he care now? He had plenty of time.

He had not. He had only ten days.

They quite lost all trace of him for the next two days. And thereafter they only found trace of him with the greatest difficulty. For a day or two the ground would be soft, so carefully and craftily he disguised his tracks. When he had to approach a sandy or muddy waterhole he would walk backwards upon his own tracks until he got back to hard ground again—thus, with many a puzzle bringing the trackers to a sulky halt again and again. And Hamilton and Murray, too, knew it was useless hurrying the exasperated trackers when they were puzzled by a difficult tracking. They could grow sullen, and then would not try. Yet Hamilton at last could not help asking, 'Which way he been go now?"

Peter would stand erect, his screwed-up eyes opening like those of a man awaking from sleep; reflectively he would take off the hat that shaded his black, wrinkled forehead.

"Me think it he plurry well *fly* away!" he would growl with an "I've had it" air of absolute finality.

This would be when the tracks stopped dead; it would take time and much patient effort to prove that here Terry had walked backwards upon his own track, having made moccasins of euro skin and walking on the fur. When an expert walks without pressure and with his feet loosely encased in skin with the furry side underneath, then it is difficult indeed to find trace of such a track. And if he walks backwards—well, then, if you do find some faint little scrape upon the earth, or a dislodged pebble, or faintly bruised grass-tuft, how the blazes are you to tell for sure whether that faint sign is the track of a man? And if so, whether he is coining or going?

As the days and nights passed, Terry, in between travelling, dodging the patrols, bamboozling the trackers, and finding his water and tucker, improved upon this idea by attempting to make a pair of Kurdaitja shoes. He did not have those perfect materials, emu feathers, though he had the glue—his own blood. These are the Witch-doctor's shoes when he walks as the evil spirit seeking to kill in the night. Those short, "fluffed" feathers, hound together with coagulated blood, are the most perfect thing known to conceal tracks, and on certain grounds to leave no faintest track at all These shoes are quite shapeless, so that it is impossible to tell whether the wearer has been coming or going where an impression is purposely left, when the Witch-doctor wishes to terrify. He can even cross over sand without leaving a track, should those feather shoes have been made by an expert, and worn by an expert.

Thus walks the Devil-man, he who wears the Kurdaitja shoes and comes to kill in the night.

XXXVI

THE HEAT IS ON

Terry came down on to flat country purposely to find and shoot an emu for food and to make real Kurdaitja shoes. To his surprise he learnt he had not the time—learnt that a hunted man is living on borrowed time. For swiftly, to his bewilderment, a bullet flying past his ear advised him it was not only the emu that was being hunted. He leapt for cover quicker than any hunted emu.

It was a miner, so I was later told, firing from his lonely hut who had given Terry the hint. For by now the few scattered men had been warned that Terry was "out" with a rifle, and had already freely used it.

However, Terry fashioned for himself a yet better pair of quite serviceable shoes of euro fur, torn pieces of his shirt, fluffed-up fragments of papery bark, and portions of an old chaff-bag that carefully he tore into ragged strips. Shapeless moccasins of such materials expertly made and worn by an expert can delay the craftiest tracker for many valuable hours. And they can 'lose' a tracker who is not an expert, as old Peter was.

"Where the blazes he been go now?" asked Hamilton wearily as a magnificent sunset blazing down from the Red Gorge brought them to what looked like another dead-end night.

They'd tracked him down into a gorge where tracks vanished in the low country. It had a sandy bed, too, so tracks should have been plain. But not a sign. The trackers rode along to one of the precious wells. Here stock at sunset had already come in for water, station stock of cattle and horses, teamsters' horses, miners' horses. Impossible, surely, to see a hunted man's tracks, even if any were here, the sand all churned up by many hooves. And yet Peter and George dismounted and slowly, carefully, deliberately, were walking over that churned-up morass of sand, staring down under those frowning, bushy eyebrows. Then old Peter pointed, George strode to him and stared down, they both straightened up and laughed.

"He walkem all-a-same colt!" called old Peter to Hamilton. And Hamilton rode to them with relief, knowing now they had found Terry's track where he had followed the horses to water, with his feet cleverly disguised as a young horse's. Every here and there, just in a very few places where the returning horses and cattle had not ploughed over the imitation track, the trackers pointed out Terry's clever deception.

At other times he similarly came to water among the stock, making his tracks both together to look like the front and hind hoof of bullock or cow, with toes screwed up and heel up altogether off the sand and gravel, so that the "bunch" of toes sink into the sand while the rest of the foot doesn't show at all. He knew plenty of such tricks; had they not doggedly stuck to him day and night and shot back with interest when he fired at them he would have taken a lot of catching.

Within large pockets of well-grassed, mulga-timbered flat country hemmed in by those ranges nestle three pioneer stations. It was at one of these stations that Terry picked up the old chaff-bag for his shoes. At this station his sister worked. Early in the chase he crept down from the hilltops. In the dead of night his sister sleepily awoke, looked up. Knew instinctively that the blackness standing beside her was her brother. She smelled the familiar smell also. The whites of his eyes shone down into her terrified ones. She saw the gleam of his teeth. Soundlessly she arose, crept away to get him food.

He taunted her because she, his own sister, was afraid of him. Whispering, she told him that *everyone* was afraid of him, and she nodded towards the rifle. He tapped it with a satisfied grin, and vanished. So, if it had been a bundle of spears they would *not* have been afraid of him.

It was good to have a rifle.

But, wolfing his food as he strode through the night, he frowned, beginning to realize that if everyone was afraid of him then they would avoid him, would even whisper word to trackers and police so as to get him out of the way as quickly as possible. If he was to have no friends then he would have no rest, no food should the pursuit grow hot. He would he hunted the more!

Quickly he would learn he now had another enemy he had never dreamt of—nerves! Ah, he had *not* realized what it meant to be "civilized".

Very soon he was travelling only at night, a Black Phantom now in dead earnest. Yet again and again they flushed him out.

He came through the one gap in the Red Range, high up among the rocks. Hamilton had posted a tracker down in the gap, but Terry crawled over the gap top, silent as a slithering snake, invisible. Hamilton was waiting at Bloomfield's Soak, in a nice little possy that the hunted man must pass if he came down from the Red Range.

He didn't

At the well an old blackfellow was pulling water for thirsty police horses. Keeping him company was an aboriginal shepherd watering his mob of goats for a near-by station. It was night-time, but those police horses, after a heavy day's patrolling, had to be watered. Not one sign had been seen of the elusive bad man, Terry.

Suddenly a rock whizzed by the aboriginal shepherd's ear. Both aborigines sprang erect, eyes fearfully staring out into the night. Not a sound but the thirsty drinking of the horses. A stilly night, with the smell of splashed water and sweaty horses, animal tang of goats.

'Whizz! Whizz!" as two rocks flew past the two listening men. One raced for the police camp; the shepherd abandoned his goats and ran for the station homestead. Both men were terrified by age-old superstitions of the night; if a "spirit" had appeared before them in Kurdaitja shoes neither would have uttered a sound, they would merely have dropped dead of fright.

The horses snorted back from "blackfellow smell" as the shadowy Terry stepped amongst them for his fill of water. Then he collared a goat, making sure it was a fat one. Then vanished into the night.

He would kill that goat, carry it up the rocky hills near by, and cook it in some sheltered nook. He would feed well, and sleep well between now and the dawn.

Hamilton, silently listening out into the night as he awaited Terry at *his* well, only two miles away, did not sleep. Terry did not care. Neither did he keep that appointment so desired of by Mounted Constable Hamilton. Well, not that night.

As the chase went on Terry grew savage. He prowled again his White Range, inhaled the acacia-scented air of his beloved Arltunga, saw his own people—from hide-outs. Saw them walking along tracks, the well-known tracks he had walked as a hunting boy, or saw them at work at some miner's, or station camp. And saw that they were frightened of him, quite often saw by some quick, suspicious gesture of man or woman that they were afraid of him, afraid of their own tribesman Terry who had grown up with them, afraid of Terry stepping out of the bush beside them. At first he had grinned at their fear, it gave him a feeling of power. But now came an increasing bitterness.

Then one day he *did* step out—from behind a rock—with his rifle at his uncle's chest.

The man nearly died of fright; his primitive black visage slowly seemed to turn into a dirty green, he stood there trembling, gibbering.

"Where pleece?" snarled Terry.

But the uncle could only mouth queer spitty sounds over and over again—he was remembering how he had helped give his savage nephew the father of a hiding.

Terry lowered the rifle, laughed, sneered. Then threw the leg of an euro at the uncle's feet.

"I shot it this morning!" he said in his tribal language. "Shot it stone cold—I'll do the same to you if you dare say a word about meeting me! You take it to camp and cook it and eat it and think of me—think it is dead meat and you'll be dead meat, too, if you talk about me! And now, pull yourself together. Where are the pleece? The white pleece Hamilton and Murray, and where are Hamilton's trackers riding? And where are Murray's? And where is the pleece car? Tell me all you know and watch your memory or I'll blow your teeth down your guts with a bullet!"

Of course the frightened man told his erring, forceful nephew all he knew. After which he forgot all about whatever his business might be and, wheeling round, hurried fearfully back to his own camp. On the way he had to pass the Arltunga police camp, on which both patrols had happened to converge seeking news and stores. A tracker speculatively watched him sneaking by.

"Terry's uncle him bin see *something}.*" the tracker called to Murray.

"Bring him in right away!" ordered Murray.

When the tracker called out to the uncle to come back into the station the uncle hurried on, shamming deaf. The tracker had to race out and catch him. By then the uncle was wobbling at the knees in sheer terror.

"Where is Terry?" demanded Murray.

"I bin see him!" stuttered the uncle, and pointed. But he was so terrified he was incapable of explaining, could only stutter and point.

They crowded into and clung to the police car, Hamilton and Murray, and trackers Peter and George, Ned and Wyndham Jack, then, just as they were moving off, a gory vision leapt grinning to cling to the running board—black Printy, gripping a bloodstained butcher's knife; he had been killing a goat for the patrol's meat. The uncle was now really speechless, but he tried to guide them, and as they were passing a clump of rocks a startled Terry jumped out from a cleft and raced across into a dense clump of tea-tree beside Kangaroo Gully.

"All out! Quick-feller!" shouted Hamilton, and directed his men to race out in a wide circle round the tea-tree thicket, then quickly but cautiously enter it and flush out the runaway.

"With a bit of luck we have him!" exulted Hamilton. "Get him," he called to the trackers, "but be careful—keep under cover all you can!"

XXXVII

"FINISH!"

As they raced for cover to surround that clump of timber Terry unhurriedly climbed down from a tree licking his chops at thought of just what he would do to uncle when he should catch him in some nice, lonely place. Then he saw Wyndham Jack as Jack saw him.

"Put down that gun!" shouted Jack in surprised alarm.

"Right!" shouted Terry as he whipped up his rifle and fired.

Wyndham Jack fell over backwards in startled fright and vanished.

Terry laughed his scorn aloud, then his face hardened in savage doubt

He had missed! Missed a standing man, at that distance! Had it been a euro he would have hit it.

He walked on, frowning uneasily, then nearly turned green as he came almost face to face with a black "creeping" face, eyes bulging from fiendish head, a long, bloodstained knife clutched in sinewy black hand—Printy, with his butcher's knife, coming running to intercept him.

If Terry almost "dropped his bundle" from sheer maniacal fury it was then. He simply whipped up his rifle and blazed away.

Printy leapt back into the timber as if a devil were at his heels.

Terry missed again, and fired at what now were but sounds of a frantic retreat.

But a few days later at the Alice it was told me (the gossip with a laughing gusto came from the jail yard, as a matter of fact) that Terry's sorriest memory of those ten wild days and nights was the hopeless wish that he had waited just another second or two until Printy had got so close he must have flattened him with a bullet in the guts. Then, oh, then—just what *wouldn't* he have done to Printy with his very own butcher's knife!

But now Terry, in imminent danger of losing liberty if not life, nearly went to pieces; no doubt that creeping black face and the bloodstained butcher's knife had jangled his nerves, already unhappily alarmed by his bad shooting. With a tense effort he pulled himself together to fight his way to a running escape. Racing up a steep gully that offered shelter and also, as he knew, led to the hilltops, he turned and fired two shots at tracker George, whose quick eyes had spotted him. George ducked behind the rocks to the whine of the bullets and Terry was away again. He was well up the gully when he saw Peter peering from a gully head right opposite where Constable Hamilton was emerging. Dropping behind a rock exactly as Peter did, Terry fired, then leapt up the gully to take cover as Peter fired. Terry swiftly wheeled to fire back at this persistent Peter yet again. His old ally, darkness, soon now would favour him, but he must last until it did come. Grimly he hurried on, though now even he was gasping for breath. But let the bullets come—they all seemed to be seeing him now, shouting to one another his whereabouts, while the sheltering arms of dusk were swiftly reaching out to envelop her primitive son. He leapt up and over the gully bank and doubled up as a swift shadow might move, leapt across to plunge into yet another gully, and vanished from his pursuers' sight.

Thus forced again into a cold wariness, he climbed, dead tired but in a shivery triumph, the rocky wall of a precipitous defile. They would find no tracks here when the dawn should come. He made for his own country, to the very spot where he was born.

And from now on he was that Black Phantom in earnest, for he travelled only by moonlight. Appeared here, only to vanish, to reappear but for a moment miles away, only briefly seen on such occasion as he wanted something. The two pursuing patrols were now co-operating, Hamilton's from the Alice, and Murray's from Arltunga. And despite their two groups of trackers, as well as natives they pressed into willing service, they found they were chasing a Will-o'-the-wisp. As one constable's terse report to headquarters:

> When told to put down his rifle at Jessie Gap he replied, "I will shoot whites, blacks, or half-castes. I will shoot all you b——— b——
> —s!" We have not had the opportunity of seeing him on level ground as he has not travelled five miles on soft ground since he left Alice Springs but has kept to the ranges. As he is travelling in the moonlight and leaving few tracks the difficulty of locating them then following over miles of bare rocks is difficult indeed and sometimes impossible as he constantly changes direction, thus often working round behind us at night. Yet we must cling to what tracks we do find, while making every effort to keep him away from the natives and miners' camps, thus preventing him doing harm to them and also from getting further supplies of arms and ammunition.

Terry vanished into his favourite White Range, that ever and anon gleams like snow-capped hills. For numerous ridges are massed with white quartz reefs, milky-white from the presence of huge quartz outcrops that make up most of the country here, with the granitics and conglomerates and the red, black, and yellow "ironstony" rocks, with the pyrites and gossans, the sandy clays which combine to help make up this rough but highly interesting mineralized belt.

A favourite look-out of Terry's, known well since boyhood, was the rocky mass known as Corbin's Bluff, with its walls in places sheer cliffs of milky quartzite pressurized on grey granite. From here he enjoyed a wonderful view across to the favourite gold workings, and could also laugh at anyone coming to scale the bluff to get him. Any man so foolish would be a sitting shot. Leisurely then he could stroll away to the cosiest of get-aways on southward, a fantastic ravine nearly four hundred feet in depth, cutting sheer through a ridge, its gloomy bed a raging torrent during storms, its quartzite walls well over three hundred feet in thickness. Similar masses of this white rock, jutting plentifully in rugged outcrops from the hilltops, give this picturesque locality its name, the White Range. Had Terry's "friends" stuck to him, had he become firmly established in such a natural labyrinth, there's no telling what damage he would have done, or how long before the police would have got him. Within this area was the main gold-mining camp, consisting only of about forty or fifty men spread out in twos and threes over some fifteen miles of gold-bearing country. East of this wild tangle of small, rocky ranges is a strip of near-desert country to the Queensland border. To the north, he could have lost himself. Some three hundred and thirty miles south is Oodnadatta, with a further six hundred and eighty-eight miles south to Adelaide. But only seventy miles nor'-west is the Alice.

Terry had plenty of country to roam in, but now sullenly he holed up in his beloved White Range, his own tribal country.

Towards one red sunset both weary patrols, with near-exhausted horses, converged upon the little Arltunga police camp. They were thankfully ready for the sunset meal when a blackboy came hurrying to the goat-yard to kill a goat and excitedly whispered to tracker Peter, "That boy with rifle over there!" and jerked his chin violently across the bush.

The patrol leapt for the police cars, both were luckily there and in action. With trackers clinging to the cars they were off, Hamilton anxious because yet again there was but little daylight left. Murray with some of the trackers drove swiftly around one side of Terry's hide-out, Hamilton and Peter round the other. Then all jumped out and ran to flush out the quarry.

Terry first saw his old friend Wyndham Jack, whipped up his rifle, fired, and—missed. Peter copied Terry's own tactics and hurried straight up the side of the nearest hill, then wheeled to gaze down—and away below saw Terry bent low as he ran in criss-cross fashion between rocks. Difficult indeed to pick him out away down there, let alone hit him when dodging among the rocks thus. But the runaway was sighted, and the now excited Peter, gazing down with the sun shedding its rays downward, could plainly follow the warily moving figure. Peter fired. Terry leapt behind a rock like a scalded cat; a rifle bullet splattering with a whine of fragments against a rock beside him will make any man leap, especially when it is fired unexpectedly from above. Terry, knowing that now all hands would be racing towards him directed by Peter's high-pitched shouts and shots, raced desperately for cover farther ahead. Peter fired again and missed. Peter was thoroughly excited now, but he could only see Terry as an occasional leaping shadow down there in the now dimming rays of the swiftly setting sun. He got one more shot in, but then Terry vanished into thick bushes in that fast-gathering gloom.

Wearily the patrols collected themselves to return to Arltunga and camp.

Wearily, too, though savagely and bewildered, Terry crawled into his hole in the rocks. This particular hole smelt strongly of euro, though that did not offend Terry's keenly primitive sense of smell, in fact it smelt homely and friendly in his now fast developing feeling of resentful loneliness. But if that tough old buck euro had left any of his ticks in here then even the Stone Age man's thick hide would make him painfully aware of it before he slumbered long. It was still far from Terry to consider himself a primitive man, but in bewildered fashion he was beginning to feel that this being civilized was not all he'd thought it to be. It was miserably lonely and he seemed to be missing out on something.

The ticks *were* there. Cursing in a fiendish anger, he leapt out into the open night to yank those vicious devils off his tortured body. Believe me, the euro tick is pretty awful.

Terry knew only too well now that every man's hand was against him — white, black, brown, and brindle. It was his treasured rifle that did it, the weapon he so far had failed to use properly. For they knew he felt "sulky-feller" towards them. With a rifle in hand and in his nasty mood he was a dangerous man, dangerous to friend and foe.

Terry now had no friends — in his own country!

Both patrols harried him ceaselessly, day and night. They had the men and sympathizers to help do it, while he was only the one hunted man. And he must sleep, with every murmur in his now tortured ears a tracker's footstep. And by now also, by the hunt or thieving from the lonely camps, he must find food to eat, in a near panic now, that either method must swiftly betray his presence in the vicinity. The report of a rifle shot echoing up those gorges and deep ravines would bring the scattered patrol men converging at the gallop should the locality be suitable for swift horse work. Whereas ratting a camp would alarm the owner when he returned from work. Lest worst befall him he would send a blackboy running to find the nearest police patrol.

At this rate, Terry's nerves would soon be "shot to pieces". He had by now shot quite a number of times at men and had not hit one — how he would brighten up if he could only kill one man! He had not even hit one man, while he had been hit himself—and above all by that most despised of all his trackers, Wyndham Jack!

True, it was only a slight wound, a nick in the left forearm. Still, so close that but an inch to either side and the bullet would have torn into his body. The upset to Terry was that the grinning, slinky Wyndham had hit *him* and he had failed to hit Wyndham!

The police as yet did not know of Terry's close call, would not know until he was caught and admitted the scar was a bullet from Wyndham Jack's rifle one day while he was slinking through the bush making for the Black Angel, at which little mine was working a tribesman whom he hoped might not be too frightened to be a friend. By way of variety, here is that particular little skirmish as described by tracker George later on at the official inquiry:

> "Me hear Wyndham Jack sing out, 'Look out! He run over there!' Me ran back along the gully and meet him and shout, 'Stop!' He fired and jumping back fired again and I fired and then again and he ran back over the 'Jump Up'. Printy ran past me after him an' Terry fired at him and made him jump down. Wyndham sang out, 'Look out, Peter! He over there!' Terry fired at Peter then ducked and jumped down a gully and got away."

The two patrols dared not let up on seeking him. He was ripe to start a line of tragedies at any moment.

Peter picked up his tracks at the police station well and they were after him again, now into the very heart of the White Range. About midday, as if in derisive defiance, he stood right atop of a snow-white quartzite hill, a chocolate-black statue bathed in sunlight below a deep-blue sky. Deliberately he levelled his rifle. Murray accepted the challenge and aimed and fired, but the distance was too far. Terry was no foolhardy fool.

Where the country became too rough for horse, let alone car, the trackers slowly followed on foot, persistently, grimly. Next day they were following the faintest of tracks, they guessed making for White Range Well, and there they saw plainly that he had drunk thirstily, and had not bothered to disguise the fact, which brought a suspicious frown to the dinosaur visage of Wyndham Jack. Wyndham had a face like a hunk of black tar trodden on by a bull elephant, but it could still register suspicion at any apparent false move by his vicious enemy, Terry. Wyndham had quite a lively idea of horrid little pleasantries that Terry would play upon him if only he could get him helpless in some lonely gully.

They tracked him towards a red quartzite hill, constantly changing to rose and purple in colours of tremulous glory as the Supreme Artist played his magic brush upon it, the rays of the sun dipping through fairy mist from the drifting clouds. Through ten miles of this ever-changing beauty arduously they tracked Terry; he appeared to be making for Claraville mining camp ten miles north-east of Arltunga, where they knew he had a girl-friend.

Even a Stone Age Antony may be caught through his Cleopatra.

Very cautiously they planted such a clever little ambush within the scrub round her camp. But that cunning Romeo, Terry, did not come that night. He was miles away, making for the sanctuary of the native well, Ooyah-leeulah.

Next day they rode out for five miles and circled, and cut his tracks at a waterhole. They followed right to Cavanagh's sheep camp. To a lubra working there Peter demanded, "Where Terry? That feller man with gun?"

Fearfully she pointed. Peter knew that away out in that direction was camped a lone blackboy shepherding a little mob of sheep, out there towards the Wheel of Fortune gold show.

Hopefully, very carefully, they rode away to change direction and ride so that they would near that lone camp after dark. Then they would advance quietly on foot, then stealthily surround the lone shepherd's camp—and wait.

And Terry did come, as a shadow, about eight o'clock. He was very tired, lonely, hungry, and thirsty. So as not to frighten the shepherd too much he hid his rifle, he knew now that the mere sight of it in the hands of the so-feared Terry would frighten the lonesome blackboy into gibbering uselessness.

Which was what happened—but not *that* way. The shepherd did not know that a soul was within miles until a black phantom was beside him with softly spoken, smiling greeting. And then———

A black figure fairly flung itself upon Terry and they were snarling on the ground as to Peter's half-strangled yell others came running to hurl themselves into the now maniacal fight. They were all over him, then a click of handcuffs, and Terry was caught.

I finished up with "bad boy Terry" for several reasons, all seeming good to me. Firstly, I think we're all a bit interested, nationally and in our own way, in the old abo. Secondly, Terry went on the rampage at a time that was particularly interesting throughout the entire continental back-country, when the internal-combustion engine was fast taking over from the horse, the mule, the camel, and the little old donk. And, believe me, those sturdy-hearted teams of little donks for many years hauled great loads to and from for far northern stations and tiny settlements from the Territory into and throughout the Kimberleys, and away throughout the Nor'-west back of Port Hedland and elsewhere. At about the same time, too, the aeroplane was just starting out to annihilate distance and time. At this same time also, over huge areas where it had not previously happened, numerous tribes were fast becoming detribalized, these various happenings strangely coming together. Relatively so, anyway. All these momentous happenings, piling up while the others and I in this book were straggling along the pathway of Fate, brought Terry in with us at the last, that is, the temporary last. Another good reason, to me, for finishing up with Terry was that he was lugged back to durance vile while I was in the Alice district. And thus, while he was still "sulky-feller", I got the personal stories from whites and blacks within a few days—of all those closely concerned, anyway.

How I've always hated taking these seemingly everlasting notes of incidents that have drifted across the wandering track of my simple little life! But how handy they have turned out to be! Here is a full book written up from notes laboriously jotted down at the time. Look at this one book—could I have remembered a hundredth part of these incidents after all these years? Not on your life I couldn't.

Well, there you are. Now you know why I ended up with Terry.
Just a moment. It suddenly struck me you might be a bit puzzled at the mention of shepherds during Terry's little adventures. Because shepherds, of course, have gone out with the dodo. Almost certainly to you they suggest Biblical times. Well, my early boyhood days, so far as memory goes, saw the very last of the old shepherds in far western New South Wales. The invention of iron wire for fencing, also settlement and the swift increase of little flocks to great mobs of sheep, finally and inexorably relegated the shepherd to the past. Anyway, he had a long spin, and no doubt he's done a very good job since long before Abraham and Jacob and the boys tended their tiny, precious flocks round about the hills and valleys of the Holy Land.

However, up to Terry's day I hadn't even given it a thought, hadn't given the shepherds a thought in that tiniest of lost worlds deep within those rugged Arltunga hills. For just here and there was a grizzled old aboriginal shepherd tending his little mob of sheep or goats. Thus shepherding did not really go out in Australia until that obliterator of so many phases of life took over, the internal-combustion engine.

Blessed if I'd thought of it before, that shepherding also went out when the motor-car came in!

I was writing these sentiments on 15th February 1961 when Bill Harney blew in from Ayers Rock, full of beans as usual, happy as a wild duck in a thunderstorm. Bill, as you know, is probably the best-known "down to earth" authority on his beloved aborigines. And now he is Guardian of the Rock, and looks like it, for his granitic old visage is as deep-lined as the weather-beaten face of the Rock itself - and looks as if it's going to last as long. He's seen a lot of wear and tear, has Bill.

"Hullo, Bill! What Willy-willy blew *you* in from the Centre?"

"Big-feller blow, Jacky—dust-storm big-feller *too* much! No more find 'im witchety grub longa gum-root now. Me go walkabout longa Brisbane, this feller time, go yabber-yabber tribesman belonga me longa Queensland! Anyway, what are you polishing off now, Jack?"

"Oh, just a yarn of a Kimberley trip, then a run down the Centre, about the time the Tennant's broke out. Found proper-feller, anyway. Writing up these old notes, Bill, has brought forcibly to mind that we've lived through a wonderful era, from the horse and buggy days to the internal-combustion engine, the aeroplane, wireless, and now the sputnik."

Bill blew out that nuggety chest of his.

"Yeah!" he declared. "And we've seen it all—and still going strong! That's the amazing part when you come to think of it—those of us who've survived have just taken it in our stride. Hardly noticed it—it's been just one darned impossible miracle invention after another. We must have got used to them happening. And we're keen for more. But all the same, Jack, when I'm squatting out there by the campfire and a plane happens to drone overhead I do wonder sometimes if I haven't slipped into life from the days of the Dream-time straight to the Moon Gods, taken it all in a stride as it were.

"Yes," I said, grinning, "outlived Life and Progress from the lily lagoons to the big-gun tourist man of Ayers Rock."

"Yes," chuckled Bill, "and out there when I'm drinking in that lonesome moonlight that appears to me the most amazing thing of all. Who in all the world would ever have thought that that prehistoric rock of ages would ever become a *tourist* magnet? And me a glorified shepherd of tourists?"

I laughed; I hadn't thought of that either. For Bill has lived life in the raw, very raw at times. From the Fields of France back to the Land of the Buffalo and the Lily Lagoons, and tough living ever since.

"What on earth do they think of you, Bill—all these car- and bus-loads of city visitors?"

"They reckon I'm the biggest attraction in the Centre," he chuckled, "next to the Rock. They come to see the good God knows what—and they see me!" And Bill's weather-beaten visage rocked in a puckered amazement. "They reckon they've seen everything then," he declared. "They're quite satisfied with their trip to the Centre. They go back home and advise all their friends to tour out to the Rock and see what's camped by the waterhole there."

"We're both a bit moth-eaten," I said. "A bit long in the tooth, too—what we've got left of them. We could both do with a bit of re-thatching also. And I'm afraid our hooves aren't quite what the old grey mare's used to be."

"But look at our hearts, Jack!" declared Bill. "No one knows what noble innards beat with their chests."

"We're lucky there, Bill," I agreed. "The old tickers have seen us across many a dry gully. And still going strong. Anyway, you weather-beaten old hunk of prehistoric memories, you really look the part of Guardian of the Rock. You look damn' near as tough as that weird old monolith of the plain. Yes, who ever would have thought of tourists seeing it?"

Thinking back on the recent utterly desolate isolation of that particular area of Centralia made me realize the wonderful change.

"Of course," said Bill soberly, "it was the internal-combustion engine did it. Came just at the right time to change the entire development of the whole continent. Maybe some of us old-timers are sorry to see the old times go. But it's mighty interesting being in the swim to keep on keeping on ahead. I wouldn't be dead for a million quid, would you, Jack?"

"Not for two million," I agreed decidedly. "I'm going to take a bit of mustering before the angels rope me up there into the Heavenly Paddocks."

"I'm not too sure what paddock they've got ready for me to browse in," chuckled Bill. "I've got a sort of feeling the skids might be under me—I might slide down instead of fly up. Anyway, we're not there yet. Are you writing up early Tennant days, Jack?"

'Yes. What little I know. Luckily I took notes at the time." Like a lightning stroke a memory hit me.

"Stone the crows, Bill! You remember O'Brien, the bloke who was shot in that gunfight?"

"Yes, Jack."

"Well, those dashed goats—he drove them across country from Mount Isa!"

"Yes, for old Fazil Deene the Afghan."

"Yes. Did he have a motor-truck?"

"I dunno, Jack. There were very few motor-trucks those days, and they were only two-tonners if so. Who'd remember, anyway? And why?"

'Well, I've written him up as droving those goats per hoof across that track and distance. And you know how waterless it was! It practically meant death to stray half a mile from the track if man or beast could not find his way back. What if he had a truck to help him? It was a tough job, as you know, in those days. And, as we were saying, it was just the time the motor was invading the back-country. Do you think maybe the drover of goats had an old truck of sorts to help him?"

Bill wrinkled up his ironstone brow, his twinkling eyes closed up in a screw, those gullies and canyons and ravines of his tough old face screwed up in a mighty effort of memory. At last he relaxed with a gusty sigh.

"Haven't a clue, Jacky!" he declared brightly. "And, anyway, what does it matter? As Einstein says, everything is relative. O'Brien brought those goats, somehow or other, across that hellfire of a track, to the good content of that hungry, horny-handed old Afghan. Then he went and got himself mixed up in a gunning feud. He couldn't care less now *how* he brought those goats across. Same with me. Same with all the other boys, whether they're pushing up the daisies or not. Why should *you* worry? Put finis to that bally old book of yours and come out and show me where the Sydney glamour boys hang out now. I feel like a whiff of Sydney brew and a witchety grub or two. I could eat the leg off a hopping bandicoot at one bite—if I could catch him hopping past. Come along!"

Well, and there you are, the end of the journey, until we pick up the swag again.

So long,

Ion Idriess.

Michael Terry looking at Lasseter's message, Lake Christopher, 1932.